REPRESENTING SPACE IN THE REVOLUTION

The novel understanding of the physical world that characterized the Scientific Revolution depended on a fundamental shift in the way its protagonists understood and described space. At the beginning of the seventeenth century, spatial phenomena were described in relation to a presupposed central point; by its end, space had become a centerless void in which phenomena could be described only by reference to arbitrary orientations. David Marshall Miller examines both the historical and philosophical aspects of this far-reaching development, including the rejection of the idea of heavenly spheres, the advent of rectilinear inertia, and the theoretical contributions of Copernicus, Gilbert, Kepler, Galileo, Descartes, and Newton. His rich study shows clearly how the centered Aristotelian cosmos became the oriented Newtonian universe, and will be of great interest to students and scholars of the history and philosophy of science.

DAVID MARSHALL MILLER is Assistant Professor of Philosophy at Iowa State University. He has published articles in journals including *Philosophy of Science* and *History of Science*.

REPRESENTING SPACE
IN THE SCIENTIFIC
REVOLUTION

DAVID MARSHALL MILLER

CAMBRIDGE
UNIVERSITY PRESS

CAMBRIDGE
UNIVERSITY PRESS

University Printing House, Cambridge CB2 8BS, United Kingdom

Cambridge University Press is part of the University of Cambridge.

It furthers the University's mission by disseminating knowledge in the pursuit of education, learning and research at the highest international levels of excellence.

www.cambridge.org
Information on this title: www.cambridge.org/9781107624719

© David Marshall Miller, 2014

This publication is in copyright. Subject to statutory exception and to the provisions of relevant collective licensing agreements, no reproduction of any part may take place without the written permission of Cambridge University Press.

First published 2014
First paperback edition 2016

A catalogue record for this publication is available from the British Library

Library of Congress Cataloguing in Publication data
Miller, David Marshall, author.
Representing space in the scientific revolution / David Marshall Miller.
pages   cm
ISBN 978-1-107-04673-3 (hardback)
1. Science – History – 17th century.   2. Science – Philosophy.
3.   Space.   4. Space and time.   I. Title.
Q125.2.M55   2014
530.1–dc23
2014007595

ISBN 978-1-107-04673-3 Hardback
ISBN 978-1-107-62471-9 Paperback

For my family

Contents

Figures

Preface

This book pays homage to Alexandre Koyré, one of the founders of the intellectual history of science, who coined the term "Scientific Revolution," and whose work originally excited my own interest in the field. From its inception, this project has been motivated by a conviction that Koyré gave precisely the wrong answers to exactly the right questions. In particular, I have been fascinated by Koyré's idea, expressed in *From the Closed World to the Infinite Universe*, that changing conceptions of space were an essential catalyst of the Scientific Revolution. I was sure, though, that the story Koyré told about the metaphysics of space could not be correct. At bottom, this is an attempt to follow the trail Koyré blazed to a more satisfactory conclusion. The old questions are still worth asking.

Though it retains relatively little of the text, the ideas expressed in this book originated in my doctoral dissertation, written while I was a student in the History and Philosophy of Science department at the University of Pittsburgh. I am grateful for the guidance and support of my mentors, Peter Machamer and Ted McGuire. Through their eyes, I first discovered the lasting perplexity of the Scientific Revolution. Important inspiration also came from Hasok Chang and the late Ernan McMullin, who demonstrated how history and philosophy could be woven into scholarly material whose value transcends disciplinary bounds. John Norton, John Earman, Jonathan Hodge, Paolo Palmieri, Jonathan Scott, Zvi Biener, Greg Frost-Arnold, Jim Tabery, and Brian Hepburn also served as early interlocutors and made lasting contributions.

In the many years since, this project has had the support of many institutions and individuals, for which I am very thankful. I have worked on this book while affiliated with the University of North Carolina at Chapel Hill and Oxford College of Emory University. I was also a Mellon Postdoctoral Fellow in the Humanities at Yale University, where Matthew Smith, Barbara Sattler, Verity Harte, Michael Della Rocca, Ken Winkler, Tamar Gendler, and Sun-Joo Shin graciously offered comments and counsel. At Duke University, I enjoyed the wisdom and friendship of Seymour Mauskopf and Andrew Janiak, both of whom provided invaluable comments on the completed manuscript, and without whom this book could never have been completed. In addition, I spent a productive summer at the Max-Planck-Institut für Wissenschaftsgeschichte as part of the Modern Geometry and the Concept of Space working group, led by Vincenzo De Risi, alongside Marius Stan, Delphine Bellis, Valérie Debuiche, and Michael Friedman, all of whom made significant and helpful suggestions, especially for the Descartes chapter. At the same time, I had the pleasure of discussing Galileo with Jochen Büttner, Rivka Feldhay, Alison Laywine, and Daniel Warren.

Along the way, I have benefitted immensely from generous criticism by Tad Schmaltz, Dan Garber, Maarten Van Dyke, Eric Schliesser, Michael McVaugh, Maurice Finocchiaro, Stephan Blatti, Patrick Boner, Adela Deanova, and anonymous referees. Samuel Schindler, Helge Kragh, and the science studies reading group at the University of Aarhus provided useful comments on the Copernicus chapter. Conversations with a multitude of audiences refined my thoughts and improved their expression. For particular points of assistance, I offer additional thanks in the footnotes to the text. I am also indebted to my wonderfully excellent colleagues at Iowa State University, particularly Jonathan Tsou and Patrick Connolly.

With guidance from Owen Gingerich and translation assistance from Nicholas Jardine and Paolo Palmieri, a version of the Kepler chapter was published as "*O Male Factum*: Rectilinearity and Kepler's Discovery of the Ellipse," *Journal for the History of Astronomy* 39 (2008), 43–63. I am grateful to Michael Hoskin and Science Publications Limited for permission to reproduce that material here. Thanks are also due to Hilary Gaskin, Kanimozhi Ramamurthy, and all those working with Cambridge University Press for their extraordinary care in seeing this book through publication.

Finally, I owe the deepest love and appreciation to my family. My parents, grandparents, and brother offered a remarkable and mystified enthusiasm that buoyed me over innumerable obstacles, while my four-legged relations reminded me that naps and walks are what are really important. Above all else, there is Dana LeVine, whose support of me and my obscure toil has long been steadfast. She is a model of dedication, energy, sympathy, and caring. I could never thank her enough.

Note on texts

For quotations from well-known texts, I have provided references to standard translations. In cases where a text is not well known, I have cited both the translation quoted and the original source, in most cases including the latter in a footnote. Where no translation is available for a text, I have provided my own, citing the original and including it in a footnote.

CHAPTER I

Introduction: centers and orientations

The historiographical problem

It is something of a commonplace to say that the seventeenth century witnessed a shift from viewing the natural world as fundamentally spherical to viewing the universe as fundamentally rectilinear. This move toward rectilinearity is evident in the emergence of all the hallmarks of "classical" science. The dissolution of the heavenly spheres, the replacement of equilibrium by collision as the model of mechanical interaction, the abandonment of Aristotelian natural place, and the all-important development of rectilinear inertia to supplant natural motion and impetus all display the general trend. Nevertheless, while these developments have been extensively studied individually, the conceptual shift common to all has not been satisfactorily addressed. Though most scholars would immediately recognize and acknowledge the existence and importance of the adoption of a rectilinear framework in the early modern physical sciences, none has satisfactorily detailed how this came to pass.

Many scholarly studies have sought answers to this question in the metaphysical understanding of space during the period.[1] According to these accounts, a rectilinear framework was somehow adopted alongside a shift in the understanding of space considered as a substantial thing. Their focus, therefore, is on the history of debates about space's ontological properties – its infinitude, eternality, vacuity, absoluteness, and so on. However, as I argue more extensively below, this emphasis is misplaced. Abstract speculation about the nature of space was too divorced from the changing explanations of the behavior of bodies that formed the physical core of the Scientific Revolution. The move toward rectilinearity was a change in the understanding

---

[1] Classic treatments include Jammer (1954), Koyré (1957), Grant (1981). See also Burtt (1954), Butterfield (1957), Dijksterhuis (1961),Toulmin and Goodfield (1961), Koestler (1968), Huggett (1999), Barbour (2001). To be fair, Jammer's treatment of the ancient and medieval periods focuses on the epistemic import of space. In fact, Jammer's work constitutes an appropriate prelude to my own. Nevertheless, his treatment of the early modern period veers toward the metaphysical.

of phenomena *in* space, not the nature of space itself. For example, sometime in the early modern period, authors decided that rectilinear translations were instances of uniform change. This decision was not determined by their views about the plenitude or immobility of space. Rather, it came about in their construction of theoretical knowledge about the behavior of physical objects. What is needed, then, is not another history of spatial ontology, but a history of spatial *epistemology*. This is what I attempt in the following.

In particular, this book will argue that *representation of space* is the appropriate unit by which to analyze the development of rectilinearity in classical science. As will be expressed more precisely below, a representation of space is part of a descriptive framework by which spatial properties and relations are described and explained. Thus, the "something" that changed during the seventeenth century was the prevailing representation of space. The shift that accompanied the emergence of modern science can be described as a move from a centered representation of space to an oriented representation of space. Authors described and explained spatial properties spherically, in relation to centers, at the beginning of the period and rectilinearly, in relation to orientations, at its end.

So baldly stated, this thesis seems blatantly and perniciously anachronistic. It imputes a contemporary notion of my own devising into the work of historical authors, and thus threatens to distort the resulting historical account. I am compelled, therefore, to offer a preliminary defense of the analytical frame I use to approach the history of the Scientific Revolution. The thoroughgoing argument in favor of my approach will be the analysis itself. The coherence and accuracy of the account presented in the rest of this volume will be the justification of my claims and the measure of their success. In the meantime, however, I must show that the authors here examined made use of what I am calling representations of space, such that they are appropriate objects to seek and characterize in historical work, and not mere anachronistic figments. There are two ways I might accomplish this task. The first is to identify pieces of text in which authors explicitly state their representations of space. This path is not available, since explicit expressions of a representation of space are very rare, though not entirely absent, in the work of early modern natural philosophers. This is not surprising. Indeed, it will be argued below that explicit statements regarding representations of space should not be expected of *any* author, since a representation of space comprises commonly held, "ordinary" concepts that seem obvious in most contexts. Hence, authors usually do not need to elaborate a representation of space in order to effect meaningful communication.

The second path, which I will follow, is to argue that a representation of space is a necessary part of any physical understanding of the natural world, and thus an essential part of the work of any natural philosopher. If I can establish the *a priori* expectation of finding a representation of space implicit or explicit in any attempt to provide physical understanding, I can then reasonably seek the representation of space contained in the work of early modern authors, or any other for that matter. One need not fear pernicious anachronism due to the illicit distortion of historical texts. Notice, however, that establishing the necessity of a representation of space makes a claim about physical understanding in general that transcends temporal period. It entails a *philosophical* argument proceeding from basic intuitions about the nature of scientific understanding. The remainder of this introduction sketches just such a philosophical argument.

The philosophical argument for the necessity of representations of space does not complete the historiographical project, however. One must also show how the proposed unit of analysis is to be identified in historical texts, especially since it is usually implicit. This introduction proposes a method for identifying representations of space by textual interrogation. Finally, it must be demonstrated that representations of space are actual. That is, it needs to be shown that representations of space in fact describe the historical phenomenon in question: the shift from a spherical to a rectilinear worldview. The latter demonstration proceeds in the course of the following narrative.

It follows that this will be a work of integrated history and philosophy of science. On the one hand, the subject is philosophical. I will examine the spatial epistemology of early modern natural philosophy. In particular, I will suggest that physical theories necessarily contain descriptive frameworks that coordinate their explanatory principles with phenomena, and that representations of space are part of these descriptive frameworks. On the other hand, the argument itself will be historical. I will detail how a shift in descriptive frameworks occurred in the work of several seventeenth-century authors by offering a chronological reconstruction based on the examination of representations of space. These aims are meant to be mutually reinforcing. Representations of space form the analytic framework for the historical account, and the historical account establishes the constitutive and causal role of representations of space in physical thought. The coherence and likelihood of the historical narrative will support the plausibility of the philosophical analysis by which it is constructed, and *vice versa*. The aim is to make the philosophical and historical case *at the same time*.

Explanations, descriptions, frameworks, and theories

This is not the place for an extended philosophical disquisition. The bulk of my argument for the epistemology of science I am here proposing will reveal itself in the course of the narrative to follow. However, in order to identify the analytical tools with which I am working, I must first offer a sketch of my view of the structure of scientific theories. At this level of generality, I take my account to be non-controversial (if there is such a thing) and in keeping with current trends in philosophy of science.[2] The details are more contentious, naturally; I hope eventually to offer an expanded exposition of my position, using the present work as evidence, but I leave that for another venue.

Science offers explanations of the natural world. Any scientific theory, that is, purports to explain the phenomena within its domain. However, explanations necessarily rely on descriptions. In order to construct an explanation, one must first specify the phenomena to be explained with a definite description. Moreover, explanations themselves must involve at least some descriptions of phenomena. If an explanation is meant to show how the properties and relations of objects account for the feature of the world to be explained, then those properties and relations must be described in the course of the explanation. For example, an explanation might include descriptions of the initial conditions that occasion the target phenomenon; or it might include a description of the physical context in which the phenomenon took place (the forces acting and so on).[3] The ability to explain depends on the ability to describe.

The latter ability, in turn, is provided by a descriptive framework that coordinates descriptions with the features of the phenomena they represent. This framework consists of the criteria by which the propriety of the application of a description is judged – i.e., the verification conditions of the description. It specifies which phenomena count as instances of a description. To illustrate, consider the description 'the apple falls down'. This statement describes the behavior of a physical object. It specifies an

---

[2] The layered epistemology outlined here has its roots in the Fregean distinction between sense and reference. On my account, a description gets part of its meaning from its sense relative to the explanations provided by the theory and part from its reference in the phenomena as determined by the coordinative framework. Versions of this layered view, based on a similar semantic distinction, are widespread. I take my coordinative framework, at least in general terms, to be a reflection of Poincaré's (1905) conventional definitions, Reichenbach's (1920, 1958) relativized *a priori* and coordinative definitions, Carnap's (1950) linguistic frameworks, Putnam's (1962) framework principles, Kitcher's (1978) reference potentials, van Fraassen's (2008) representing-*as* (opposed to a theory's representing-*that*), and Friedman's (1999, 2001) constitutive *a priori*.

[3] For classic perspectives on descriptions in explanations, see Davidson (1967), Levin (1976), Woodward (1993).

object – the apple – as well as its behavior – a particular form of motion, falling. The statement also specifies the direction of the motion – down. Altogether, then, 'the apple falls down' can be comprehended as a meaningful description of a phenomenon. It specifies a certain phenomenon or fact about the world: the behavior of the apple – i.e., its motion in a particular manner in a particular direction. The meanings of 'apple', 'falls', and 'down' in this description, however, are not transparently intelligible. These terms must be coordinated with features of the phenomena in order for the meaning of the description to be made patent. 'Apple' must be coordinated with a particular object or set of objects. The term 'falls' must be coordinated with a particular kind of accelerated motion. 'Down' must be coordinated with a specific direction or trajectory. Such coordinations, taken together, constitute a descriptive framework. Thus, the descriptive framework enables an interpreter of the description 'the apple falls down' to identify the phenomenal objects described. For instance, the coordination of 'falls' allows the interpreter to understand that the apple undergoes an accelerated motion, while the coordination of 'down' picks out which direction is meant by the term. Similarly, an observer of a falling apple would employ his or her own coordinations of 'apple', 'falls', and 'down' in order to generate the description 'the apple falls down'.

Interpreters and generators of descriptions can only operate within the context of a descriptive framework that includes the coordinations of the elements of their descriptions. Put simply, the very possibility of description relies on the coordinative framework that links descriptive representations to the phenomena described. Only by using a descriptive framework can a generator of a description decide which terms adequately describe the phenomenon, or can an interpreter decode the resulting description. By the same token, users of a language hoping to communicate must share roughly similar descriptive frameworks. The possibility of communication breaks down when interlocutors possess different or radically divergent frameworks. Thus, if one were to say, on observing the falling apple, that "The apple falls umpwise," an interpreter of that description lacking the coordination criteria of 'umpwise' would be unable to understand the utterance. Likewise, if an interpreter's notion of "down" coordinated it with the direction toward the center of the sun, he or she would deny that 'the apple falls down' is an acceptable description of the phenomenon.

Theories offer explanations of phenomena, but, as we have seen, explanations include descriptions. It follows, therefore, that explanations can only be carried out in association with a descriptive framework. Since explanations require descriptions, and any description requires a framework by which the description is interpreted, explanations require coordinations. The coordinations contribute meaning to the descriptions that constitute the explanation. They establish the referential links between the explanation and the phenomena it purports to explain. Descriptive frameworks are necessary to bring phenomena under explanations, and thus necessary to make them intelligible.

Scientific theories must therefore contain two distinct epistemic levels. On the one hand, a theory provides explanatory resources that can account for the phenomena in its domain. On the other hand, a theory contains a descriptive framework that coordinates its explanations with those phenomena. Theories explain nothing without a descriptive framework in the context of which they are interpreted. Explanatory principles have no explanatory force – they are not explanations of anything – unless they are coordinated to some feature of the world by a description. Water, chemistry explains, is a certain combination of oxygen and hydrogen, but chemistry says nothing at all if does not also specify that 'water' signifies the stuff here in my glass or there in the river. Physics tells us that gravity causes an object to fall, but it also must tell us which motions count as 'falling'.

Representations of space

It remains to show that a *representation of space* is a necessary part of any *physical* theory. This is accomplished simply by definition: a representation of space is the subset of coordinations in a descriptive framework that concern spatial properties and relations. It includes, among many others, the coordinations of 'up', 'down', 'above', 'below', 'far', 'near', 'straight', 'curved', and so on. A representation of space is therefore the set of coordinations that underwrites descriptions of directions, locations, sizes, shapes, distances, and any other spatial property or relation. Hence, a representation of space is an essential element of the explanation of physical phenomena, insofar as such phenomena occur in physical space and physical explanations concern their behavior in that space. If an explanation refers to spatial properties and relations (and all the physical explanations I am interested in do), it calls upon a representation of space.[4]

---

[4] Kant used the term 'representation of space' to refer to the "form of outer intuition." In the Transcendental Aesthetic, he argued that a representation of space is the means by which sensory experience is ordered and thereby rendered intelligible (1998, 175). Though I do not agree with Kant that a Euclidean, oriented representation of space is a *necessary* feature of human cognition, I do think some representation of space is a necessary, *a priori* element of theoretical understanding. Hence, I conscientiously adopt Kant's term in order to refer to something very similar to what he seems to have had in mind.

A representation of space, however, can be characterized as more than just a bare set of coordinations. The coordinations in a representation of space are not held *in vacuo*, one by one. Various coordinations relate to the same objects, forming coordinative complexes and structures. For example, "up" is (usually) the opposite of "down." If 'down' is coordinated with the direction toward a stipulated location, 'up' is directly away from the same location. Also, the coordinations of 'above' and 'below', 'top' and 'bottom', etc., will refer to the same location, such that if "above" is further from the location, "below" is nearer, "top" is furthest, and "bottom" is nearest. The interrelations between the coordinations included in this representation of space form a coherent structure, built around a single presupposed location in relation to which each coordination is established.

These structured interrelations among coordinations make it possible to characterize the "shape" of a representation of space. If the coordinations in a representation of space all relate to a presupposed, privileged location, then directions, such as "up" and "down" will converge or diverge toward or away from the presupposed location. That is, the directions an observer employing this representation of space will describe as "down" will converge toward the central point his or her coordination criterion for 'down' relates to. Each region of space may also be conceived with a determinate privileged orientation – e.g., the direction toward or away from the privileged location. The observer will be able to say without any ambiguity which way is "up" or "down." And different regions of space will be distinguishable from one another by their distance from the privileged location. The observer, therefore, will be able to describe regions of space as "higher" or "lower." Put another way, a representation of space that presupposes a single privileged location is convergent, anisotropic, and heterogeneous. This is a *centered* representation of space.

Consider, by contrast, a representation of space in which terms are coordinated by relation to an arbitrary line or axis, rather than a privileged location. In this case, to describe spatial properties and relations, one must first specify the orientation to which descriptions are referred. 'Down' might then be coordinated with the direction parallel to the orientation in one sense, 'up' with the direction parallel to the orientation in the other. Similarly, 'above' would be further along the orientation in the "up" direction, 'below' would be further along the "down" direction. Here, directions described similarly will be parallel to each other. The direction described as "up" or "down" in one part of space is parallel to the direction described as "up" or "down" in another.

Moreover, without a presupposed privileged location by which locations could be uniquely specified, there would be no way to determinately distinguish different parts of space. There is nothing inherently distinguishing about the way any location is described. No feature of the descriptive framework allows a unique specification of place. One region of space might be correctly described as "higher" than another, but it could also be described as "lower" than a third. An observer can describe locations only relative to other locations. Consequently, descriptions of locations require the prior arbitrary stipulation of a reference point whose location is not itself specified. In sum, an *oriented* representation of space is isotropic, self-parallel, and homogeneous.[5]

This discussion is not meant to suggest that representations of space fall neatly into two categories: centered and oriented. There could be many other varieties of representation of space, as well as countless variations within each kind of spatial framework. Each author one encounters might employ a slightly different descriptive scheme. The point here is simply that it is possible to characterize the general shape of a representation of space. It makes sense to talk about a "centered" or "oriented" representation of space. In particular, one can meaningfully assert that the development of classical science included a shift from a prevailing centered representation of space to a prevailing oriented representation of space. This is a claim open to historical investigation.

A representation of space has special significance for the theoretical treatment of motion. Representations of space determine the phenomenal import of descriptions of directions and distances. In particular, they determine what counts as the same direction and the same distance in different locations and times. Consequently, a representation of space picks out what can be described as "the same motion" from place to place and moment to moment. As will be seen in relation to the historical examples discussed later in this chapter, this function of a representation of space is essential to any physical theory, since it identifies which features of the phenomena stand in need of explanation by a theory. Newtonian physics, for instance, says that motion is conserved. Yet the theory also coordinates 'conserved motion' with bodies moving uniformly along straight lines. The representation of space associated with the theory picks out the phenomena described as conserved motions and explicable as such.

Along these lines, it helps to point out the contemporary correlate of this historical discussion. What I am after is the *affine structure* of pre-modern and

---

[5] This kind of spatial framework is commonly called *Euclidean*, since its structure is similar to that of "Euclidean" geometry. The label, however, is misleading, since Euclid himself was ecumenical in his approach to geometry. His methods presupposed, on an equal footing, both lines, in the form of the straight edge, and central points, in the form of the compass point. Someone trying to describe phenomena could appeal to Euclid's proofs, whether his own representation of space was centered, "Euclidean," or otherwise.

classical physics. In relativistic physics, an affine structure determines what counts as the "same" direction through space, and it fixes, in turn, the inertial trajectories of bodies. Thus, the affine structure specifies what phenomena are described as "simple motions" – motions that are unchanging and need no explanation other than the conservation of prior motion. Calculation of the affine structure is part of the solution to the Einstein field equations determined by the distribution of mass and energy. The affine structure is therefore *a posteriori* in the sense that it depends on the actual distribution of matter and energy in a spacetime manifold. By the same token, determination of the simple motions is an explicit part of the physical theory, and the representation of space implied by the theory can be discovered by a straightforward inspection of its mathematical expression. The coordination of explanations with phenomena is a part of the theory itself. A physicist must state from the outset what his or her descriptions of motions *mean*.[6]

Of course, before the advent of relativity, representations of space were *a priori* in that space was presumed to have a certain structure within which bodies moved. Einstein's essential realization, which was partly the result of influence by Poincaré and Mach, was that the structure of space (and time) is not fixed, but affected by the bodies in it. In other words, he realized that the representation of space was part of physics, not a background assumption. Einstein did not create the notion of affine structure or the question of representation of space out of whole cloth. He simply made it a subject of empirical investigation. By the same token, though, the representation of space was an essential part of pre-relativistic physics. There is a pre-history of affine structures – a history of representations of space.

Representations of space are not anachronistic figments. They are a necessary part of any physical understanding, since they enable the phenomena to be described and explained *in space*. Though representations of space can be constrained by the context of a phenomenon, they are not trivial. Therefore, the historian of scientific understanding can and should seek the representations of space associated with physical explanations of phenomena. That is what I attempt to do in this book.

Interrogating texts

At this point, however, one encounters a difficulty. One should not expect to find explicit statements of an author's representation of space in his or her texts. More often than not, the representation of space goes without stating.

---

[6] See, e.g., Sklar (1974), Friedman (1983).

On the one hand, descriptive frameworks can be very complicated, and, since they are prior to the use of a description, they are not themselves expressible. One might talk *about* the coordinations, and thus one might attempt to describe a descriptive framework, but the framework itself is beyond expression. Furthermore, some descriptive coordinations may refer to exemplars – particular objects – that cannot appear in sentential rules. One might have in mind one's own dog when judging whether another object can be described as "a dog."[7] Other criteria might be simply heuristic and subject to inexpressible exceptions. It can be difficult even to *try* to express the conditions that constitute a description's coordination and thus hard to identify precisely the phenomenal extension of that description.

On the other hand, and equally problematic, is the fact that failures of communication caused by divergent descriptive frameworks are rare and limited to extreme cases. In the case of neologisms and obscure terms, an author is expected to provide explicit definitions – one should state clearly the meaning of 'umpwise' before expecting an audience to agree that an apple falls umpwise. However, the vast majority of coordinations are anything but novel or obscure. In normal communication, one can assume that competent users of a language have learned, through the process of language acquisition, a coordinative framework similar to one's own. Thus, explicit definitions are seldom called for, and authors, even in science, can typically describe phenomena without explicating the frameworks they employ.

This is especially true in the case of representations of space. A representation of space is necessary for and prior to the description and explanation of physical phenomena, but it is, on the one hand, itself difficult to express (as are all descriptive frameworks), and, on the other, often obvious or simply conventional. We all have "ordinary" notions of "up," "down," and so on, even if these are not the precise notions used in physical explanations. Thus, readers already have some sense of an author's meaning when it comes to descriptions of spatial properties and relations. Explicit definitions of such terms would seem redundant. Moreover, particular physical situations usually present obviously privileged objects and a convenient geometric structure. These tend to constrain our "ordinary" spatial frameworks to a limited set that are similar enough to allow meaningful communication. We tend, for example, to employ a centered representation of space when observing the

---

[7] This is a particularly simple example. In fact, exemplars may be quite technical and complicated. Galileo's appeal to the behavior of bitumen on a hot iron pan, for example, helped make his description of sunspots intelligible. Similarly, he often used the lever to generate descriptions of phenomena, as in the cases of floating bodies and inclined planes. Machamer (1995) calls these exemplars "models of intelligibility." See also Feldhay (1995).

stars, but an oriented one when describing objects in a room. It simply makes sense to use a centered representation of space to represent the vault of the heavens in relation to an observer and an oriented framework in a room with flat walls, floor, and ceiling at right angles to one another.

At the same time, most spatial descriptions are very tolerant of ambiguity. Even individuals with different spatial frameworks are usually able to communicate effectively. Consider two people, one of whom conceives of "down" as the direction along the head-to-toe axis and the other as the direction toward the center of the earth. Even though they have different definitions of "down," both would agree that a falling apple is moving "downward." In other words, their descriptive frameworks are congruent in this context since applying either set of criteria yields descriptions and explanations that are effectively indistinguishable. They become distinguishable only when the representations of space are directly compared or when they are extended to other contexts, such as when one of them is prostrate, where the descriptions and explanations they generate diverge.[8] Hence, an author can usually appeal to ordinary spatial frameworks that the audience already possesses, that are usually apparent in the given context, and that need only be congruent, not identical to his own in that context. As a result, spatial descriptions are often adopted without comment.

Nevertheless, representations of space are not opaque. Texts can be interrogated in order to discover implicit representations of space. Notice that the overall geometry of a representation of space can generally be distinguished by the geometrical entities that must be stipulated in order to generate and interpret the descriptions appearing in the textual expression of a theory. A centered representation of space, for example, presupposes a center. As a result, the coordinations in the representation of space will use that center as a privileged reference point. An oriented representation of space, meanwhile, presupposes a rectilinear orientation. Its coordinations will relate to that straight line. Therefore, one way to characterize an author's representation of space is by noting which geometrical entities are stipulated by his or her descriptive scheme. A privileged point or location indicates a centered representation of space; a privileged line suggests an oriented representation of space (though, again, this does not exhaust the possibilities). Hence, the historian can ask several specific questions of a text

---

[8] One might be tempted to say that congruent conceptual frameworks constitute a *paradigm*, with all that implies, including the incommensurability of different frameworks. This temptation should be resisted. The possible divergence of congruent frameworks is one reason. Though the two individuals employ different coordinations, they are able to effectively communicate in some circumstances. Their descriptive frameworks are not necessarily incommensurable. This is a much more fraught issue than I can tackle here. See Kitcher (1978), Lakoff (1987), Brigandt (2010).

in order to discover its underlying representation of space. Most importantly, what are the basic geometrical elements of spatial descriptions? Does the author presuppose centers or lines? Does he or she presuppose fixed points or not? We might also ask how an object is located in space. That is, how is an object's location specified? What geometrical presuppositions are necessary for the specification?

The description of directions by an author is also useful for discerning a representation of space, especially by examining how the author describes the similarity of directions. In a centered representation of space, directions are specified in relation to the spatial center. Thus, two directions will be described similarly – that is, identified as "the same" direction – if they bear the same relation to the center. For example, two directions might be described as "down" if they are both directed toward the presupposed center. In an oriented representation of space, by contrast, directions are specified in relation to the spatial orientation. Two directions will be described similarly if they bear the same relation to the orientation. This entails that directions will be called the same if they are parallel in the same sense, since two parallel lines bear the same relation to a third. This method of investigation will be put to use below.

Representations of space are necessary for and prior to the description and explanation of phenomena, even if they usually go without stating. By interrogating a text, one can reveal the implicit representation of space.

Examples: Aristotle, Epicurus, and Newton

Having argued that representations of space are possible objects of historical inquiry and given some indication of how they can be investigated, I can finally put all of this together to suggest how representations of space might be *worthwhile* objects of study, especially with regard to the development of classical science in the early modern period. Of course, the ultimate proof will be in the narrative – the history I can construct using representation of space as a unit of analysis in the remainder of this book. For now, three specific examples will have to suffice.

Consider first Aristotle's description of the "simple motions" in *De Caelo*:

> Now revolution about the center is circular motion, while the upward and downward movements are in a straight line, 'upward' meaning motion away from the center, and 'downward' motion towards it. All simple motion, then, must be motion either away from or towards or about the center.[9]

---

[9] *De Caelo* I.2 (Aristotle 1984, 1:448).

Aristotle describes directions in relation to a presupposed privileged location, namely, the center of the universe, which coincides with the center of the earth. This center is a primitive feature of Aristotle's representation of space. The location is presumed in order to make descriptions of direction intelligible. 'Downward' means toward the center. 'Upward' means away from it. In other words, Aristotle is representing phenomena using a *centered* representation of space structured spherically around a single, privileged location.

This centered representation of space allows the description of three "simple motions" – upward, downward, and circularly around the center. Why are these motions simple? In a centered representation of space, the direction of the motion along these paths is always described the same way. A body circularly orbiting the center, for instance, always bears the same relation to the center – it moves perpendicularly. Thus, the direction of the body's motion is described as unchanging. That is, it is simple. The "simplicity" of the motion, however, depends on the centered representation of space by which direction is described and, thus, how the motion is described.

The explanatory consequences of this centered representation of space in Aristotle's physical theories are well known. First, Aristotle distinguishes different regions of space, or "places," by their distances from the center. This heterogeneity of space allows the use of locations as *termini a quo* and *termini ad quem* in physical explanations. Aristotle can claim that bodies naturally move towards their proper places, which are inherently distinct from one another. He also argues that, since they are simple bodies, the elements should move simply – with simple motions. The heavy elements earth and water naturally move "downwards," seeking their "place" near the center. In turn, this entails that the earth's center and the geometrical center of space, though distinct, must coincide. The earth remains motionless at the center of the moving heavens, since its parts are all "balanced" upon the center, and there is no cause of additional motion. If the earth were in any other place at some distance from the spatial center, it would fall towards the center.[10] Meanwhile, the light elements, fire and air, move "upwards," toward the periphery of the terrestrial realm. The celestial bodies, already in their natural places, possess only circular rotation around the center – motion "in place." In sum, the heavy and light elements move linearly toward and away from the center, respectively, and the heavens rotate circularly around it. These natural motions in turn form the basis of

---

[10] *De Caelo* II.14 (Aristotle 1984, 1:487–89).

Aristotle's physics. As we have seen, though, Aristotle's description of "simple motions" depends on his centered representation of space.

Consider, by contrast, the oriented representation of space employed by Epicurus in his "Letter to Herodotus":

> Moreover in speaking of the infinite we must not use 'up' or 'down' with the implication that they are top or bottom, but with the implication that from wherever we stand it is possible to protract the line above our heads to infinity without danger of this ever seeming so to us, or likewise the line below us (in what is conceived to stretch to infinity simultaneously both upwards and downwards in relation to the same point).[11]

Epicurus applies 'up' and 'down' in relation to a line protracted "above our heads" and "below us" – i.e., the extrapolation of the head-to-toe axis. "Up" is along the line in one direction, "down" along it in the other. "Above" is further "up"; "below" is further "down." The coordinations in his representation of space therefore relate to a presupposed straight line that serves to orient the space – a rectilinear orientation. Moreover, similarly described directions will be parallel to each other throughout the space described, since they retain the same relation to the line extended above and below us. Each "up" is parallel to every other "up"; each "down" is parallel to every other "down."

Epicurus, an atomist, held that space is an infinite void. This infinite space, he argued, could have no boundary and no center. As a result, he explicitly rejects any appeal to privileged locations in his conception of space. "Up" and "down" are directions *simpliciter*. They are not to be conceived as toward a "top" or "bottom." There is no *terminus a quo* or *terminus ad quem* by which directions or other spatial concepts can be designated. Directions stretch to infinity:

> Therefore it is possible to take as one motion that which is conceived as upwards to infinity, and as one motion that which is conceived as downwards to infinity, even if that which moves from where we are towards the places above our heads arrives ten thousand times at the feet of those above, or at the heads of those below, in the case of that which moves downwards from where we are. For each of the two mutually opposed motions is none the less, as a whole, conceived as being to infinity.[12]

There is no "place above our heads" such that motion towards that place is "up." When an object moving upward reaches those "places above our heads," it continues to move "upward" (in the infinite void) even though, having arrived at and passed any given place, it moves away from, rather

---

[11] Epicurus (1987, 10).   [12] Epicurus (1987, 10).

than toward, any point we might use to identify "up." The same is true for "downward" motion. The directions are "conceived as being to infinity," not toward (or away from) a location. As Epicurus writes, "For this [i.e. that there should be a top and a bottom] is unthinkable." The Epicurean representation of space, therefore, is self-parallel, anisotropic, and rigorously homogeneous.[13]

This representation of space, of course, is important for Epicurean physics, which holds that the atoms have weight, which causes them to forever fall "downwards" through the void. This assumes that the physical space inhabited by the atoms is already oriented such that "downwards" is determinable. In other words, the explanation that atoms naturally fall "down" is based on the oriented representation of space that gives meaning to the description 'downwards'.

The rectilinear structure of space also led to explanatory trouble for Epicurean philosophers. Since "down" is everywhere parallel to itself, atoms simply falling "down" would never encounter one another, and the world would never change. As Lucretius wrote, "everything would be falling downward like raindrops through the depths of the void, and collisions and impacts among the primary bodies would not have arisen, with the result that nature would never have created anything."[14] An additional explanatory principle, the famous *clinamen* or "swerve," had to be introduced to bring about collisions between atoms that could bring about observed change. However, these random, spontaneous sideways "swerves" were themselves inexplicable, a cause for much criticism.[15]

Finally, consider Book I, Proposition 1 of Newton's *Principia*, which proves that "The areas which bodies made to move in orbits describe by radii drawn to an unmoving center of forces lie in unmoving planes and are proportional to the times [in which they are described]."[16] In other words, Newton shows that Kepler's second law of planetary motion – orbiting bodies sweep out equal areas in equal times – holds for any body moving under the influence of a centrally directed force. This proposition is crucial to Newton's argument for universal gravitation, since it establishes the basic kinematic effects of an attractive force.

The demonstration of the proposition proceeds by deriving the path of a body through several equal, infinitesimal moments, where the body receives

[13] Epicurus (1987, 10). As Max Jammer (1954, 13) puts it, Epicurus "conceived space as endowed with an objectively distinguished direction, the vertical. It is in this direction in which the atoms are racing through space in parallel lines. According to Epicurus and Lucretius, space, though homogeneous, is not isotropic." See also Shapere (1964), Furley (1976), Hahm (1976), Machamer (1978), Clavelin (1983).
[14] Lucretius (1987, 11).   [15] See Furley (1976, 96–98).   [16] Newton (1999, 444).

an instantaneous, center-directed impulse at the beginning of each moment. In each moment, then, the body's motion is a combination of the inertially continued motion from the previous moment and the motion due to the percussive action of the attractive force. To find the resultant motion, Newton simply constructs a parallelogram composition of the two motions. In each infinitesimal moment, the body is carried between diagonal vertices of a parallelogram, the parallel sides of which describe the body's inertial and centripetal motion. Having shown this to be the path of the body, Newton then proves that the area swept out in each moment is always the same, and the proposition follows.

Newton's use of a parallelogram composition of motions here is telling, since it only makes coherent sense in an oriented representation of space. As Newton's own justification of the parallelogram composition shows, it assumes that the direction of either of the two motions is everywhere parallel to itself.[17] That is, the parallel sides of the parallelogram must signify motion in *one and the same* direction. Only if this is the case will one of the motions carry the body between the two parallel, straight lines describing the other motion. As we have seen, this assumption indicates that Newton describes and explains the phenomenon – the interaction of inertia and attractive force – using an oriented representation of space.

Someone assuming a centered representation of space, by contrast, would object to Newton's treatment of the moving body. He or she would complain that parallel sides of Newton's parallelogram do not bear the same relation to any center, including the center of force, and therefore do not signify motion in one and the same direction. For example, the side of the parallelogram describing the motion caused by the attractive force at the beginning of the moment is directed toward the center of force, but its pair is not. Thus, the parallel sides represent, Newton's interlocutor would claim, different motions. Newton's presuppositions about how direction is described would be seen as illegitimate.

This example, finally, returns us to the broader historical question. Newton's proposition assumes that both inertial and attractive/gravitational phenomena are described using an oriented representation of space. Yet natural philosophers working in the Aristotelian tradition at the beginning of the seventeenth century described and explained such phenomena on the basis of a centered representation of space. This, then, is the first part of the thesis to be defended in this book: the seventeenth century witnessed a profound and rapid shift in the representation of space used by natural

[17] Corollary I of the Laws (Newton 1999, 417–18).

philosophers to understand the physical world. A convergent, heterogeneous, and anisotropic representation of space was replaced by a self-parallel, homogeneous, and isotropic framework. Descriptions of spatial phenomena were centered at the beginning of the period and oriented at its end.[18]

Reciprocal iteration

Beyond establishing *that* a shift in the prevailing representation of space actually occurred during the early modern period, I can try to say something about *how* that shift came about. How, that is, were inertial and gravitational phenomena brought into an oriented framework by early modern authors? How were inertia and gravitation *rectified?* I will tell this story in what follows. To prepare the ground for my narrative, though, I should first describe in general terms the intellectual mechanism that produced the new representation of space.

As I have argued, theories consist of two distinct epistemic levels, the explanations provided by a theory, including the descriptions contained therein, and the descriptive frameworks that enable their production. The former are propositional. They represent some fact about the world in some representational language and attach that fact to some explanatory principle upon which the theory is based. Descriptive frameworks are *coordinative*, linking a description with its phenomenal extension. Successful theories provide explanations of phenomena via description of those phenomena. That is, the phenomena are represented by descriptive explananda that can be linked to the available explanantia. The physical explanation applies to the description, and the description is coordinated with the observed phenomena. A complete, satisfactory theory thus makes phenomena intelligible.

By the same token, however, a theory can fail at two distinct interfaces: that between phenomena and description and that between description and explanation. In the first case, the descriptions of phenomena derivable from the theory – i.e., the predictions generated by the theory – fail to correspond to experience. This is an empirical failure. In the second case, the phenomena are described in such a way that they cannot be satisfactorily explained. The physical principles, as explanantia, do not lead to the descriptions, as explananda. This is an explanatory failure. We shall see instances of both failures in what follows.

---

[18] For a more (mathematically) rigorous characterization of various authors' representations of space (and time), see Earman (1989).

In the face of either kind of theoretical failure, a theorist can attempt to improve a theory in two ways. He or she might alter explanations to make phenomena intelligible, or he or she might alter the descriptions of the phenomena to bring them into line with existing explanations. In particular, he or she might describe phenomena in such a way that what lacked explanation before no longer stands in need of explanation, though the explanatory principles remain unchanged. To change a theory is to alter either epistemic layer within it. Altering either the descriptive framework or the explanatory principles generates a new theory. In both cases, the phenomena are made intelligible anew.[19]

Of course, altering a theory at either level raises the possibility, indeed the likelihood, of opening new gaps between the levels – new empirical or explanatory failures. These problems will then lead to new adjustments, and the process will repeat. Altogether, this suggests a *reciprocal iteration* model of scientific change, where the epistemic levels constituting a scientific theory slide across one another, each shift at one level supported by fixity at the other. There will be numerous examples of each mode of theoretical change in the historical account given here.[20]

Elsewhere, I have argued that a reciprocal iteration model offers a defense of the rationality of scientific change against post-Kuhnian worries about incommensurability.[21] The present project, however, is not an attempt to comment generally on the problems related to conceptual change in science, and the historical account I will elaborate is specific to the investigation of representations of space. Hence, I will not claim that the reciprocation follows any strict pattern. The adjustments made at each of the levels by the authors discussed are, for the most part, unique and peculiar to the circumstances. In particular, I do not offer an account of the scientific and cognitive values by which a theory is judged satisfactory. By outlining a process of reciprocal iteration, I only mean to suggest that the process of conceptual and theoretical change can be traced through the

[19] Emily Grosholz (2007) gives a similar account, involving non-verbal representations in particular. She argues that divergence between the "symbolic" and the "iconic" modes of a representation allow for "productive ambiguity" leading to scientific progress. The symbolic mode of a representation captures its relationship to the theory in which it is embedded, and is comparable to the conceptual role of the representation. The iconic mode relates the representation to the object represented, and is analogous to the coordinative definition. Grosholz's notion that the two modes can shift with respect to one another is thus aligned with my own suggestion of reciprocal iteration.

[20] Hasok Chang (2004) suggests a similar model of iterative progress, in which change is effected by successive corrections to theories. He calls this "epistemic iteration," "a process in which successive stages of knowledge, each building on the preceding one, are created in order to enhance the achievement of certain epistemic goals" (45).

[21] Miller (2011a).

works examined. It is open to investigation, rather than buried in the inscrutable workings of genius.[22]

I will argue that the process of intellectual development by which physics adopted an oriented representation of space was reciprocal iteration. The development of physical understanding at the level of explanation was both enabled by and a cause of the shifts in descriptive frameworks I aim to illustrate. Changing representations of space allowed the development of novel physical explanations, and the development of explanations brought about the shifts in representations.

The epistemology and the metaphysics of space

I must forestall a looming misapprehension. Representations of space are not depictions of *space itself*. A representation of space does not describe space *qua* entity. Rather, a representation of space is the set of coordinations by which the spatial features of phenomena are formulated into a descriptive representation. It is part of the process of *representing* spatial facts in some expressive language, verbal or otherwise. When I say, for example, that an author uses a centered representation of space, I am not asserting that the author believes that space has a center or is anisotropic, etc., though he may do so. I am merely asserting that the author uses a stipulated central location in order to describe phenomena occurring in space, and thus represents spatial phenomena *as* anisotropic. Thus, 'representation' here is an action-noun, not an object-noun. It refers to the "representing"; for instance when two motions through space are represented by the description "the same motion" or "motion downwards." A representation of space is the con-struction of spatial representations, not itself a spatial representation.

By focusing on representations of space, therefore, I am limiting my subject to spatial epistemology, excluding spatial metaphysics. I am inter-ested in the epistemic role of the representation of space in physical theories, not in the properties of space itself. These lines of inquiry pose rather different questions. I will ask how an author generates descriptions of locations, directions, motions, and so on. I will not ask if an author believes space to be infinite, eternal, void, a plenum, absolute, relative, etc.

This is not to say, though, that spatial metaphysics and representations of space are completely independent, nor that the authors I discuss did not

---

[22] Of course, nothing prevents this project from being used as evidence for a general model of theoretical or conceptual change. This historical study can establish desiderata such models might be expected to satisfy. Models can then be tested against the actual theoretical and conceptual changes described here. The historical account is grist for the philosophical mill.

have anything to say about the ontology of space. Questions about the ontology of space spawned significant lines of inquiry in natural philosophy leading up to and throughout the period examined here. In particular, authors like Nicholas of Cusa, Bernardino Telesio, Francesco Patrizi, Giordano Bruno, Thomas Digges, Thomas Campanella, and Henry More laid the foundation for oriented representations of space by suggesting the infinitude of space. It is hard to imagine how a finite space might be limited if one employs an oriented representation of space, because that representation does not offer privileged places, so any spatial limit would be arbitrarily located. A centered space, by contrast, befits spatial finitude, since the limiting bound could be located at a certain distance from the center.[23] Later, Descartes, Newton, Leibniz, Huygens, and others, drawing upon the scientific theories discussed below, vehemently disputed the existence of void space and whether space had an absolute existence *per se* or was merely the set of relations between bodies.

Nevertheless, these philosophical considerations were tangential to the construction of physical theories. Metaphysical considerations only applied external constraints on the explanatory projects faced by natural philosophers. Certain kinds of explanation might be ruled in or out on metaphysical grounds. Within these constraints, however, natural philosophers still had to go about the task of actually fitting explanations to phenomena, which called upon a representation of space. As I hope to show, early modern physicists altered their representations of space not in response to metaphysical commitments regarding space itself, but because of explanatory difficulties they encountered while trying to understand nature. In my view, what is more important for the history and philosophy *of science* is the way space was incorporated *in the science*. But this is just to say that the focus of investigation should be the representations of space that make up the coordinative frameworks in the scientific theories proposed by historical figures, insofar as they were acting as scientists.[24] My concern is exclusively with the way representations of space are used in scientific theories. I leave speculations about the metaphysics of space aside.

Therefore, as noted at the outset, this project covers significantly different territory from most of the literature on early modern space, which emphasizes more abstract metaphysical questions. Consider, as a case in point, Alexandre Koyré's seminal *From the Closed World to the Infinite*

[23] Thanks to Benjamin Hill and Henrik Lagerlund for raising this point.
[24] Julian Barbour (2001, 49) offers a relevant admonition: "We must be prepared to encounter the concepts of space and motion of both the philosopher and the natural scientist and realize that they need not be the same – even when one and the same person is involved."

Universe, which argues that the central development concerning space in the Scientific Revolution was the "destruction of the Cosmos," by which Koyré meant the "disappearance ... of the conception of the world as a finite, closed, and hierarchically ordered whole ... and its replacement by an indefinite and even infinite universe."[25] For Koyré, then, the key to the emergence of classical science was an acceptance of an infinite, homogeneous space. However, as Koyré himself notes, Kepler believed that space was finite and Galileo had nothing to say one way or the other. As a result, for Koyré's historical thesis, Kepler is a recalcitrant anomaly and Galileo is irrelevant.[26] Yet nobody was more important to the theoretical developments of the period! By focusing on representations of space and the shift from a centered to an oriented spatial framework, I can better account for the significance of their contributions. I can also focus on the physical theories of Gilbert, Kepler, Galileo, Descartes, Newton, *et al.*, for which the period is rightly famed, as opposed to the speculative philosophies of Cusa, Telesio, Patrizi, Bruno, Digges, Campanella, More, *et al.*, which figure so prominently in the existing literature, Koyré included.

On the other hand, this project *is* continuous with studies of space-time for the post-Newtonian period leading to Einstein, which include a focus on what amounts to representations of space in the emerging consideration of affine structure.[27] Representations of space are more obvious in this context because the "shape of space" becomes a more explicit part of physical explanation in the move toward general relativity.

Caveats and qualifications

There are some other thorny issues that can be set aside at the outset. These concern technicalities that might form stumbling blocks for the more philosophically specialized, but might not be of interest to the general reader, who should feel free to skip this section.

First, note that I am using 'description' in a very loose sense. I use the term to refer to any representation of a (putative) fact about the world. This need not take the canonical form of a description-sentence, 'x is p', where x is some definite or indefinite term and p is some predicate clause.[28] Indeed, 'description' in my sense can also apply to non-verbal representations of phenomena, such as charts, graphs, pictures, diagrams, and so on. The

---

[25] Koyré (1957, 2).   [26] See Koyré (1957, chs. 3 & 4, esp. 95).
[27] In particular, I refer to the work of Robert DiSalle (2006). See also Nerlich (1976), Earman (1989), Nerlich (1994), Brown (2005).
[28] See Ludlow (2004).

argument applies to these cases, as well, since they also require some descriptive framework to coordinate elements of the representation with features of the phenomena represented. A "term" in those instances is an element of the representation that can be coordinated with a feature of the phenomena.[29] By defining descriptions in this manner, I want to avoid the concern that legitimate explanations can be provided in which no sentential descriptions appear.[30] My interest is not the syntactic form of a description, but its content – whether and how it specifies a phenomenal fact.[31]

Note that descriptions are relativized to the context in which they are generated and interpreted. The status of a description does not depend on the actual existence or observability of the entities it purports to describe. Suppose, for example, a magician explains the fall of an apple by appealing to malign astral influences. His putative explanation would include descriptions of astral influences and their behavior – even though, so far as we know, astral influences do not really exist. Nevertheless, legitimate descriptions can be generated according to the magician's descriptive framework. He must have in mind a set of criteria under which he takes the application of the terms of his descriptions to be appropriate. Similarly, a physicist standing over a cloud chamber can legitimately point to a vapor trail and say "that is an electron," even if the electron itself is not observable. The physicist, by dint of training and experience, has learned the conditions under which the description is applicable. Descriptive frameworks can permit the description of non-existent and unobservable things.

On the other hand, philosophers of science usually require that the statements constituting an explanation be *true*, in some relevant sense. In the case of descriptions, they require that they accurately reflect facts about the world, however that accuracy is measured.[32] The historical aims of my project require the relaxation of this requirement. This is a historical study of outdated theories. It would be anachronistic to say that because the theories turned out to be wrong, the accounts of phenomena their

---

[29] On representation in science, see Van Fraassen (2008).

[30] For instance, Paul Humphreys (1989) has suggested that explanations can be legitimately invoked that have noun-clauses as explananda. He suggests that explanations can be given for "the increase in volume of a gas maintained at constant pressure; of the high incidence of recidivism among first-time offenders; of the occurrence of paresis in an individual; [etc.]" These possible explananda are not sentences. Nevertheless, these terms do specify facts about the world. In Humphreys's words, they specify "usually explicitly, sometimes implicitly . . . the occurrence or change of a property associated with a system" (298). Hence, they would qualify as descriptions in my sense.

[31] See Scriven (1988, 65–66).

[32] Otherwise, one is forced to accept the "awkward consequence" that "originally [an] explanatory account was a correct explanation, but that it ceased to be one later, when unfavorable evidence was discovered" (Hempel 1965, 248).

proponents provide are not explanations. Instead, so long as an account is proposed as an explanation, I will treat it as an explanation. I require only that an author accept, given whatever resources he or she has to hand at the time, that his or her assertions adequately account for the phenomenon in question. (The principle of charity will lead me to assume that this is usually the case.) I will say that, whether or not an explanation is correct, it is still an explanation.[33]

This does not imply that anything goes; there are constraints. In particular, despite my argument that explanations necessarily include descriptions, I do not mean to suggest that explanations are merely descriptions. Explanations are distinct from descriptions insofar as they evince some sort of active principle or entity. In other words, an explanation, by either its structure or content, should relate the phenomenon in question to some underlying productive *cause*.[34] Suppose that it is possible to deduce, from a series of descriptions of the present behavior of a physical system, any past or future behavior of that system. Unless the deduction appeals to causes, I would not count the deduction as an explanation of the system's behavior. A prediction or retrodiction, in other words, does not an explanation make.[35] A seventeenth-century case in point is the distinction between astronomy and physics. In general, most commentators thought astronomy was primarily concerned with providing *descriptions* of the motions of the heavens, which could then be used to predict and retrodict planetary positions. The astronomical systems of Ptolemy and Copernicus alike were seen as calculating methods, not explanations of the motions they described. To *explain* celestial phenomena, even after Copernicus, philosophers relied on Aristotelian physical theories, which appealed to the nature of celestial matter as the *cause* of its motion.[36] Explanations include an appeal to causes. Descriptions can include causes, but need not.[37]

---

[33] For a more extended discussion of this historiographical issue, see Skinner (1988, 246–47), Garber (2001, ch. 1).

[34] With this caveat, I am again following most post-positivist philosophers who have cautiously rejected Humean skepticism about the epistemic accessibility of causal relationships. My intuition is that, in the words of Wesley Salmon (1989, 46), the "commonsense notion of explanation seems to take it for granted that to explain some particular event is to identify its cause and, possibly, point out the causal connection."

[35] For a contemporary take on this matter, see Salmon's distinction between explanatory and descriptive knowledge (1989, 126–35).

[36] See Chapter 2. As we shall see in Chapter 4, Kepler broke with this tradition and tried to unify physics and astronomy. See Westman (1975), Jardine (1984), Barker and Goldstein (2001). For more general accounts of early modern causal reasoning, see Jardine (1976), Wallace (1981, 1988), Dear (1998), Nadler (1998).

[37] I leave it as an open question as to *how* causes can appear in explanations. It is entirely possible that causes appear *in* descriptions. That is, part of the explanans might consist of *descriptions of causes* and

Note, though, that the seventeenth-century palette of acceptable "causes" was much broader than today's. One effect of the Scientific Revolution has been a severe limitation of what can count as a cause.[38] Though modern philosophers do not agree on what should and should not count as a cause, most would reject many of the causes proposed by early modern philosophers. Chief among these are the "natural," teleological causes central to Aristotelian accounts of nature, as well as the myriad "harmonies," "sympathies," and appeals to God's will. We will encounter a particularly idiosyncratic explanatory strategy in Kepler's appeal to planetary minds, for instance. While the status of these as causes was questioned during the early modern period, there is no reason to dismiss them out of hand. Throughout the following, I will not advance any unified theory of causation, modern or otherwise. Instead, I will respect what each author himself considered a legitimate cause or legitimate causal explanation.

Plan of chapters

What follows can be read as a series of connected vignettes, each of which illustrates the layered structure of scientific understanding, the importance of representations of space, and the process of reciprocal iteration. I begin Chapter 2 with a discussion of Nicolaus Copernicus, who recognized a deep conflict between Aristotelian explanatory principles and the mathematical descriptions of planetary phenomena in Ptolemaic astronomy. Copernicus attempted to rectify the situation by replacing the Ptolemaic descriptions with his own, which he thought could be reconciled with Aristotelian explanations. Nevertheless, Copernicus's new astronomical hypotheses raised difficulties at both the explanatory and descriptive levels, with which subsequent authors were forced to deal.

Copernicus's successors thought that he had not provided an adequate explanation of the phenomena he described. They sought ways to fill this explanatory hole in his theory. Moreover, Copernicus described astronomical phenomena by presupposing "many centers." That is, he employed at least two different representations of space, each constructed around its own center. Though each of these frameworks was centered, they could not be brought together into a single descriptive framework applicable to all phenomena. Copernicus's successors were forced to adjust their

---

the ways they operate. I do not wish to prejudge this issue by claiming that descriptions, as a rule, do not include appeals to causes (though *mere* descriptions, by definition, do not). I only wish to claim that explanations *do*.

[38] See Joy (2008) for a survey of developments in early modern explanation.

representations of space to render his descriptions commensurable with themselves and with the explanations they provided. These difficulties were especially well illustrated by the "third motion" of the earth, which was a problem of significant interest to those following Copernicus.

Chapters 3 and 4 examine the rectification of celestial and (ultimately) gravitational phenomena, beginning with the work of William Gilbert. I provide a detailed exposition of Gilbert's *De Magnete*, where he employs what I call a *geographical* representation of space appropriate to his subject matter. My main interest, though, is Gilbert's treatment of the "third motion." Unable satisfactorily to explain this "motion," Gilbert re-described it as a stasis. To do so, though, Gilbert added a presupposed rectilinear orientation to his representation of space. This simplified Gilbert's explanatory task, and constituted a move toward an oriented representation of cosmic space.

Johannes Kepler, as I discuss in Chapter 4, sought a reconciliation of astronomical explanations and descriptions. This project, as Kepler describes in a 1605 letter to David Fabricius, was frustrated by a problem similar to that posed by Copernicus's "third motion." At a crucial juncture, Kepler was inspired by Gilbert's solution to that difficulty. The solution, though, entailed the use of an oriented representation to describe and explain an important aspect of the planetary motions.

Turning to the effect of Copernicanism on inertial phenomena, the work of Galileo is examined in Chapter 5. Galileo sought to explain phenomena on a moving earth. To do so, he added an inertial principle to the theory of motion. Over the course of his career, he eventually coordinated this with a centered spatial framework. However, he used an oriented framework to generate approximate descriptions of some terrestrial phenomena.

In Chapter 6, I show that René Descartes, perhaps influenced by his early work in optics and geometry proper, adopted as fundamental an oriented representation of space in order to describe and explain inertial phenomena, thereby reversing Galileo's approximation. He used this descriptive framework to describe and explain small-scale phenomena – the collisions between individual bodies, which he took to be the sole physical interactions in the natural world. This representation of space was also associated with metaphysical considerations about the basis of physical laws and our knowledge of them. Descartes, however, did not know how to extend his oriented treatment of individual collisions to the behavior of ensembles of bodies. As a result, he continued to use a centered framework when dealing with large-scale phenomena, including cosmic vortices. Nevertheless, we find in Descartes's work, for the first time, a space that is self-parallel, homogeneous, and isotropic. I then describe how Pierre de Fermat and

Gilles Personne de Roberval picked up on these essential features of Descartes's system. In particular, Fermat and Roberval introduced the use of the parallelogram rule for the composition of motions, which depends upon an oriented representation of space.

In Chapter 7, I discuss the work of Isaac Newton, who, after a critical interaction with Robert Hooke, finally synthesized the celestial and terrestrial developments into a universally applicable oriented representation of space. This modern synthesis is exemplified in the use of the parallelogram rule mentioned above. A short conclusion then follows.

One final disclaimer. Obviously, there is no way a book such as this one could be a complete history of representations of space, even in the Scientific Revolution. I have only skipped a stone across the surface. It has picked out certain points that exemplify the story I wish to tell, but I have yet to follow the interlacing ripples emanating from those points. Much more can be said about each of the authors I have discussed, and it is possible to tie their thoughts to others I have not mentioned. This is a preliminary sketch. The picture is still bare.

CHAPTER 2

Pluribus ergo existentibus centris: *explanations, descriptions, and Copernicus*

Why a new astronomy?

Historians of science have extensively examined the ultimately affirmative reception of Nicolaus Copernicus's heliocentric astronomy in the Scientific Revolution it helped bring about. Yet any study of a revolution must inevitably inquire after its cause, and here remains something of a puzzle. Namely, what motivated Copernicus to propose an alternative to the Ptolemaic geocentric theory in the first place? Ptolemy's system had been accepted for over a millennium, unaltered in essence and successively refined in application since first set down in the second century. Yet, at the beginning of the sixteenth century, Copernicus saw Ptolemaic astronomy as somehow inadequate. There was some problem with the geocentric system that Copernicus took it upon himself to solve. What was that problem?[1]

My purpose in raising this question is not to delve into the technical details of the genesis of Copernican heliocentric astronomy, which have been well documented elsewhere.[2] Rather, my interest is in the intellectual motivations that led Copernicus to question the Ptolemaic *status quo*. As it happens, Copernicus could not have been motivated by empirical failures in Ptolemaic astronomy, since there were none serious enough to merit drastic revision. Instead, Copernicus's innovation emerged from a resurgent

---

[1] Robert Westman (2011) calls this the "Copernican Question." He argues that Copernicus sought an alternative to Ptolemy in order to defend astrological prognostication from a specific criticism (raised by Pico della Mirandola): astrologers could not agree on the proper ordering of the planets. Heliocentrism helps in this regard because the planets are patently ordered by their periods. This may indeed be part of the story. However, Westman himself admits that the evidence for this view is sketchy, at best: "we know of no horoscopes that he [Copernicus] cast, no prognostications that he issued, and no orations in praise of astrology such as were commonplace in his lifetime" (104–05). Swerdlow (2012) has shown that this is not quite true – there is indirect evidence of Copernicus's interest in astrology – though he also harshly dismisses Westman's view, as does Heilbron (2012). For a summary of competing accounts, see Westman (2011, 56–60).
[2] See, e.g., Swerdlow and Neugebauer (1984).

Averroism in the Renaissance university contexts in which he was schooled. Copernicus was thus a participant in a debate about the priorities of astronomical research stretching back through the medieval period to antiquity.

My argument for this claim affords an opportunity to introduce several themes related to the overarching view of science and scientific change expressed by this book. First, the history of Renaissance astronomy reveals the structure of scientific knowledge. Scientific theories are constituted by the explanations that make phenomena intelligible and the descriptions that convey those explanations to the world. A successful theory, therefore, satisfactorily interfaces *both* descriptions to the world *and* explanations to descriptions. Conversely, scientific theories can be judged unsatisfactory either because they fail to describe experience, or because they describe experience in a way that is not compatible with available explanations. Failures at either interface motivate scientific change. While Ptolemaic astronomy was conscientiously concerned with reconciling theory and experience, the Averroists focused on the epistemic interface within the theory and insisted Ptolemaic astronomy could not reconcile descriptions with explanations. This was the explanatory problem Copernicus sought to address.

Second, the discussion illuminates the importance of representations of space in the physical sciences. One of the Averroists' crucial criticisms of Ptolemaic astronomy concerned its description of spatial properties – its representation of space. As noted in Chapter 1, Aristotle's physics depended on a representation of space related to a single, universal center. It could not be made to account for the Ptolemaic descriptive system, which posited a multiplicity of motions around a multiplicity of centers. Averroists insisted that this was a fundamental and insurmountable obstacle to Ptolemaic astronomy's reconciliation with the Aristotelian physics meant to explain celestial motions.

Finally, the episode begins to show how scientific change can come about via a reciprocal iteration among the epistemic levels constituting scientific knowledge. Renaissance Averroism renewed interest in the interface between descriptions and explanations and the problem of multiple centers, and Copernicus was among several astronomers who again sought to reconcile observational astronomy with physics. However, Copernicus was not a radical Averroist who rejected Ptolemy outright, as did some of his peers. Instead, he remained faithful to Ptolemaic astronomy as far as he could. He was also primarily a mathematical astronomer, in the end mostly unreflective about physical explanations. Thus, Copernicus did not solve the problem Averroës had raised. Like Ptolemy, he posited a multiplicity of centers, contrary to the demands of Aristotelian physics.

This difficulty was especially evident in Copernicus's description of the "third motion," which accounted for the fact that the earth's rotational axis remains parallel to itself as the earth orbits the sun. The description of this phenomenon *as a motion* is a consequence of Copernicus's representation of space, but such a motion could not be readily explained. That is, a new gap between explanations and descriptions opened as a result of Copernicus's heliocentric astronomy. Subsequent authors struggling with this problem were led to novel and ultimately non-Aristotelian explanations of the heavens and the natural world. The "third motion," that is, brought about a reciprocal iteration among the epistemic levels of scientific knowledge. A change of descriptions to save explanations led to changes of explanations to save descriptions.

The problems of astronomy

What caused Copernicus to question Ptolemy? On many interpretations, theoretical innovation is motivated only by failures at the interface between the theory (taken as a whole) and experience, so new theories are generated only in the face of anomalous or recalcitrant phenomena.[3] However, Copernicus cannot have been motivated by empirical failure, since the corpus of astronomical observations he sought to accommodate had remained largely unaltered since the Alfonsine Tables were compiled in the thirteenth century. A handful of observers, including Copernicus, had added a few new observations since, but these were insignificant in comparison to the voluminous recordings of planetary positions handed down from antiquity. In any case, all observations available at the time of Copernicus could be and were accommodated to the Ptolemaic view. There was no outstanding, extensive set of problematic observations, either newly discovered or slowly accumulated, that demanded novel explanation.[4] Indeed, even in the end, the Copernican system did not appreciably improve

[3] Most famously, this is the view of Thomas Kuhn (1996), who argued that new scientific "paradigms" are adopted when anomalies overwhelm predominant theories. But this view is also perhaps the most enduring legacy of twentieth-century empiricism in the philosophy of science. It was a core tenet of logical positivism that theories succeed insofar as they "save the phenomena," and even the post-positivist Quine held that science is tested by the "tribunal of sense experience" (1951, 38).

[4] There were some predictive errors. For instance, as a student in 1500, Copernicus observed a conjunction of Saturn, Jupiter, and Mars where he noted a discrepancy with the Ptolemaic Alfonsine Tables of over two degrees for Mars and one and a half degrees for Saturn (Gingerich 2004, 59). But these empirical failures were by no means decisive, since Ptolemaic parameters could be adjusted, and Copernicus's ultimate system would do just as poorly.

predictive accuracy over its predecessor. Certainly, Copernicus himself never suggested his system was empirically superior.[5] Nor could Copernicus have been motivated by descriptive simplicity. The supposition that Ptolemaic astronomy had become too cumbersome as subsequent refinements added "epicycles on epicycles" in order to improve its empirical accuracy has been shown to be a modern misconception, and the Copernican system was not appreciably simpler than Ptolemy's.[6]

Copernicus, moreover, was not alone in thinking there was a problem with Ptolemaic astronomy. In fact, he was one of several astronomers of his generation to propose alternatives to the Ptolemaic system, as we shall see. Copernicus's work also generated a great deal of interest even before the publication of his *magnum opus*, *De Revolutionibus Orbium Coelestium*, in 1543.[7] An early treatise setting out the rudiments of heliocentrism, the *Commentariolus*, circulated widely in manuscript. A Lutheran scholar, Georg Joachim Rheticus, was inspired by rumors of Copernicus's system to leave Germany in order to throw himself at the feet of the Catholic canon at Frauenburg, in northern Poland, and later to publish a "first report," the *Narratio Prima*, of Copernicus's ideas. Rheticus and others also spent years cajoling Copernicus into publishing the *De Revolutionibus*, which was read attentively, if sparsely, throughout Europe.[8] Thus, Copernicus's contemporaries attributed, even before it was widely understood, great significance to his view, which is to say they took it seriously as a possible solution to some problem. Again, what was that problem?

The excitement of Copernicus's peers points to the broader context of astronomical science. There was something about the Ptolemaic system that bothered scholars. But how could an astronomical theory, such as Ptolemy's, fail? How, that is, could there be a problem in astronomical science? This is a question about the structure of astronomical knowledge, and to respond one must turn to the history of astronomy to understand its first constitution as a science.

The natural philosophers of antiquity ascribed uniform rotations to the heavens. This motion, it was explained, resulted from the near perfection of the celestial bodies themselves. The rotation of a circle or sphere in place was the least amount of change a physical body could undergo, and thus was the closest thing to immortal and complete being in the physical cosmos. The heavenly bodies, forever returning to their previous positions in the sky, neither came to be nor perished, never changed in shape, size,

---

[5] See Goldstein (2002), Gingerich (2004, 57–60).   [6] See Gingerich (1975), Swerdlow (2004).
[7] Copernicus (1543, 1976, 1978, 2002).   [8] On the book's reception, see Gingerich (2004).

color, or any other quality, and had nowhere outside their own orbits to go. They constituted, in Plato's words, "a moving image of eternity,"[9] far different and apart from the corruptible bodies of the terrestrial realm, which were always altering their appearance and moving about from place to place.

For Aristotle, the heavens were the realm of divine, intelligent, infinitely powerful beings manifesting as much perfection as possible. They were subject to some change, since they were material and thus contained some potency (as opposed to, for example, a non-material and strictly unchanging Platonic Form). However, change in the heavens was the simplest change possible, since for Aristotle, perfection consisted in the complete actualization of potential, and change was a transition from potency to act. If they underwent anything but the barest minimum of change, the heavenly beings' potential would be sometimes less than optimally actualized and this was inconceivable. It followed that the celestial bodies were necessarily spherical, the simplest, most homogeneous shape. They were also eternal, since any generation or corruption required unactualized potential from which or into which the sphere might change. The heavens all consisted of one essence – the "quintessence" or aether – because the spheres could not suffer change of quality, since this, too, would require unactualized potential. Nor could the spheres change their places at fixed distances from the center of the universe, since this would require unactualized locations, the mere potency to be someplace else. The only change available to a celestial sphere, then, was rotation in place around the center of the universe – a movement of itself into itself, of actuality into actuality. And this rotation would have to be uniform, since alteration of speed also required the sometimes unactualized potential to move faster. Uniform rotation of the heavens around the center was therefore a direct consequence of the privileged role of the heavens in Aristotle's (and most ancients') cosmology. Their near perfection, their almost pure actuality, entailed their uniform rotation.

Of course, uniform rotation is the most apparent motion of the heavenly bodies. The stars, sun, moon, and planets all traverse the dome of the sky from east to west once a day, parallel to the equator. Indeed, most stars move *only* this way, returning to the same positions night after night. But this is not the only motion visible among the celestial bodies. Against the background of the uniform rotation of the "fixed" stars, the sun, moon, and planets can be seen to move about in periods longer than a day. These additional motions all generally follow the ecliptic, the path of the sun's

---

[9] *Timaeus* 37c–e (Plato 1997, 1241).

motion through the constellations of the zodiac at a 23½ degree angle to the equator, and they all usually progress from west to east, contrary to the diurnal motion of the stars.

Here, however, the generalities end, for the motions of the planetary bodies exhibit several "anomalies" – irregular digressions from uniform circular motion. In longitude, parallel to the ecliptic, their motions speed up and slow down. The sun, for instance, moves at different speeds in the course of a year, so the seasons are of different length. Some of the planets even stop, reverse their direction entirely, and "retrogress" from east to west, before becoming stationary again and then continuing along as before. And all of these motions are compounded by similar irregularities in latitude, perpendicular to the ecliptic. Moreover, the heavens also display some striking changes of appearance. This was most notable in the phases of the moon, but the apparent sizes of the moon and Mars (and perhaps Venus[10]) were known by the ancients to vary, as well. Obviously, the heavens did not display the minimum of change – uniform rotation – expected on the ancients' understanding of their nature.

This, then, was the problem facing the early astronomers: how to coordinate that which could be explained – uniform rotation – with the irregular appearances of the heavens. This coordination was to be carried out by a descriptive system. A successful astronomical theory, then as now, would enable the application of explanatory power from the physical principles to the observed phenomena via the description of those phenomena. By the same token, an astronomical theory could fail in two ways. The descriptions might deviate from the phenomena – what I have called an empirical failure. Or the explanatory principles might fail to fit with the descriptions generated by the descriptive framework – an explanatory failure. I will argue that Copernicus altered his descriptions of the phenomena in the face of what he thought was the explanatory failure of Ptolemaic astronomy, though Copernicus inspired subsequent authors to generate new explanations to solve the explanatory failures in his own theory.

Eudoxus, Aristotle, and Ptolemy

In practice, ancient astronomers seeking to explain the celestial appearances had to introduce a diversity of motions into the heavens, contrary to the supposed perfection of the celestial realm. The irregularity observed in the heavens could then be described as the summary effect of multiple uniform

[10] Bowen (2002, 161–62).

rotations, which were each individually explicable by the nature of the heavens. By late antiquity, there were two leading astronomical theories along these lines.[11] They shared the physical principle that natural motion of the heavens was uniform rotation in place. They differed in the way uniform rotation was ascribed to the heavens.

In Eudoxan astronomy, first espoused by Eudoxus of Cnidus in the fourth century BC, the irregular motions of the planetary bodies were described as the conjoined action of concentric spheres. Each sphere rotates uniformly around its own axis, but the poles of the axis are embedded in the sphere just outside it, and are thus carried about by the uniform rotation of the outer sphere. A series of such interconnected spheres could account for irregular and retrograde motions of a planet located at some point on the innermost sphere. In Eudoxus's own system, the stars were carried by one sphere, and each planetary body required three or four interlocking spheres.

The success of the Eudoxan theory lay primarily at the interface between explanation and description. Its description of the heavenly motions as the result of interlocking spheres corresponded well with the explanation provided by physical theory: the uniform rotation of spheres concentrically arranged around the center of the universe. The irregular motions of the planetary bodies did demand some diversity in the heavens, thus reducing their perfection, but there was at least no diversity in the *kind* of motion in the heavens. All motions were uniform rotations around a single center, and they only differed in speed and the relative direction of their axes. Indeed, Aristotle himself adopted Eudoxus's theory as the foundation of his own.

The problem with the Eudoxan system lay at the other interface – that between experience and description. The Eudoxan system, that is, suffered empirical failures. One problem was the fact that the changing apparent size of the planetary bodies could not be accounted for. Since the planets themselves did not change, this had to be caused by the optical effect of changes in distance to the planets. However, the planets were all supposed to move on concentric spheres centered on the earth, so their distance from the earth was constant, according to the theory. Eudoxan astronomy, therefore, predicted no change in the apparent diameter of the planets. Yet such changes were observed. This objection, it seems, was raised by

---

[11] I have ignored the Pythagorean astronomical system of Philolaus and the geokinetic theories of Heraclides and Aristarchus. While these theories are interesting in the light of Copernicus, since they held that the earth moves and the fixed stars are stationary, they failed to gain much attention after Ptolemy. Thus, they did not play a large part in motivating Copernicus, though he found encouragement in them once he began seeking alternatives to Ptolemy. For the sake of brevity, I leave them out of the narrative. See Dreyer (1953, chs. 2, 6), Neugebauer (1957), Copernicus (1978, 4–5).

Autolycus and helped bring about the general abandonment of Eudoxan astronomy.[12]

Another problem, which was to have more significance later, was that, though a system of concentric spheres could account for the irregularities in the heavens in principle, it was impossible for such a system to yield anything like tolerably accurate predictions of planetary motions. Eudoxan spheres could account for the qualities of planetary motion; they could be made to produce irregular and retrograde motions. They could not, however, produce the *actual* motion of a planet across the sky.

The main difficulty here, it is worth noting, was that the Eudoxan system did not allow many degrees of freedom in its representation of a planet's motion. In the four-sphere account of a planet's motion, the outermost sphere always represented the diurnal motion, and the second outermost the mean ecliptic motion of the planet. Thus, all the irregularities in a planet's motion had to be accounted for by the motions of the two innermost spheres, which were entirely determined by the angle between their axes and the difference between their rotational speeds. (On some reconstructions of the theory, even this latter parameter had a fixed value, such that the two spheres were supposed to rotate at the same speed in opposite senses.) Thus, for example, if the parameters of a four-sphere system were set to account for Mars's regression in longitude, the same system predicted motion in latitude such that the planet would be found outside the zodiac, where it was never observed. Three-sphere systems were even more constrained. Eudoxan astronomers could introduce more degrees of freedom by adding spheres to a planetary system – indeed, Calippus improved Eudoxus's system in this manner – but the improvement was marginal and calculationally cumbersome.[13]

On the other hand, this empirical failure of Eudoxan astronomy was not readily recognized. There was no Greek tradition of precise astronomical observation before the third century BC. Eudoxus and his immediate successors therefore had no extensive set of planetary observations against which to test the predictions of the theory. Planets were known to move

---

[12] Goldstein and Bowen (1983). See also Bowen (2002). There is some dispute as to the significance of this objection, and the exact causes of Eudoxan astronomy's fall from favor have not been clearly determined. Other factors might include the rise of Stoic philosophy, and the Greeks' encounter with Babylonian astrology in the centuries after Aristotle. Goldstein and Bowen argue that Babylonian arithmetical methods for planetary position predictions far surpassed the precision of the Greeks', and the Greek astronomers struggled to emulate their achievement. This may have been reinforced by Stoicism, which demanded one learn to predict phenomena in order to conform one's behavior to them. In any case, it does seem that some empirical deficiency told against the Eudoxan system.

[13] Yavetz (1998).

irregularly and retrogress, but that was all. Hence, there was essentially no need for descriptions of experience beyond the rough, qualitative characterizations generated by Eudoxan representations. Given the close agreement between explanatory principles and descriptive system, the Aristotelian–Eudoxan astronomy was complete and satisfactory. It *could* explain the motion of a planet, even its irregular and retrograde motion, described in general, qualitative terms like "irregular" and "retrograde."

The empirical failure of the Eudoxan system was not felt until the third century BC, when observers working at Alexandria began compiling detailed catalogues of stellar and planetary positions.[14] Once this concerted program of quantitative, observational astronomy got up and running, it became possible to test astronomical descriptions against an extensive set of observed motions. The Eudoxan astronomy was then definitively seen to fail, and new astronomical descriptions that better represented experience were devised. Thus, there began a shift away from "physical astronomy," which was primarily concerned with the explanation of celestial phenomena, toward "mathematical astronomy," which was primarily concerned with generating representations of celestial motions that allowed accurate calculations of observed planetary positions. That is, the emphasis among astronomers shifted from bridging the gap between explanation and description to bridging the gap between description and experience.

In this context arose the astronomical system brought to maturity by Ptolemy, who was active at Alexandria in the second century AD. Ptolemy, following a path blazed by Apollonius and Hipparchus, described the motions in the heavens as the conjoined motion of circles, each of which rotated uniformly around some, though not necessarily the same, center. In Ptolemaic astronomy, the longitudinal motion of a planet is typically accounted for by locating it on a small circular epicycle rotating around a center that is itself rotating around a larger circle, the deferent. The deferent, meanwhile, is an eccentric – its center does not coincide with the center of the universe (a point coincident with the center of the earth). Furthermore, the rotation of the deferent carrying the epicycle is not uniform with respect to its own center, but to a third center, the "equant point," such that the deferent follows the motion of a point uniformly rotating on a third circle centered on the equant. Each geometrical device – epicycle, eccentric, or equant – introduces some irregularity into the planet's motion.

The advantage of the Ptolemaic theory was its ability to accurately describe observed phenomena and generate precise predictions. Epicycles,

---

[14] Goldstein and Bowen (1983).

eccentrics, equants, and other such devices allow an extensive parameterization of the descriptive representation, since the relative sizes, speeds, and
central locations of the various circles can all be independently determined.
As a result, the Ptolemaic astronomical descriptions could be (and were)
carefully tuned to match observations. In the face of recalcitrant observations, parameters could be adjusted or new devices could be added to the
system to produce a better fit. The description, that is, could be engineered
to correspond with experience. This made the Ptolemaic system enor-
mously useful, given the numerous practical uses of astronomical predictions, most importantly in judicial and medical astrology.

On the other hand, the Ptolemaic astronomy did not carefully respect the
physical principles meant to explain celestial motions. The circles rotated
uniformly, but not around one and the same center, let alone the center of
the universe, and, in the case of equants, not even around their own centers.
Nor could the circles represent the equators of solid aethereal spheres, since
the circles (such as an epicycle on its deferent) interpenetrated. In the
Mathematike Syntaxis (*Mathematical Treatise*; better known by its
Latinized Arabic name, *Almagest*), Ptolemy explicitly acknowledges that
his ultimate aim is not a theoretical explanation of planetary motion, but a
description adequate for prediction:

> Rather, if we are at any point compelled by the nature of our subject to use a
> procedure not in strict accordance with theory . . . or [if we are compelled] to
> make some basic assumptions which we arrived at not from readily apparent
> principle, but from a long period of trial and application, or to assume a type
> of motion or inclination of the circles which is not the same and unchanged
> for all planets; we may [be allowed to] accede [to this compulsion], since we
> know that this kind of inexact procedure will not affect the end desired,
> provided that it is not going to result in any noticeable error; and we know
> too that assumptions made without proof, provided only that they are found
> to be in agreement with the phenomena, could not have been found without
> some careful methodological procedure, even if it is difficult to explain how
> one came to conceive them.[15]

Thus, for Ptolemy, the "end desired" was the absence of "noticeable error."
Mathematical expedients found by "trial and application," without basis in
theory or "readily apparent principle," were acceptable so long as the results
were "found to be in agreement with the phenomena." The ultimate goal
was empirical accuracy – accurate description of planetary positions, so that
the planet is, quite simply, where one predicts it to be at any given moment.
Explanation by appeal to first principles is of lesser importance to the

---

[15] Ptolemy (1984, 422–23).

descriptive project. Ptolemy was satisfied even if his models required some loosening of their ties to physical explanations. Whereas Eudoxan astronomy fastened description to explanation at the expense of empirical failure, Ptolemaic astronomy fixed description to experience at the expense of explanatory failure.

Note that the friction between Aristotelian physics and Ptolemaic astronomy arises from their respective representations of space and the resulting descriptions of motions. In Ptolemaic astronomy, circular motion at a constant angular speed around *any* center is deemed uniform. However, eccentric motions necessarily change a body's distance to a stipulated universal center. Since a body's place is described in relation to the universal center in Aristotelian physics, this entails that such rotations are changes of place – the body is sometimes moving higher and sometimes moving lower. Rotations around any center other than the center of the universe, on this view, *cannot* be a uniform motion – one can distinguish different parts of the motion. The Aristotelian representation of space does not allow rotations around multiple centers to be described as "simple" or "uniform" motions. Consequently, Aristotelian physics cannot explain such rotations as the natural motions of heavenly bodies, which are necessarily simple. By describing the planetary motions as the result of a multiplicity of eccentric motions, Ptolemaic astronomy offers descriptions of the phenomena that cannot be linked to the available explanations.

The trouble with Ptolemaic astronomy, then, did not lie at the interface between experience and theory, i.e., descriptions and explanations taken together. Rather, the difficulty lay at an interface *internal* to the theory: that between the description of the observed phenomena and their explanation. Ptolemy's astronomical descriptions were not compatible with the Aristotelian explanations by which celestial phenomena were to be understood. This was a problem with the Ptolemaic theory that vexed astronomers and philosophers from antiquity. Yet, how was that problem passed down to the time of Copernicus? How, that is, did it emerge among the Renaissance astronomers? It is to this history that I now turn.

The Ptolemaic compromise

The practical usefulness of epicycles, eccentrics, equants, and so on in Ptolemaic astronomy ensured that most astronomers of late antiquity and the Middle Ages adopted them. However, their loose connection to physical explanation, especially to the Aristotelian explanations that eventually came to predominate, remained problematic. Celestial appearances could not be made intelligible without some grounding in physical theory. As a result, astronomers and natural philosophers worked out something of a compromise as a way of cordoning off the difficulty.

In the first place, astronomers developed *physical* descriptions of the heavens to instantiate the mathematical representations used to calculate positions. The physical representations consisted of uniformly rotating spheres and could, on this score, be considered physically plausible. The mathematical representations were thus shown to correspond to physical representations, thereby linking them to physical explanation, at least in principle.

Ptolemy, for instance, was careful to maintain the principle of uniform rotation, even around several centers:

> [F]or, when uniform circular motion is preserved for all without exception, the individual phenomena are demonstrated in accordance with a principle which is more basic and more generally applicable than that of similarity of the hypotheses [for all planets].[16]

Uniform rotation renders the mathematical descriptions "demonstrable" by physical principles, even if the various models for the planets are not governed by more specific principles that make them all similar to one another. Ptolemy then provides a "demonstration" connecting the mathematical models to physical principles in a separate text, the *Planetary Hypotheses*. This begins where the *Almagest* leaves off:

> We have worked out . . . the models of heavenly motions through the books of the *Mathematical Syntaxis*, demonstrating by arguments, concerning each example, both the logicality and agreement everywhere with the phenomena, with a view to a presentation of uniform and circular motion, which necessarily was to arise in things taking part in eternal and orderly motion and that are not capable to undergo increase or decrease in any way.[17]

The text then proposes physical models for the *Almagest*'s geometrical representations. A planet is thought of as a sphere embedded in the rim of a solid "sawn-off piece" – a disc-like truncated sphere – that rolls around the inside of a larger hoop-like truncated spherical shell, like a cymbal in a tambourine rolling around the inside of a wagon wheel. The rotation of the smaller disc reproduces the motion of the epicycle, and its motion along the inside of the outer shell reproduces the motion of the deferent.[18] Using similar constructions, Ptolemy could connect his geometrical descriptions to the uniform rotation of solid (truncated) spheres, and from there to the

---

[16] Ptolemy (1984, 423).   [17] Hamm (2011, 44). See also Goldstein (1967).   [18] Murschel (1995)

physical principles of celestial motions. He could, in this way, explain the phenomena.

Ptolemy's *Planetary Hypotheses* was just one instance of a broader tradition of physical astronomy. A similar, widely adopted system completed Ptolemy's truncated spheres. Thus, an epicycle was identified with the equator of a small (complete) sphere turning in the space between inner and outer spherical shells. This spherical space, however, was not concentric with the center of these shells (so they varied in thickness), and thereby corresponded to an eccentric path. So as not to leave a void in the heavens, this space was also filled by another spherical shell, within which the epicylcic sphere was embedded "like a pearl in a ring."[19] Each planet, therefore, was carried about by a system of three or four solid, eccentric spheres. This physical system was also commonly used to compute distances from the earth to each planet's orbit, on the supposition that the outer surface of each planet's outer shell formed the inner surface of the next planet's inner shell, filling the heavens with nested solid spheres.[20]

A system along these lines was outlined by Theon of Smyrna, a near contemporary of Ptolemy. The idea then passed into the Arabic world and appeared in the work of Ibn al-Haytham (Alhazen) in the tenth and eleventh centuries, and then with thirteenth-century Marāgha and fourteenth-century Damascene astronomers. Eccentric spheres reappeared in the Latin West as the *theorica* tradition stemming from the late-thirteenth-century translation of Arabic scholarship, including al-Haytham, and bore its most famous fruit in Georg Peurbach's *Theoricae novae planetarum*, published numerous times after 1472.[21] The physical models showed the physical plausibility of descriptions of the heavens in terms of epicycles, eccentrics, and equants, and this mere plausibility was sufficient for astronomers to continue using and developing their geometrical representations as legitimate descriptions of the heavens. By pointing to these physical models, astronomers could insist that their science was complete. Astronomy explained the heavens, even if the details of the explanation were postponed or left for others.[22]

---

[19] Abu 'l Faraj in Dreyer (1953, 260).

[20] Ptolemy's *Planetary Hypotheses* were equivalent to this standard system, except he discarded the parts of the spheres where the planets never appeared as unnecessary, thus truncating ("sawing off") the spheres at the planets' maximum latitudes.

[21] Swerdlow and Neugebauer (1984, 48–50).

[22] Grant (1978, 280–84). For instance, Apollonius first proposed epicycles partly to account for the changing apparent diameter of the planets, since an epicycle ascribed a motion toward and away from the earth, but the representation was not generally accepted until Theon's system made it physically plausible (Dreyer 1953, 160).

The link between description and explanation was tenuous, however. The details of these physical systems were never worked out to the same degree of detail as the geometrical descriptions, so not all features of the latter could be "made physical" in terms of the former.[23] Moreover, these physical systems still required a large diversity of spheres and a multiplicity of centers, both violations of the supposed near-perfection of the heavens. In sum, the eccentric spheres were a gesture toward physical explanation to make the empirically successful Ptolemaic system palatable as a complete science. As Bruce Stephenson has put it, "The solid-sphere planetary models were really not so much a celestial physics as a reason why no one had ever developed any celestial physics."[24]

The second feature of the "Ptolemaic compromise" was the delineation of disciplinary boundaries between "astronomy" and natural philosophy. On the one hand, practical astronomers were responsible for "mathematical astronomy" – the collection, description, and prediction of celestial observations using mathematical representations. On the other hand, philosophers or "physical theorists" (*physikoi*) were responsible for "physical astronomy" – the explanation of the celestial phenomena by causal powers (*dynamē*). Thus, bridging the interfaces between experience, description, and explanation became, in effect, separate disciplines. This division had its roots in Aristotle's own distinctions among the sciences, particularly between mathematics and physics,[25] and was already in place by the turn of the modern era. Geminus of Rhodes is quoted as saying, in the first century BC:

> For, in general, it is not for astronomers to know what is by nature at rest and what sorts of things are moved. Instead, by introducing hypotheses [i.e., geometrical representations] of some things being stationary, others in motion, they investigate from which hypotheses the phenomena in the heavens will follow. But astronomers should take as first principles from physical theorists that the motions of the celestial bodies are simple, smooth, and orderly, and through these [principles] they will demonstrate that the choral dance of all [those bodies] is circular, with some revolving in parallel circles, others in oblique circles.[26]

The task of astronomers, in other words, is to describe phenomena, that of physicists to explain them.

We have already seen Ptolemy's separation of the descriptive *Almagest* from the explanatory *Planetary Hypotheses*. In the Middle Ages, this

---

[23] Murschel (1995, 50), Barker (1999, 345).   [24] Stephenson (1994, 26).
[25] *Physics* II.2 (Aristotle 1984, 1:330–32).
[26] Simplicius, *Commentary on Aristotle's Physics*, in Bowen (2007, 344). See also Dreyer (1953, 131–32).

disciplinary boundary was further entrenched by the advent of school curricula organized around the trivium and quadrivium in the fourth and fifth centuries, which made practical astronomy one of the quadrivium subjects, but left physics to "higher" learning in theology. Later, in the universities, mathematical astronomy was a practical science, relegated to the lesser Arts faculties, or to technical instruction outside the university altogether. Here the focus was on the application of astronomy, mainly in astrological prediction and medicine, making accuracy of the utmost importance. Physical astronomy, concerned as it was with the nature of things, was associated with the more prestigious Philosophy and Theology faculties, who were not equipped with the mathematical skills needed to address the empirical aspects of the subject. There was little interest in the practical applications of astronomy, and little interest in empirical accuracy. Hence, there was less and less cultural pressure for or intellectual interest in reconciling the two projects.[27]

Still, the two sides of the astronomical discipline never completely lost touch with one another. The persistence of the physical systems of solid spheres alone belies this suggestion. Rather, the different approaches reflected only a difference in emphasis on which epistemic interface took precedence.[28] Astronomers continued to recognize that the purpose of their science was to explain the observed phenomena – to make them intelligible. This required that descriptions be *both* accurate *and* physically plausible. The Ptolemaic astronomers that focused on descriptions were concerned with "saving the phenomena," but only in a way that could be grounded in physical principles. Hence, they accepted "as first principles from physical theorists that the motions of the celestial bodies are simple, smooth, and orderly."

In general, the Ptolemaic compromise remained the state of the astronomical art throughout the Middle Ages. Professional astronomers focused on refining the Ptolemaic geometrical devices to achieve ever-greater observational accuracy, while natural philosophers developed explanations, however tenuous, for Ptolemaic descriptions of the heavens.[29] Mathematical

---

[27] Blair (2008) provides a useful overview of disciplinary bounds in the early modern period.

[28] Pedersen (1978, 321).

[29] Contrary to some authors, this implies that mathematical astronomy was not "instrumentalist" or "fictionalist." Rather, it was realist insofar as it held that its models represented *possible* mechanisms of celestial movement, though skeptical insofar as these mechanisms were hypothetical, based on probable reasoning, and the actuality of the mechanisms was not supposed. The "instrumentalist" position that astronomical models were mere calculating devices for predicting observations, without any relevance to physical possibility or actuality, most notably the "Wittenberg interpretation" exemplified by Andreas Osiander's unsigned preface to the *De Revolutionibus*, was primarily an early modern innovation, though Petrus Ramus did set an earlier precedent. See Westman (1975), Jardine (1979), Westman (1980).

and physical astronomy were two practices within one astronomical science that continued to develop throughout the medieval period and into the Renaissance.[30]

The Averroist challenge: where is the center?

The Ptolemaic focus on mathematical astronomy was seriously challenged by medieval Arabic astronomers, most notably by a school of physical astronomy that emerged in Arabic Andalusia during the twelfth century, the leading figure of which was Ibn Rushd, known in Latin as Averroës. This Averroist school insisted on the priority of physical explanations of the natural world. Closing the explanatory gap, for them, took precedence over closing the empirical one. In particular, they insisted on the literal truth of Aristotle's natural philosophy. This ruled out of hand Ptolemy's system, since it could not, even in principle, be reconciled with Aristotle:

> For to assert the existence of an eccentric sphere or an epicyclic sphere is contrary to nature. As for the epicyclic sphere, this is not at all possible; for a body that moves in a circle must move about the center of the universe, not aside from it; for it is the revolving thing itself that produces the center. Thus if a revolution about a center other than this center were to take place, then a center would exist other than this center, and there would exist an earth other than this earth. But all this has been shown to be impossible in natural science.
>
> It is similarly the case with the eccentric sphere proposed by Ptolemy. For if many centers existed, we should have a multitude of heavy bodies outside the place of the earth, and the center would cease to be unique, and it would be extended and divisible. But all this is not possible.[31]

Eccentrics and epicycles require the rotation of celestial bodies around centers other than the center of the universe. In Aristotelian physics, however, there can be only one center, which corresponds to the center of the earth. Ptolemy's multitude of centers violates the necessary simplicity of the celestial motions, contrary to the near perfect nature of the heavens.[32]

Averroës' objection hinges on the incompatibility between Aristotle's and Ptolemy's representations of space – the way they describe spatial properties and relations, such as directions and locations. Aristotle describes directions in relation to a presupposed privileged location – *the* center of the universe.

---

[30] See, for instance, Galileo's distinction between "pure astronomers" (*puri astronomi*) and "philosophical astronomers" (*astronomi filosofi*) in the *Sunspot Letters* (2010, 95). See also Westman (1980).

[31] Averroës, *Commentary on Aristotle's Metaphysics* [*Tafsir*], in Sabra (1984, 141).

[32] Ibn al-Haytham had raised similar difficulties in the tenth century (Swerdlow and Neugebauer 1984, 44–45).

This center is a primitive and unique feature of Aristotle's representation of space to which descriptions of directions and locations refer. "Down" means the direction directly toward the center. "Up" means the direction directly away from the center. This centered representation of space also entails the description of three "simple motions" – upward, downward, and circularly around the center. These are "simple" because these motions do not change their relation to the stipulated center.[33]

As noted above, in Aristotle's view, the heavens are (nearly) perfectly simple, and must therefore exhibit one of the "simple" motions. In fact, they exhibit rotation around the center, because this is the only motion that does not change the description of a body's place. Places are also described relative to the center; they are distinguished by distance from the center. Hence, a body rotating around the center at a fixed distance from it – i.e., circularly – is moving simply and in place. This, then, is the motion appropriate to the heavens, precisely because directions, locations, and thus the simplicity of motion are described in relation to a single center. The centered representation of space makes the descriptions of phenomena compatible with the explanations.

Averroës objected to Ptolemy's eccentrics and epicycles because they suppose several distinct centers of "simple motion" instead of the single center comporting with Aristotle's explanations. Motion around multiple centers is not simple, as the celestial motions must be, since uniform rotation around one center is not described as the *same* motion as uniform rotation around a different center. Multiple centers would also imply several locations for the earth, since earth, as a heavy body, would tend to fall toward each of the centers. Both implications are absurd, hence eccentrics and epicycles cannot be true descriptions of the heavens. Aristotelian explanations are only compatible with a uniquely centered representation of space. Hence, Ptolemaic descriptions referring motions to several centers could not be reconciled with Aristotelian explanations, even when made physical as a series of solid eccentric spheres. Aristotelian physics supposed a single center. "Where," Averroës essentially demanded, "is Ptolemy's center?"

Averroës rejected Ptolemaic astronomy precisely on the grounds of this explanatory failure:

> We should therefore embark on a new search for this ancient astronomy [i.e., a Eudoxan system], for it is the true astronomy that is possible from the stand-point of physical principles. . . . For nothing of the [true] science of astronomy

---

[33] *De Caelo* I.2 (Aristotle 1984, 1:448).

exists in our time, the astronomy of our time being only in agreement with calculations [i.e., the phenomena] and not with what exists.[34]

The elaborate system of epicycles, eccentrics, and equants *could not* be a satisfactory description of the observed phenomena, even if it was empirically successful. At most, it is a mathematical calculating tool that generates accurate descriptions of planetary positions, but it is not itself a description of the heavens. The explanatory failure *implied* an empirical one, regardless of the theory's predictive success. Since Aristotelian explanations were true, Ptolemaic descriptions had to be false.

Averroës advocated a return to a Eudoxan system of concentric spheres around a single center, which would better conform to Aristotle's physics, as well as to the letter of his texts. He also held out hope that the empirical failures of Eudoxan astromomy could be overcome. Averroës himself said he intended to take up this project in his youth, though he did not do so. Some of his contemporaries, most notably al-Biṭrūjī (Alpetragius), a fellow disciple of Ibn Ṭufayl (Abubacer), made some headway by introducing additional devices by which uniformly rotating concentric spheres could produce more irregularities in the motion of an orbiting body. Nevertheless, the empirical adequacy of the Ptolemaic system remained superior, and the Averroist challenge to Ptolemy petered out.

However, once the Renaissance brought the works of the ancients and their Arabic commentaries to the scholarly attention of the Latin West, the old astronomical compromise began to falter, and the reconciliation of Ptolemy and natural philosophy once again became a pressing question. This was in large part due to the influence of Averroës himself, whose extensive commentaries were Aristotle's primary conduit to the Latin universities, but whose insistence on the truth and priority of Aristotelian philosophy (over, say, religious doctrine and Scriptural testimony) made him instantly controversial. As much as Averroës was "the Commentator" to Aristotle "the Philosopher," his ideas were also repeatedly condemned,[35] and the merit of the Averroist interpretation of philosophy relative to religion was a central locus of intellectual debate. This was especially true in the universities of Northern Italy, where an Averroist movement emerged by the end of the fifteenth century. At the universities in Bologna and Padua, the controversy, carried out by Averroist professors and their opponents, occupied intellectual life. At Padua, for instance, the initially Thomist Pietro

---

[34] Averroës, *Commentary on Aristotle's Metaphysics* [*Tafsīr*], in Sabra (1984, 142).

[35] Averroist doctrines were famously condemned at Paris in 1270 and 1277, but also again by the Fifth Lateran Council in 1513.

Pompanazzi debated with the Averroists Antonio Fracasciano and Alessandro Achillini for several years, ending with Pompanazzi's partial conversion in *Tractatus de Immortalitate Animae* (1516) and the subsequent burning of the book for violating the most recent ban on Averroist doctrine.[36]

Not surprisingly, Averroës' influence extended to the study of astronomy, and Renaissance astronomers renewed his criticism of Ptolemy. Following Averroës' own suggestion, this was accompanied by renewed interest in Eudoxan systems of concentric spheres as a more physically plausible alternative to Ptolemaic astronomy. For instance, Regiomontanus, who had completed Peurbach's *Epitome* of the *Almagest*, the book that reintroduced Ptolemy to the Latin world, died while travelling and lecturing in Italy, having begun to develop a concentric-sphere alternative to his mentor's *theorica*.[37] A self-styled student of Regiomontanus, Domenico Maria Novara, would then go on to become Copernicus's teacher at Bologna and perhaps relayed this interest to his student. At about the same time, also in Bologna, Alessandro Achillini (who was later to debate with Pompanazzi in Padua), lectured on Aristotle and repeated Averroës' criticisms of Ptolemy in his commentaries. These were subsequently published as *De Orbibus* (1498), which Copernicus is likely to have known of, if not read.

The Averroist critique of Ptolemaic astronomy on physical grounds reached its climax in Copernicus's own generation with the work of Girolamo Fracastoro and Giovanni Battista Amico. Fracastoro was a professor of astronomy who arrived in Padua in 1501, at about the same time as Copernicus. In 1535, he published *Homocentricorum, sive de Stellis*, which restated the Averroist view of Ptolemy's explanatory failure:

> Astronomers have professed to have great difficulty rendering the causes of all the things that appear amongst the stars. There are two ways to render the causes of these; the one by those orbs which are called homocentric [i.e., concentric], the other by those called eccentrics. Each threatens its hardship, its obstacle. If homocentrics are used, the appearances will not be demonstrated. If eccentrics [are used], these [appearances] will seem to be better demonstrated, but these divine bodies will be understood erroneously and in a certain way impiously, for figures and positions will be given to them that

[36] Barker (1999, 351). Averroism was not the only factor leading to the breakdown of the Ptolemaic compromise. Another important development, particularly evident in Northern Italy, was the advent of medicine as a subject of post-baccalaureate study in the universities. This included courses in medical astrology, of course, and astronomical science enjoyed a concomitant increase in prestige. On this aspect of the wider social and intellectual context of Renaissance humanism, see Westman (1980, 118–21), Donahue (2008), Garber (2008).

[37] Regiomontanus did note empirical failings of the Ptolemaic system, but his main concern was reconciling description with natural philosophy – as in Averroës and al-Biṭrūjī, whom he cited (Shank 1998, Swerdlow 1999).

do not suit the heavens. . . . Hipparchus was amongst the first to choose to accept eccentric orbs over mistaking what appears. Ptolemy and soon nearly all followed him. But against this [astronomy] (as much as it pertained to eccentrics) all of Philosophy – even Nature and the great orbs themselves – have always protested. Until now, no philosopher has been found who could accept that these monstrous spheres exist amongst the divine and most perfect bodies.[38]

Amico, though several years younger, also studied at Padua and, in 1536, published *De Motibus Corporum Coelestium Iuxta Principia Peripatetica, Sine Excentricis et Epicyclis*. This complained that:

Astronomers assign all that appears around the bodies above to eccentric orbs and the little spheres called epicycles. But they reduce those effects to these causes poorly, and it is no surprise they would err; any reduction, says Aristotle in the first book of the *Posterior Analytics*, is difficult when one reduces to false principles. If nature does not admit eccentrics and epicycles, as Averroës rightly holds . . . we are to reject them; and that more willingly since the motions ascribed to eccentrics and epicycles . . . (in my opinion) do not belong to the quintessence at all.[39]

Eudoxan, concentric astronomy may fail to "demonstrate" appearances, but Ptolemy suffers the graver, "impious" error of incompatibility with the "divine and most perfect" nature of the heavens. The simple nature of the heavens could not be compatible with a multiplicity of motions around a multiplicity of centers.

---

[38] (Duhem 1969, 49–50). "Astronomica sunt professi, omnes semper in reddendis eorum causis, quae circa sydera apparent, magnam habuisse difficultatem. Duae enim quum essent viae eas reddendi causas, altera per orbes illos, quos Homocentricos vocant; altera per eos, quos appellant Eccentricos, in utraque quidem suus labor, suus scopulus impendebat. Si in Homocentricis uterentur, apparentia non demonstrabant. Si vero Eccentricis, melius quidem demonstrare videbantur, sed iniq; & quodammodo impie de divinis illis corporibus sentiebant, situsque illis ac figuras dabant, quae minime coelum deceant. . . . Hipparchus vero inter primos maluisse Eccentricos orbes recipere, quam iis, que apparebant, decesse. Que Ptolemeus Phaeludiensis & ab eo mox penè omnes secuti sunt. Venim enim vero adversus hosce [?] (quantam ad Eccentricos pertinebat) omnis semper Philosophis, imò ipsa Natura magis ac orbes ipsi semper reclamavere. Nemo in qui Philosophus esset, hactenus inventus est, qui inter divina illa & perfectissima corpora monstro fas spheras statui audire posset" (Fracastoro 1584, 1r–1v).

[39] Duhem (1969, 50–51). "Astrologi vero per eccentricos orbes, quos primi omnium (ut testatur Nicomachus) invenere Pythagorei, et sphaerulas quasdam qui epicycli dicuntur, assignant ea omnia, quae in superioribus corporibus perspiciuntur. Male tamen effectus illos ad has causas resolverunt. Sed quod in resolvendo errarint mirum non est. Omnis enim resolution, ut ait Aristoteles in priori libro Posteriorum Analyticorum, difficilis est, propter falsa principia quae resolventibus occurrunt. Si igitur eccentricos et epicyclos non agnoscit natura, ut recte sentit Averroes in Comentariis suis primi et secundi libri De Coelo et duodecimi Primae Philosophiae, nobis reiiciendi sunt; et eo libentius quo motus quosdam epicyclis atque eccentricis ascribunt . . . nullo pacto (ut opinor) quintae naturae convenientes." (Amico 1536, ch. 7).

The solution, Fracastoro and Amico held, was to reject Ptolemy entirely. In his place, they proposed Eudoxan systems of concentric spheres, which they attempted to make represent the observed phenomena, though their results in this regard were somewhat less than satisfactory. The empirical failings of Eudoxan astronomy persisted. Nevertheless, the explanatory failure of the Ptolemaic system and the resulting need for reconciliation between astronomical descriptions of the heavens and Aristotelian physics was clearly a well-recognized problem among astronomers at the turn of the sixteenth century, especially in Italy. Amico and Fracastoro were not mathematical astronomers, but this was precisely their point: physical astronomy must take priority over "saving the phenomena." Moreover, the priority of explanatory problems over empirical ones was one aspect of a broader debate over Averroism that exercised the intellectual community of Europe.[40]

Copernicus's solution: a new center

Copernicus was schooled in the midst of the Averroist controversy. After completing his undergraduate degree at Cracow,[41] Copernicus went to Bologna in 1497 in order to study canon law. After a sojourn in Rome, where he likely lectured on mathematics and astronomy, and a trip home to Poland in 1500, Copernicus returned to Italy to study medicine at Padua, where he probably studied astronomy under Fracastoro as part of his medical training. In 1503, Copernicus took a degree from Ferrara and returned to Poland, but his studies had put him at the epicenter of the debate over Averroism, in general, and in astronomy, in particular.[42]

It is unsurprising, then, that Copernicus embraced the Averroist challenge to Ptolemy in *De Revolutionibus*. Like Fracastoro and Amico, he laments the explanatory failures of the Ptolemaic astronomy:

> [T]hose who devised the eccentrics seem thereby in large measure to have solved the problem of the apparent motions with appropriate calculations.

[40] Fracastoro and Amico themselves cited several other figures who shared their views in astronomy. Fracastoro even claims that his text simply reports the ideas of one Iohannes Baptista Turrius (Giovanni Battista Della Torre), who died before he could see his work into print (Fracastoro 1584, IV; Dreyer 1953, 297).

[41] One of Copernicus's professors at Cracow, Albertus de Brudzewo, discussed the Averroist challenge to astronomy (Barker 1999, 347).

[42] Copernicus is also tied to the Paduan astronomical "school" by his use of the "Ṭūsī couple" in some of his astronomical models. While the transmission of this device from the Marāgha astronomer Naṣīr al-Dīn al-Ṭūsī remains mysterious, the fact that Copernicus, Amico, and Fracastoro all employ it suggests a common source, and thus a communal interest, if not direct contact, between them. See Swerdlow and Neugebauer (1984, 48), Di Bono (1995).

But meanwhile they introduced a good many ideas which apparently contra-
dict the first principles of uniform motion. Nor could they elicit or deduce
from the eccentrics the principal consideration, that is, the structure of the
universe [*mundi formam*] and the true symmetry of its parts. On the contrary, their experience was just like someone taking from various places
hands, feet, a head, and other pieces, very well depicted, it may be, but not
for the representation of a single person; since these fragments would not
belong to one another at all, a monster rather than a man would be put
together from them. Hence in the process of demonstration or "method," as
it is called, those who employed eccentrics are found either to have omitted
something essential or to have admitted something extraneous and wholly
irrelevant. This would not have happened to them, had they followed sound
principles. For if the hypotheses assumed by them were not false, everything
which follows from their hypotheses would be confirmed beyond any
doubt.[43]

Echoing Geminus's maxim, Copernicus notes that the Ptolemaic descriptions fail to respect the "first principles" of astronomy: uniform rotation of
the heavenly bodies. The cobbled-together "monstrosities" used to describe
the celestial motions in Ptolemy are, on the face of it, physically implausible.
If these descriptions could be reconciled with explanatory principles, at the
very least similar motions would have similar explanations, and thus similar
descriptions. But the Ptolemaic system is, by design, *ad hoc*, and otherwise
similar irregularities are accounted for by epicycles in some cases, eccentrics
or equants in others. Even if experience does match its predictions,
Ptolemaic astronomy cannot be a true theory of the "form of the world."[44]

   Copernicus adheres, meanwhile, to the Aristotelian explanation of celestial motion. The celestial bodies are carried circularly about on uniformly

---

[43] Copernicus (1978, 4).

[44] Copernicus cites a specific instance of disagreement among astronomers as a reason to reject existing
astronomical systems: "For, in the first place, they [astronomers] are so uncertain about the motion of
the sun and moon that they cannot establish and observe a constant length even for the tropical year"
(1978, 4). This is a reference to the reform of the calendar. There was a slight discrepancy between the
Julian calendar year then in use (365.25 days) and the tropical year (the time it takes the sun to return
to an equinox or solstice point; about 365.2425 days). Over the centuries since Caesar, this caused a
slow movement of the equinoxes through the calendar year, such that by the sixteenth century, the
vernal equinox fell in early March. This problem eventually led to the reform of the calendar under
Pope Gregory XIII later in the century. Strictly speaking, this is an empirical failure of the calendar,
not of astronomy, but Copernicus points out that the tropical year is a parameter in Ptolemaic
astronomy, and astronomers cannot agree on its actual value. What is significant for Copernicus,
though, is not the empirical failure, but the fact of disagreement among astronomers. He takes this as
further evidence of an explanatory problem. Were astronomers to employ systems answerable to the
physical principles by which the natural world operates, they would agree upon a value for this
invariant property of the solar motion. Physical considerations would ensure "commensurability"
between descriptions and the natural world. Incidentally, this is precisely the objection Ptolemy had
set aside in order to reach "agreement with the phenomena," as discussed above.

rotating spheres. Other kinds of motion, Copernicus insists, simply cannot be explained. There is no possible way to account for nonuniform motion:

> [A] simple heavenly body cannot be moved by a single sphere nonuniformly. For this nonuniformity would have to be caused either by an inconstancy, whether imposed from without or generated from within, in the moving force or by an alteration in the revolving body. From either alternative, however, the intellect shrinks [*abhorreat intellectus*]. It is improper to conceive any such defect in objects constituted in the best order.[45]

The celestial spheres are (nearly) perfect simple bodies, without part or joint. They do not have, therefore, any internal "unevenness" that could explain irregular motion. Nor can irregular motion be attributed to the source of a sphere's motion, since the spheres move only according to their internal, simple, and therefore (again) uniform nature. Hence, celestial motions are only explicable if they are described as uniform: "It must be agreed [*consentaneum est*], therefore, that their [the celestial bodies'] uniform motions appear nonuniform to us."[46] The complicated, irregular motions of the planets can only be properly *explained* if they are *described* as compositions of uniform, circular motions. Copernicus, like Averroës, holds that Aristotelian explanation of celestial motion must take precedence, and must be adhered to. A description is only acceptable if it is physically plausible.

However, Copernicus was a conservative critic of Ptolemy – a moderate Averroist. More radical Averroists had advocated the complete overthrow of Ptolemaic astronomy. In their view, epicycles and eccentrics could not be reconciled, even in principle, with Aristotelian physics. They rejected out of hand the foundation of Ptolemy's system. Copernicus, on the other hand, was unwilling to completely abandon the Ptolemaic system in favor of Eudoxan concentric spheres. Averroës (and Fracastoro and Amico) thought Ptolemy's explanatory failures insurmountable and the empirical failings of a Eudoxan system tractable. Copernicus was not so sanguine:

> For although those who put their faith in homocentrics showed that some nonuniform motions could be compounded in this way, nevertheless by this means they were unable to obtain any incontrovertible result in absolute agreement with the phenomena.[47]

Eudoxan systems could only get as far as producing the *qualities* of the heavenly motions, such as retrogression and irregularity. They could not,

---

[45] Copernicus (1543, 3; 1978, 11).   [46] Copernicus (1543, 3; 1978, 11, translation slightly altered).
[47] Copernicus (1978, 4). Though he does not mention them by name, it seems that Copernicus aims this remark at Fracastoro and Amico.

however, describe the *actual* motions of the celestial bodies. Even if the rotations of concentric spheres were physically explicable, they were empirically unsatisfactory, and work to improve such systems showed little promise.

Rather than overthrowing Ptolemy entirely, Copernicus pursued a moderate program of salvaging what he thought physically plausible in Ptolemy.[48] In particular, Copernicus was willing to admit eccentrics and epicycles as physically explicable descriptions of the heavens. Though they did not rotate around a single center, they at least exhibited the uniform rotation natural to the heavens. Moreover, they allowed the extensive parameterization needed to adequately account for the appearances.

Equants, however, were another matter. These, in Copernicus's view, were a mathematical conceit by which one calls uniform that which is not uniform at all.[49] In the *Commentariolus*, Copernicus complains:

> [T]he theories concerning these matters that have been put forth far and wide by Ptolemy and most others, although they correspond numerically [with appearances], also seemed quite doubtful, for these theories were inadequate unless they also envisioned certain *equant* circles, on account of which it appeared that the planet never moves with uniform velocity either in its *deferent* sphere or with respect to its proper center. Therefore a theory of this kind seemed neither perfect enough nor sufficiently in accordance with reason.[50]

The equant allows one to mathematically describe the appearances, but it is explanatorily abhorrent, disconnected from any causal principle "in accordance with reason."

In *De Revolutionibus*, Copernicus writes of Ptolemy's description of lunar motion, which includes an epicycle moving about an eccentric deferent with a motion uniform only at an equant point:

> [W]hat shall we say about the axiom [*axioma*] that the heavenly bodies' motion is uniform and only apparently seems nonuniform, if the epicycle's apparently uniform motion is really nonuniform and its occurrence absolutely contradicts an established principle and assumption [*principio & assumpto*]? But suppose you say that the epicycle moves uniformly with respect to the earth's center, and that this is enough to safeguard uniformity. Then what sort of uniformity will that be on an extraneous circle on which

---

[48] Zilsel (1940) has detailed Copernicus's adherence to the "teleological conception of nature" that is the hallmark of Aristotelian explanation, especially with regard to celestial motions.

[49] In this view, Copernicus followed the Marāgha astronomers, who were also particularly concerned to eliminate the equant from Ptolemaic astronomy, and used variations of the Ṭūsī couple to do so. However, just as with the Ṭūsī couple itself, it is difficult to say what direct influence, if any, this had on Copernicus and his peers. See Swerdlow and Neugebauer (1984, 46–47), Di Bono (1995).

[50] Swerdlow (1973).

the epicycle's motion does not occur, whereas it does occur on the epicycle's own eccentric?[51]

Ptolemy's "regular" motion, Copernicus argues, is not regular at all. For Ptolemy has an epicycle rotating uniformly only with respect to an equant, which is neither the center of the heavens, nor the center of its orbit (the deferent). Thus, the epicycle may sweep equal arcs of a circle centered on the equant in equal times, but this is not a truly regular motion, since the epicycle itself will travel unequal arcs of the deferent in equal times. Ptolemy might be satisfied that the motion is regular about *some* point, but this is a perversion of the meaning of uniform motion. Copernicus claims Ptolemy has violated Aristotle's fundamental "axiom" of planetary motion, circular uniform motion, by misapplying it to motion around an equant.

Unwilling to countenance Ptolemy's mathematical expedient, Copernicus tried to close the gap between explanations and descriptions caused by the equant:

> [A]s they [the ancients] admit, a circular motion can be uniform with respect to an extraneous center not its own. ... But (in my opinion) I have already refuted this idea in connection with the moon [in the passage just quoted]. These and similar situations gave me the occasion to consider the motion of the earth and other ways of preserving uniform motion and the principles of the science [*principia artis*], as well as of making the computation of the apparent nonuniform motion more enduring.[52]

The equant model of planetary motion was incompatible with Aristotelian explanations, which required uniform celestial rotations resulting from the simple and (near) perfect nature of the heavenly spheres. It could not be used to coordinate appearances with physical causes. Eliminating the equant was thus a "means for preserving regularity and the first principles of our science." Copernicus considered the "mobility of the earth" as a way of doing just this.

Copernicus, then, sought to produce empirically successful descriptions of the phenomena that employed only eccentrics and epicycles. In Ptolemaic astronomy,[53] planetary longitudinal positions were calculated on the basis of the planet's mean motion and its total irregularity or

---

[51] Copernicus (1543, 99v; 1978, 176). The centrality of this "axiom" was not lost on Copernicus's readers. On the title page of his copy of *De Revolutionibus*, Erasmus Rheinhold added the note "Axiom of Astronomy: Celestial motion is uniform and circular, or composed of uniform and circular" (*Axioma Astronomicum: Motus coelesti aequalis est et circularis vel ex aequalibus et circularibus compositus*) (Westman 2011, 151).

[52] Copernicus (1543, 140v; 1978, 240).

[53] In the following discussion, I am ignoring Ptolemy's discussion of the moon and Mercury. The moon, of course, really does orbit the earth, so its anomalies arise for different reasons than those of

"anomaly."[54] Given a date and time, the mean motion and anomaly of a planet (obtained from a table or by calculation) were combined to generate the position of the planet. Ptolemy, meanwhile, separated the total anomaly into two parts. The first was the synodic anomaly, which, in modern terms, accounted for the fact that the sun, not, as Ptolemy assumed, the earth, is the center of the solar system. Since this anomaly depends on the location of the sun,[55] it is the same for all the planets. The remainder of the planet's irregularity was the ecliptic anomaly, which accounted, again in modern terms, for the fact that planets orbit in ellipses with varying speeds, rather than uniformly in circles. For the superior planets – Saturn, Jupiter, and Mars – Ptolemy used an epicycle model to account for the synodic anomaly. The ecliptic anomaly, meanwhile, consisted of two corrections – one generated by an eccentric, the other by an equant. For Venus and Mercury, the ecliptic anomaly was accounted for by an epicycle, while the synodic anomaly consisted of corrections generated by an eccentric and an equant. Thus, each of the planets' anomalies was accounted for by three angular corrections to the mean motion, generated by an epicycle, an eccentric, and an equant.

To remove equants from Ptolemaic astronomy, therefore, Copernicus had to remove one of the corrections for each planet, leaving the other two to be generated by an epicycle and an eccentric. By assuming that the earth is in uniform, eccentric motion around the sun, Copernicus could describe the synodic anomaly for each planet as the result of the earth's motion, not as an irregularity in the planet's motion. This allowed Copernicus to describe the planetary orbits using just an epicycle and an eccentric deferent around the sun, each rotating uniformly around its own center.[56] The remaining irregularities in planetary motions associated with solar position could then be described as "appearances," rather than real motions. The third correction for each planet, hitherto accomplished by an equant, was no longer necessary, and the "axiom" that "the motion of the heavenly bodies is regular, except when it seems to be irregular as far as appearance is concerned" would be preserved. In other words, by putting the earth in motion, Copernicus redescribed the observed phenomena. The synodic part of the total anomaly was now just an appearance and no longer stood in

the other planets. Mercury's motion is decidedly more complicated than the motions of the other planets. The latter is an exception in both Ptolemy's and Copernicus's systems, since both resort to oscillations not found in any other planetary model in order to account for it.

[54] The mean motion of a planet is the motion it would have if it moved with constant angular velocity around the orbital center (i.e., the earth). The rate is equal to 360 degrees divided by the orbital period. The (total) anomaly is the angular deflection from the mean motion owing to the nonuniformity of the planet's actual motion.

[55] Actually, in Ptolemy's system, it depends on the mean motion of the sun.

[56] Again, excluding Mercury.

need of explanation. Only uniform rotation was ascribed to the heavens, albeit around several centers, which he thought permitted explanation by Aristotelian principles of celestial motion.[57] The part of the gap between explanation and description caused by the equant was closed.

As Bernard Goldstein has noted, Copernicus also cited a second explanatory failure of Ptolemaic astronomy as a motivation to seek a new system.[58] In *De Caelo*, Aristotle argued that the motion of the heavens was ultimately caused by the rapid, diurnal motion of the outermost sphere. This motion is corrupted by the successive spheres, such that planets further from the extremity lag further behind. Consequently, planets closer to the earth at the center should move against the diurnal motion of the fixed stars faster – their sidereal periods should be shorter. Venus and Mercury, for instance, share the period of the sun. Thus, they should be at the same distance from the earth in order to correspond with Aristotle's explanation of their motion. However, in Ptolemy's system, the planetary distances are not related to sidereal periods. Inasmuch as they are determined at all, planetary distances are consequences of the nesting of the eccentric spheres, and no two planets can be equidistant to the earth. The Ptolemaic description is again incompatible with the Aristotelian explanation.

If, by contrast, the sun is considered the center of the heavens, then the periods of the planets are properly ordered:

> [The sphere of the fixed stars] is followed by the first of the planets, Saturn, which completes its circuit in 30 years. After Saturn, Jupiter accomplishes its revolution in 12 years. Then Mars revolves in 2 years. The annual revolution takes the series' fourth place, which contains the earth, as I said, together with the lunar sphere as an epicycle. In the fifth place Venus returns in 9 months. Lastly, the sixth place is held by Mercury, which revolves in a period of 80 days. . . . In this arrangement, therefore, we discover a marvelous symmetry of the universe, and an established harmonious linkage between the motion of the spheres and their size, such as can be found in no other way.[59]

Heliocentrism, that is, allows proper explanation of the planetary periods, whereas Ptolemy does not. A heliocentric system unites the description of the celestial motions into one "form of the world," eliminating the "monstrosities" of Ptolemy's geocentrism. Note that this has nothing to do with empirical success. Rather, it has to do with how the appearances are described – as motions around the sun or as motions around the earth. A heliocentric description offers a solution to a second explanatory failure.

---

[57] For a general summary of Copernican astronomy, see Dreyer (1953, ch. 8).
[58] Goldstein (2002).   [59] Copernicus (1978, 21–22).

The point to be made here is that Copernicus's innovation was motivated by something other than empirical failure. Ptolemaic astronomy was not deemed unsatisfactory by Renaissance astronomers because it failed to accurately account for observed phenomena. Quite the contrary: the Ptolemaic theory had been conceived partly in order to match observation and was widely accepted for a millennium and a half precisely because it did so well. Ptolemaic astronomy in Copernicus's time, therefore, was successful in "saving the phenomena." There was no mounting body of recalcitrant experiences that could not be reconciled with the system. Those that challenged the Ptolemaic view, including Copernicus, never did so on empirical grounds and always acknowledged its empirical superiority over the available alternatives.

The Renaissance Averroism that surrounded Copernicus, on the other hand, renewed scrutiny of the explanatory failure of Ptolemy's system by rejecting the Ptolemaic compromise that had glossed over questions about its physical plausibility. The old question of physical plausibility was once again brought to the fore, and astronomers once again saw a need to reconcile descriptions with explanations. Copernicus was one of several scholars seeking physically grounded alternatives to Ptolemaic astronomy, and this is why his proposal was seen as a significant contribution even before its formal publication. This general concern with explanation is also seen in the specific motivations Copernicus cited, the equant and the ordering of the planets. Copernicus saw failures at the interface between descriptions and explanations as problems calling for theoretical innovation.

In the end, Copernicus's position was a moderate one. Copernicus did not try to expand or revise Aristotelian explanations of planetary motion.[60] He intended, rather, to adhere to the Aristotelian physical principles that had inspired him to pursue a novel description of the celestial motions. Copernicus remained, that is, primarily a mathematical astronomer, focused on the empirical interface between theory and phenomena. In fact, Copernicus was notoriously unreflective regarding the explanatory problems his astronomical descriptions raised. His innovation was a new description of phenomena, meant specifically to preserve existing physical explanations, but he did not consider thoroughly how his new system was to be reconciled with them. He almost never specified the causes of the

---

[60] This explains, perhaps, why Copernicus was often thought of as merely a mathematical astronomer, not concerned with physical problems. For instance, in his annotations of *De Revolutionibus*, Michael Maestlin wrote, "As for astronomy, Copernicus wrote this entire book as an astronomer, not as a physicist" (Westman 2011, 265), and Osiander's *ad lectorem* characterized the heliocentric system as a mere mathematical hypothesis. It is plain, however, that Copernicus did consider physical astronomy as a basis for his own system, at least in Book I of *De Revolutionibus*.

motions he described. He did not worry about the mixture of the terrestrial and the celestial implied by the earth's motion. He simply assumed that the "first principles" of astronomy – Aristotelian physics – could and would be applied to his system.[61] Copernicus even preserved much of the Ptolemaic descriptions, and his continued use of eccentrics and epicycles allowed, as in Ptolemy, extensive parameterization of descriptions, and, thus, a correspondence to experience comparable to the Ptolemaic system's.[62]

Copernicus says his geokinetic theory was "occasioned" by the need to remove equants from the Ptolemaic descriptions that otherwise accounted for observations. Copernicus thought his descriptions improved upon Ptolemy's because they could be better coordinated with physical explanations – because they solved, to some extent, Ptolemy's *explanatory* failure. Still, Ptolemy's empirical *success* was the standard by which Copernicus judged his own (which is why he rejected concentric spheres as inadequate).

Averroism redux

Having located Copernicus's motivation at the interface between description and explanation, one can use this insight to illuminate his influence on his successors. As it happened, Copernicus's efforts were not entirely successful. Despite his intentions, Copernicus's heliocentrism left open explanatory problems at the interface between descriptions and

---

[61] Copernicus's disciple, Georg Joachim Rheticus, reported that he was "fully convinced that for him [Copernicus] there is nothing better or more important than to walk in the footsteps of Ptolemy and to follow, as Ptolemy himself did, the Ancients and those who came before him" (Koyré 1973, 30).

[62] Gingerich (1975). Compare this interpretation to Tycho Brahe's near-contemporary diagnosis in his Copenhagen Oration of 1574: "In our time, Nicolaus Copernicus, who has justly been called a second Ptolemy, from his own observations found out something was missing in Ptolemy. He judged that the hypotheses established by Ptolemy admitted something unsuitable and offensive to mathematical axioms; nor did he find the Alfonsine calculations in agreement with the heavenly motions. He therefore arranged his own hypotheses in another manner, by the admirable subtlety of his erudition, and thus restored the science of the celestial motions and considered the course of the heavenly bodies more accurately than anyone else before him. For although he holds certain [theses] contrary to physical principles, for example, that the Sun rests at the center of the universe, that the Earth, the elements associated with it, and the Moon, move around the Sun with a threefold motion, and that the eighth sphere remains unmoved, he does not, for all that, admit anything absurd as far as mathematical axioms are concerned. If we inspect the Ptolemaic hypothesis in this regard, however, we notice many such absurdities. For it is absurd that they should dispose the motions of the heavenly bodies on their epicycles and eccentrics in an irregular manner with respect to the centers of these very circles and that, by means of an irregularity, they should save unfittingly the regular motions of the heavenly bodies. Everything, therefore, which we today consider to be evident and well-known concerning the revolutions of the stars has been established and taught by these two masters, Ptolemy and Copernicus" (Westman 2011, 244–45). Here, Tycho distinguishes Copernicus's "physical" absurdities from Ptolemy's "mathematical" ones. Copernicus's explanations are implausible, but Ptolemy's descriptions are to be rejected, especially the equants, which "save unfittingly the regular motions of the heavenly bodies."

explanations. In particular, Copernicus's new, heliocentric description of the phenomena employed a problematic representation of space.

The problem Averroës had raised against Ptolemy is even more pronounced in Copernicus: Copernicus's representation of space is incompatible with Aristotle's physics. This is not to say that Copernicus subscribed to a different *kind* of representation of space. On the contrary, Copernicus employs centered representations of space throughout the *De Revolutionibus*.[63] Motions and locations are specified in relation to presupposed centers. For example, in Copernicus's "order of the heavenly spheres," the sun is stipulated as the center. The "first and highest" of the spheres, that is, the sphere furthest from the center, is that of the fixed stars. The next sphere, closer to the center, is that of Saturn, "the first of the planets." The other planets are then described in order, each after the next. In each case, the location or "height" of a sphere is described by its distance from the center – the sun, which rests "in the middle of everything."[64]

The centered representation of space also allows Copernicus to follow Aristotle's specification of the three "simple" motions:

> Thus, according to Aristotle, the motion of a single simple body is simple; of the simple motions, one is straight and the other is circular; of the straight motions, one is upward and the other is downward. Hence every simple motion is either toward the middle, that is, downward; or away from the middle, that is, upward; or around the middle, that is, circular.[65]

Copernicus then uses these "simple" motions to describe phenomena, and this allows him to make his descriptions correspond to Aristotelian explanations. Copernicus parrots Aristotle, for example, in arguing that the celestial spheres rotate uniformly because rotation in place is the natural motion of a sphere:

> I shall now recall to mind that the motion of the heavenly bodies is circular, since the motion appropriate to a sphere is rotation in a circle. By this very act the sphere expresses its form as the simplest body, wherein neither beginning nor end can be found, nor can the one be distinguished from the other, while the sphere itself traverses the same points to return upon itself.[66]

The celestial spheres are simple bodies, expressed in the "simplest of figures." They are already and forever in their natural places, as distinguished by distance to the center. Their natural motion, therefore, is

---

[63] This is actually not surprising, since a centered representation of space was common to everyone prior to the early modern period, including Ptolemy. Indeed, the centered representation Kuhn calls "the space of the primitive" (1957, 97) and Dreyer "the peculiar habit of the ancients" (1953, 156).

[64] Copernicus (1978, 18–22).   [65] Copernicus (1978, 14–15).   [66] Copernicus (1978, 10).

motion in place – rotation about the center, just as in Aristotle. As noted above, though, this explanation only fits a centered representation of space.

Nevertheless, by setting the earth in motion, Copernicus adopted a *multiply* centered representation of space, and this raised significant problems at the interface between explanations and descriptions. Aristotle had employed a single-centered representation of space, centered on a point that coincides with the center of the earth, for descriptions of all spatial phenomena. For Aristotle, therefore, descriptions in the heavens and on the earth refer to the same point. "Down" and "lower" have the same significance everywhere. Thus, Aristotle presents, at least in this sense, a unified system. Ptolemy's cosmos, too, could be considered unified in the sense that the terrestrial center remained the primary point of reference. Copernicus, on the other hand, posits *two* fundamental centers. Descriptions of terrestrial phenomena refer to the center of the earth, while descriptions of celestial phenomena refer to the sun.[67] Heavy bodies fall "down" toward the earth, but Mars is "below" Jupiter, closer to the sun. Copernicus employs two different centers to represent space: one for the description of terrestrial phenomena, another for celestial.[68]

It is possible to generate coherent descriptions in Copernicus's multiply centered representation of space. Indeed, Copernicus is always clear which center he is using in a given context, and the reader of *De Revolutionibus* is never confused as to the significance of a description. Nevertheless, identical descriptions have different interpretations depending on the center used in their generation and interpretation. Descriptions related to different centers are incommensurate. For example, a heavy body can be described as falling "downward" in a terrestrial context, but this description loses its meaning in the solar-centered celestial context, where "downward" means a different direction in space.

One consequence is that the physical explanations generated under differing representations of space would have to be fundamentally disjointed, since the descriptions they explain are incommensurate. The explanation given for the "downward" motion of a body on the earth has no significance

---

[67] To be precise, the center of Copenicus's system is the center of the earth's orbit – a point near the sun.

[68] In the *Narratio Prima*, Rheticus quotes Bishop Tiedemann Giese, a patron of Copernicus: "If the Earth were raised to the lunar sphere, would loose fragments of Earth seek, not the center of the Earth's globe, but the center of the universe, inasmuch as they all fall at right angles to the surface of the Earth's globe? Again, since we see that the magnet by its natural motion turns north, would the motion of the daily rotation or the circular motions attributed to the Earth necessarily be violent motions? Further, can the three motions, away from the center, toward the center, and about the center, be in fact separated?" (Westman 2011, 126–27). Westman notes that these questions would be "an important heuristic for second- and third-generation Copernicans" (127), as I argue below.

or relevance to the "downward" motion of a body in the heavens. The terrestrial system centered on the earth is explanatorily distinct from the celestial system centered on the sun. This fundamentally undermines the unified ordering of all things in the Aristotelian system.[69] Moreover, the multiply centered representation of space violates the principle that nature is simple and employs the same cause for the same effect. Copernicus's astronomy ran against basic standards of intelligibility – the desiderata of science *simpliciter*.[70] Aristotelian physics had drawn a sharp distinction between the celestial and the terrestrial, but it was Copernicus who made this distinction uncomfortable. The "Newtonian Synthesis" would eventually repair this rift, but only by using a representation of space that does not presuppose centers at all, thereby stepping out of the problem.[71]

A second, more specific problem also arises in the context of Copernicus's description of a moving earth. Though it is not the main subject of his inquiry, Copernicus also adheres to Aristotelian physics when dealing with terrestrial phenomena. For Copernicus, as for Aristotle, the universe has a spatial order in which all bodies have a proper place. Bodies seek out their natural places as determined by the substantial elements that constitute them. Earthy bodies seek the "place" around the terrestrial center, watery bodies seek the "place" around the earth, and so on. When bodies are removed from these places, they tend to return to them along straight lines. Heavy bodies, like water and earth, tend toward the center; lighter ones, like fire and air, tend away from the center.

---

[69] This is what Koyré calls the "destruction of the cosmos." See the discussion in Chapter 1, above.

[70] I do not wish to imply that Copernicus himself found this problematic. His primary concern, like Ptolemy's, was a correct *description* of the planetary phenomena. His aim was not a consistent explanation of the entire universe. Thus, he was content with distinct celestial and terrestrial realms. The difficulty of reconciling this disjoint picture of the cosmos was addressed mainly by his successors.

[71] Putting the problem differently, a centered space is heterogeneous and anisotropic. Different parts of space cannot be superimposed on one another by translation or rotation (about points other than the center). A part of space near the center is qualitatively different from a part further away, and all parts possess a privileged direction toward the center that precludes rotational superposition. If a single centered structure is used to represent space, different parts of space are each homogeneous with themselves – each portion of space can be superimposed on itself. Thus, the properties and relations pertaining to that part of space will be uniquely determined. If more than one centered structure is used to represent space, however, it loses this property. A given portion of space represented in one frame is not homogeneous with the same portion as represented in another frame, even though, objectively, they are the same space. The two representations will also be anisotropic in different ways, because the privileged direction will be directed toward different centers. As a result, the spatial properties and relation found in any part of space will be described differently according to the different spatial concepts used to represent it. A body, for instance, has *two* locations – one terrestrial, one celestial. This is troublesome, though not inconsistent, since properties and relations like locations seem objectively unitary, and one usually desires them to be represented as such.

However, Copernicus's multiply centered representation of space undermines the Aristotelian explanations of terrestrial phenomena in at least two ways. In the first place, the question immediately arises as to why some phenomena are described with respect to one center while other phenomena are described with respect to another. The motion of heavy bodies cannot be simply ascribed to a "tendency to seek the center" when "the center" might not be the center of the earth. Copernicus himself stumbles on this block. He is forced to abandon the Aristotelian view that the earth is spherical because its parts all seek the geometrical center, and he subsequently proposes that bodies around the earth gravitate toward it because of a "desire" to be part of a sphere: "For my part I believe that gravity is nothing but a certain natural desire, which the divine providence of the Creator of all things has implanted in parts, to gather as a unity and a whole by combining in the form of a globe."[72] But this is not so much an explanation as a hand-waving dismissal of the problem, and Copernicus has little else to say on the matter.

In the second place, Copernicus suggests that the centers are moving with respect to one another. The "natural" motion of simple bodies cannot be simply rectilinear when they also partake of the circular motions of the earth. How, then, does one account for the "natural motion" of objects on a moving earth? How is one supposed to explain motions when there is more than one center? Copernicus haltingly attempts to solve this problem. He argues that terrestrial motion is really a "dual motion":

> We must in fact avow that the motion of falling and rising bodies in the framework of the universe [*mundi comparatione*] is twofold, being in every case a compound of straight and circular. . . . Hence, since circular motion belongs to wholes, but parts have rectilinear motion in addition, we can say that "circular" subsists with "rectilinear" as "being alive" with "being sick."[73]

Falling bodies have two motions. First, since they are out of place, they seek their proper place near the terrestrial center. But since they are part of the terrestrial globe, they take part in the rotational motion of the whole, which is caused by the globe's celestial nature and place in the heavens. The two motions subsist in one entity, just as one animal can be both alive and sick.

This solution is far from satisfactory. First of all, it ascribes a complex motion to simple bodies, contrary to Aristotle's principles. It also raises a host of other questions, none of which can be answered by Aristotelian explanations. For instance, why are the effects of the earth's (rapid) motion unobservable?[74] Why do falling bodies seek out a moving point (the center

[72] Copernicus (1978, 18).   [73] Copernicus (1543, 6r; 1978, 16–17).
[74] Ptolemy raised this question in response to early heliocentrists. See Ptolemy (1984, 44–45).

of the terrestrial globe), and why that point in particular? Why is the sun the center of the celestial motions, and not another body? And if the sun is the center of celestial motion, why does the moon rotate around the earth, not the sun, like the rest of the planets? In sum, to make use of Aristotelian explanations, one has to stipulate a unique center. Where, then, is Copernicus's center? He asks the question himself:

> Therefore, since there are many centers [*pluribus ergo existentibus centris*], it will not be by accident that the further question arises whether the center of the universe is identical with the center of terrestrial gravity or with some other point.[75]

In the end, Copernicus *prefers*, "for his part," to place the sun at the "middle of the universe."

Averroës' objection to Ptolemy applies even more forcefully to Copernicus. The multiply centered representation of space hopelessly complicates physical explanations. Aristotelian explanations rely on descriptions referring to a single stipulated center. Copernicus stipulates at least two, moving in relation to each other. As a result, the Aristotelian explanations of terrestrial phenomena are, despite Copernicus's own intentions, incompatible with the descriptions of phenomena Copernicus adopts. It is a problem he cannot solve, and it is a problem that motivated later authors to formulate a terrestrial physics compatible with the motion of the earth. As the explanatory failures of Ptolemy called to Copernicus for a solution, similar difficulties with Copernicus's view called to his successors.

The explanatory consequences of descriptions: the third motion

The incompatibility of Copernicus's representation of space and Aristotelian explanations coalesces in a very specific explanatory problem within Copernicus's astronomy. Copernicus describes three motions of the earth. The first is the daily rotation of the earthly globe around its axis, which accounts for the apparent diurnal motion of the stars, sun, moon, and planets across the sky. The second motion is the annual revolution of the earth about the sun. As noted above, this motion accounts for some of the apparent irregularities of the planetary motions. These motions, moreover, are at least made plausible on the basis of the earth's nature. Since the earth is a globe, rotation about its axis is "appropriate by nature to its form."[76] Also, since the

---

[75] Copernicus (1543, 7r; 1978, 18).   [76] Copernicus (1978, 16).

earth "can be regarded as one of the wandering stars," it is appropriate that it, as is natural for a planet, orbits the sun.

The third motion, however, is more complicated. Copernicus knew that, as the earth orbits the sun, its axis remains pointed toward the same region of the fixed stars (near Polaris, the North Star). As a result, near the summer solstice, the axis is tilted towards the sun, but near the winter solstice, it is tilted away from the sun. In other words, the direction of the axis in space changes its relation to the center of the solar system. In a representation of space referring descriptions to a central point near the sun, this relation specifies direction, so the description of the direction of the earth's axis *changes*. Therefore, the phenomenon is described as a *motion*. Specifically, the axis of the earth is said to rotate around the normal to the ecliptic, making roughly one rotation a year in the sense opposite to the earth's annual revolution around the sun. By contrast, if the earth were not to "move" this way, the axis would always point in the "same direction" – it would tilt toward or away from the sun at all times. Copernicus called this rotation of the axis the "third motion of the earth."

This is a strange motion, however. For one thing, though supposedly independent of the second motion, it follows it almost exactly, but in the opposite sense. Both the revolution of the earth around the sun and the rotation of its axis occur once every year, the first west to east, the other east to west. Thus:

> These two motions are opposite in direction and nearly equal in period. The result is that the earth's axis and equator, the largest of the parallels of latitude on it, face almost the same portion of the heavens, just as if they remained motionless.[77]

In other words, the third motion creates the appearance of motionlessness. The net effect is that the axis remains pointed at the same part of the sky.[78]

Moreover, the third motion lacks an easy explanation. The motion is not a simple rotation around an axis. It is a rotation of the axis of the first motion about another axis, like the wobble of a spinning top. In the *Commentariolus*, Copernicus comments on the third motion that "it has seemed to most persons [i.e., Ptolemaic astronomers] that the firmament has several motions in conformity with a law not yet sufficiently understood. But it would be less surprising if all these changes should occur on account of the motion of the

---

[77] Copernicus (1978, 23).
[78] Copernicus uses a slight discrepancy between the second and third motions to account for the slow precession of the equinoxes. The axis does not quite return to its orientation from year to year, such that it deviates from its former position by about one degree per century.

earth. I am not concerned to state what the path of the pole is." That is, Ptolemaic astronomers, who believed the axis of the ecliptic to move, could not account for the motion. Copernicus, who ascribes the motion to the earth's axis, likewise has no explanation, and is not even sure what the actual path of the motion really is.[79] In the *De Revolutionibus*, Copernicus does not even say this much. He leaves the third motion completely unexplained.[80]

It fell to his successors to find an explanation for this "third motion." This was no easy task. Indeed, on the modern view, this "motion" is no motion at all. It is an artifact of Copernicus's representation of space. In a centered representation of space, where direction is specified in relation to the sun, the behavior of the earth's axis is described as a *motion* – the axis turns in relation to the radius to the center. But the lack of explanation of this "motion" eventually led to the rejection of the centered representation itself. By introducing a new kind of representation of space in which descriptions do not refer to any center, later authors could say that the axis's tendency to remain pointed toward a fixed point in the sky is *not* a motion at all.[81] The new representation of space, that is, allowed authors to describe the behavior of the earth's axis as a "staying" that did not need explanation, thereby closing the explanatory gap.

As we shall see, the problem of the third motion was significant in the history of the Scientific Revolution because it catalyzed further developments in astronomical science. William Gilbert addressed the problem of the third motion, and he was the first to deploy an oriented representation of space as a result, which was adopted in turn by Kepler and Newton. At the same time, new explanations of the physical universe developed alongside the new descriptions of phenomena. The new oriented representation of space was an essential part of the revolutionary physics of the early modern period.

Conclusion: Copernicus and the Scientific Revolution

Noting the structure of scientific knowledge and the interface of descriptions and explanation as a locus of scientific change illuminates Copernicus's role in the history of science. The Scientific Revolution essentially included a fundamental change at the explanatory level. The Aristotelian explanations that had prevailed since ancient times were

---

[79] See Rosen (1937), Swerdlow (1973).

[80] In a 1590 letter to Tycho, Christopher Rothmann complains that Copernicus does not explain the third motion: "I know that in this regard Copernicus is quite obscure and is not easily comprehensible" (Westman 2011, 141).

[81] Ignoring the slow precession of the equinoxes.

replaced by the explanations of classical science. In this regard, then, Copernicus was not a revolutionary. He did not offer any new explanations of phenomena. This is not to say that Copernicus was not an important figure in the Scientific Revolution. By offering a solution to one kind of explanatory failure in astronomy, he opened up new explanatory failures, and forced others to address the same interface between description and explanation.

These are best seen through the lens of Copernicus's representation of space. Copernicus's heliocentric astronomy included a multiply centered representation of space. What in Aristotle was once a single descriptive framework centered on a single point was now a multiplex system centered on at least two, if not many centers. The Copernican hypothesis therefore required a new physical theory to explain celestial and terrestrial phenomena as they were now described, a problem exemplified by the need to explain the third motion of the earth. Copernicus had tried to reconcile his novel descriptions with existing explanations. For his successors, the task became to provide novel explanations to reconcile with the existing Copernican descriptions. A shift in descriptions to save explanations led to a shift in explanations to save descriptions.

CHAPTER 3

Non est motus omnino: *Gilbert, verticity, and the Law of the Whole*

Gilbert's response to Copernicus

In Chapter 1, I introduced the notion of reciprocal iteration between descriptions and explanations as the process by which scientific theories change. Copernicus is an illustration of this process. His adherence to Aristotelian explanations of celestial motion led him to novel descriptions of phenomena. These new descriptions, in turn, led to problems at both the descriptive and explanatory levels. One of the first authors to grapple with these new difficulties was the Englishman William Gilbert of Colchester, royal physician to Queen Elizabeth I and King James I.

Gilbert constitutes another iteration of the reciprocal process of theory change. His aim was to fill some of the explanatory gaps opened by Copernicus. To do so, he adopted an explanatory scheme originating in a particular set of phenomena, namely, those associated with magnetism. These phenomena, however, were described on the basis of a particular representation of space appropriate to the magnetic subject matter, which Gilbert then applied to the description of the earth itself. This altered description of the earth, in turn, helped Gilbert give the explanations he sought. In other words, Gilbert carried the intellectual process I have been describing full circle. A new coordinative framework led to new descriptions. The new descriptions allowed new explanations.

As we saw in Chapter 2, Copernicus left an important explanatory gap in his theory of the solar system. He showed that one can account for the apparent phenomena by describing a moving earth, but he did not offer any new causal explanations of the earth's motions. He did not say why or how the earth moves. Any follower of Copernicus had to fill this explanatory lacuna in order to answer his opponents, who, on the basis of Aristotelian physics, saw the motion of the earth as a physical impossibility. Gilbert was one such Copernican. He accepted that the earth is in motion, and he set out to explain its movement.[1]

Unlike Copernicus, however, Gilbert was not an astronomer. Save for a brief excursion at the very end of *De Magnete* (1600), his interest is restricted to terrestrial phenomena.[2] As a renowned physician with an appointment at court, Gilbert probably had little leisure to make regular celestial observations. Nor does he demonstrate the mathematical acumen necessary for any serious foray into mathematical astronomy, even by seventeenth-century standards. He may have had some facility in mathematics, having served as mathematics examiner at Cambridge from 1565, but whatever ability he possessed does not evidence itself in his published work.[3] Indeed, *De Magnete* is striking in its near complete lack of quantitative descriptions. Even Gilbert's discussion of Copernicus's theory of equinoctial precession is simply a qualitative summary of the corresponding passages of *De Revolutionibus*.[4]

As a result of this curtailed purview, Gilbert did not seek to explain *all* Copernicus's earthly motions. He aimed to explain the motions Copernicus ascribed to the earth in and of itself – i.e., the first and third motions.[5] That is to say, Gilbert tried to explain the earth's daily rotation and why the axis of this rotation remains pointed toward one region of the fixed stars. Gilbert did not, on the other hand, have anything to say about Copernicus's second motion, the annual orbit of the earth around the sun. Any investigation of this motion would require a discussion of the earth's position relative to other heavenly bodies, observations of which Gilbert was not prepared to handle. In fact, Gilbert does not explicitly affirm that the earth moves through the cosmos anywhere in *De Magnete*.[6]

---

[1] I agree with John Henry's contention, *contra* Zilsel, that "the whole point of *De Magnete* was to offer a solution to a crucial problem for Copernican theory . . . [i.e.,] Copernicus effectively left unanswered the question as to how the earth might be able to move and keep on moving" (Henry 2001, 106). See also Zilsel (1941).

[2] Gilbert's other, posthumously published work, *De Mundo Nostro Sublunari Philosophia Nova* (1651), is likewise generally restricted to terrestrial phenomena. There is some discussion of the earth's movement and the substance of the heavens, which I will touch on below, but the book is primarily concerned with sublunar phenomena, such as elemental substance, heat and cold, weather, and tides. The manuscript, compiled by Gilbert's half-brother and placed in the library of Henry, Prince of Wales, around 1607/8, was read by Francis Bacon and Thomas Harriot. The latter told Kepler about the work in 1608. Though he requested a copy, there is no evidence Kepler ever saw it. Otherwise, the book, published long after Gilbert's death, had little influence on Gilbert's successors. I will not devote much attention to it here. See Kelly (1965).

[3] Suter (1952, 271).   [4] See Zilsel (1941, 3).

[5] As well as the precession of the equinoxes, which he also attributes to a motion of the earth.

[6] He is agnostic about the earth's motion in *De Mundo*, as well. See Gilbert (1651, 196–99), Kelly (1965, 66–68).

This is not to say, though, that Gilbert did not believe that the earth moves around the sun. His project, after all, owed its existence to Copernicus, and he follows Copernicus at many points, including questioning the earth's centrality:

> But the stars or the planetary globes do not move in a circle round the center of the earth; nor is the earth the center – if it be in the center – but a body around the center.[7]

Gilbert accepts, without comment, Copernicus's conclusion that the earth is not the center of planetary orbits. As a result, like Copernicus, he wonders whether the earth really is at the center of the universe. It might be that the earth is not at the center, but revolving around another point. And even if the earth is at the center, its centrality is accidental. The center is a geometric point, unrelated to the body of the earth itself, which just happens to be "around the center." But this is as much as Gilbert will say on the matter.

Far more telling, though, is the very fact that Gilbert saw the need to explain the third motion at all. Recall that Copernicus introduces the third motion to account for the apparent stability of the earth's axis, *given* that the earth is orbiting the sun. If one assumes, conversely, that the earth does not orbit, and remains in place, presumably one would also assume that its axis remains in place, obviating any need to explain the appearance of stability. Hence, the very fact that Gilbert sees it as necessary to explain the apparent fixity of the earth's axis implies that he accepts Copernicus's second motion. One must assume that Gilbert believed the earth circles the sun.[8]

De Magnete, Book I

Gilbert begins *De Magnete* with an extensive investigation of the properties of magnets in general and spherical lodestones in particular. Book I includes encyclopedic details about: prior descriptions of magnetism; the different kinds and names of iron ore, and where they are found; how magnetism is found in iron ore and smelted and wrought iron; and the medicinal uses of magnets. Upon noticing the co-location of lodestones and iron ore in mines, the magnetism of both, and the similarity of their chemical traits,

---

[7] "nec terra si fuerit in centro, centrum est, sed corpus circa centrum" (Gilbert 1600, 227; 1958, 337–38).

[8] This is consistent with Gilbert's neoplatonic description of the sun as the source of vegetation and nourishment, which the earth "seeks and seeks again," implying (though he does not say so) that the sun inhabits the center as the source of vital energy in the universe (Gilbert 1958, 333–34). Compare this comment also to Copernicus's own neoplatonic description of the sun as the "lantern of the universe," etc. (Copernicus 1978, 22). For further support of Gilbert's heliocentrism, see Freudenthal (1983, 33–35).

Gilbert concludes "that loadstone and iron ore are the same" and their "form, appearance, and essence are one."[9]

> [T]hus loadstone is by origin and nature ferruginous, and iron magnetic, and the two are one in species . . . and the better sort of iron ore is weak loadstone, just as the best loadstone is the most excellent iron ore in which we will show that grand and noble primary properties inhere. It is only in weaker load-stone, or iron ore, that these properties are obscure, or faint, or scarcely perceptible to the senses.[10]

Lodestone and iron ore are essentially the same substance. Lodestone is just a superior form of ore, in which the special magnetic powers inhere particularly strongly.

The conclusion of Book I is presented in its seventeenth chapter, where Gilbert argues that the earth itself consists of magnetic material akin to lodestone and iron ore. Though the surface of the earth is "defaced by all sorts of waste matter and by no end of transformations,"[11] it exhibits an immutable magnetic power that influences, not only lodestones, but

> [all] sorts of fissile stone of different colors; also clays, gravel, and several sorts of rock; and, in short, all of the harder earths found everywhere, provided only they be not fouled by oozy and dank defilements like mud, mire, heaps of putrid matter, or by the decaying remains of a mixture of organic matters.[12]

Once the "dank defilements" of organic matter are removed, all earthy substances demonstrate their inherent magnetic nature. Ignoring the transformations of the imperfect organic world, then, earth's "inmost nature" and "marrow"[13] is magnetic stuff:

> Such, then, we consider the earth to be in its interior parts; it possesses a magnetic homogenic nature. On this more perfect material (foundation) the whole world of things terrestrial [is based], which, when we search diligently, manifests itself to us everywhere, in all magnetic metals and iron ores and marls, and multitudinous earths and stones.[14]

According to Gilbert, the fact that the earth consists of magnetic matter means the earth is *essentially* magnetic. For the earth is a celestial body, endowed with a peculiar and special nature.

> But the true earth-matter we hold to be a solid body homogeneous with the globe, firmly coherent, endowed with a primordial and (as in the other globes of the universe) an energic form.[15]

[9] Gilbert (1958, 59–60).   [10] Gilbert (1958, 63).   [11] Gilbert (1958, 67).   [12] Gilbert (1958, 70).
[13] Gilbert (1958, 68).   [14] Gilbert (1958, 69).
[15] Gilbert (1958, 68). "Sed terram veram volumus esse substantiam solidam, telluri homogeneam, firmiter cohaerentem, primaria, & (ut in globis aliis mundi) valida forma praeditam" (Gilbert 1600, 42).

All heavenly bodies, including the earth, have a primordial form, "endowed" by the Creator. The earth's substance, then, must partake of the earth's special form. Gilbert has shown, though, that earth-matter is magnetic. Hence, this "primordial" and "energic" form is, or at least comprises, magnetism. Magnetism is the form of the earth and earth-matter.[16]

A lodestone, therefore, shares the essential magnetic form of the earth itself, as do all other magnetic substances, in varying degrees:

> A strong loadstone shows itself to be of the inmost earth, and in innumerable experiments proves its claim to the honor of possessing the primal form of things terrestrial. . . . So a weak loadstone, and all iron ore, all marls and argillaceous and other earths (some more, some less, according to the difference of their humors and the varying degrees in which they have been spoilt by decay), retain, deformed, in a state of degeneration from the primordial form, magnetic properties, powers, that are conspicuous and in the true sense telluric.[17]

There is a real, formal affinity between a lodestone, or any other magnetic material, and the earth. They share a single form and nature. Thus, whatever is natural for a lodestone – whatever is a result of its form – will also be natural for the earth itself. In particular, Gilbert will assert, the earth's motions are natural, caused by its inherent magnetic nature:

> Thus every separate fragment of the earth exhibits in indubitable experiments the whole impetus of magnetic matter; in its various movements it follows the terrestrial globe and the common principle of motion.[18]

Experiments performed on "separate fragments of the earth" – i.e., lodestones – will exhibit the true nature of magnetic matter, including its principles of motion, "common" to lodestone and earth. Hence, whatever motions are found in the lodestone can be ascribed to the earth, as well.

Thus, in Book I of *De Magnete*, Gilbert has laid the groundwork for an explanation of the earth's motion on the basis of an investigation into the nature of the lodestone. Whatever magnetic properties exist in the lodestone will exist in the earth simply because they share a common magnetic nature.[19]

---

[16] Gilbert also favorably quotes Guillermo Cardano's proposition that "the loadstone is true earth" (Gilbert 1958, 69–70). See also Freudenthal (1983, 24–26).

[17] Gilbert (1958, 70).   [18] Gilbert (1958, 71).

[19] It is interesting to note that, in this context, Gilbert has adopted the Aristotelian structure of explanation based on substantial form. As in Aristotelian matter theory, the form is responsible for the properties of the body. In this case, however, the form is magnetism – an active principle akin to neoplatonic affinities and spirits. Gilbert accepts the notion that a form inheres in earthy matter and gives it its various attributes, but he explicitly rejects the Aristotelian view of earth as an ideal, inert, and utterly passive element. The postulated ideal earth, "Aristotle's 'simple element,' and that most

De Magnete, **Book II**

Book II begins Gilbert's investigation of the magnetic characteristics of lodestones and their motions. He focuses his attention on spherical lodestones, which he labels *terrellae*, because the spherical shape is also that of the earth. Thus, a terrella will have

> got from art the orbicular form that nature in the beginning gave to the earth, the common mother; and it is a natural little body endowed with a multitude of properties whereby many abstruse and unheeded truths of philosophy, hid in deplorable darkness, may be more readily brought to the knowledge of mankind.[20]

A spherical lodestone is most like the earth, so the properties associated with a terrella will be most like the earth's, as well. Because the forms have such close similarity, investigation of the properties of the terrella can reveal "truths of philosophy" regarding the earth.

Importantly, the phenomena associated with a terrella immediately suggest a particular representation of space to be used to describe them. This is not the centered representation of space found in Aristotelian physical theory, but the system of meridians and poles used by geographers and astronomers. Even the most rudimentary examination of a terrella – indeed, of any magnet – reveals diametrically opposed poles where the strength of the magnet's influence is concentrated. A simple procedure locates them on the surface of the sphere:

> To find, then, poles answering to the earth's poles, take in your hand the round stone, and lay on it a needle or a piece of iron wire; the ends of the wire move round their middle point, and suddenly come to a standstill. Now, with ochre or with chalk, mark where the wire lies still and sticks. Then move the middle or center of the wire to another spot, and so to a third and a fourth, always marking the stone along the length of the wire where it stands still: the lines so marked will exhibit meridian circles, or circles like meridians on the stone or terrella; and manifestly they will all come together a the poles of the stone.[21]

This method of finding the poles reveals "lines of force" marked out on the terrella. On a spherical magnet, these will, as Gilbert describes, form great circles converging at two opposing poles, "like meridians."

vain terrestrial phantasm of the Peripatetics," is merely a product of the imagination and "never appeared to any one even in dreams." Magnets, observable and active, are the true terrestrial substance. Gilbert accepts the outline of the Aristotelian theory of matter, but rejects the specific description of the earthy element. Earth is an Aristotelian element, but it is essentially magnetic, not, in Gilbert's words, "formless, inert, cold, [and] dry" (Gilbert 1958, 69).

[20] Gilbert (1958, 24).   [21] Gilbert (1958, 24).

Notice, however, that a meridian is not identifiable in a spherical representation of space constructed around an assumed center. Suppose we are presented with the claim, "the line is like a meridian." If all we presuppose is a sphere around a center, all we can determine is whether the line is a great circle of the sphere. But this is not enough to test the claim. We must also determine whether the great circle connects the poles. Thus, in addition to the sphere (and its center), we must also stipulate poles as privileged locations on the sphere to which we can refer our description. We need to include poles in our representation of space to legitimate descriptions including meridians. In other words, descriptions involving meridians can only be understood in the context of a representation of space that includes poles. The same is true, for example, of descriptions including equators, parallels, and the poles themselves.

When Gilbert says that the lines of force on a terrella are "like meridians," he is implicitly assuming that the reader knows what a meridian is and where it might lie on the sphere of the terrella. The descriptions can be understood because the reader shares Gilbert's framework that makes the descriptions sensible – a spherical representation of space with poles. The phenomena exhibited by the lodestone can then be described by reference to the sphere and its poles. I will call this the *geographical* representation of space, in virtue of its use in the geographical system of meridians and parallels.

Gilbert explicitly endorses the geographical representation of space as the proper framework for his description for magnetic phenomena:

> Astronomers, in order to account for and observe the movements of the planets and the revolution of the heavens, as also more accurately to describe the heavenly order of the fixed stars, have drawn in the heavens certain circles and bounds, which geographers also imitate so as to map out the diversified superficies of the globe and to delineate the fairness of the several regions.[22]

Gilbert, like a geographer or astronomer, will use presupposed "circles and bounds" – meridians, poles, equators, etc. – to describe the behaviors of his terrellae. This method of description is naturally suited to the phenomena, since the lines of magnetic force, for example, pass along meridians, and so on.

The presupposition of a geographical representation of space allows the specification of direction and location on the surface of the sphere. As Gilbert writes:

> And neither in earth nor in terrella do the poles exist merely for the sake of rotation; they are furthermore reference points of direction and of

[22] Gilbert (1958, 125).

position – on the one hand towards one's destination on the earth, and on the other hand as regards the angular distance between them.[23]

Position, for example, is specified as an angular distance from the pole, measured at the center – i.e., latitude. Direction is also referred to the pole as a "destination." One can be directed toward or away from the pole, or one can be directed around it, neither toward nor away. (Gilbert has in mind the compass rose. The north/south/east/west specifications of geographers are understood as toward, away from, and perpendicular to the poles.)

The description of motions – changes of direction – thus follows from Gilbert's geographical framework. Consider, for example, his description of "variation," one of the five "magnetic movements" caused by a terrella's magnetic nature. Variation is defined as "deflection from the meridian."[24] In other words, the meridian is considered the null direction. To stay in the "same direction" is to stay pointed along the meridian toward a pole. A "variation" is a change of this direction. If something, a compass needle, say, remains pointed along the meridian, it has not undergone variation. If the compass needle is deflected from the meridian to the east or west, it has moved. The description presumes a meridian between stipulated poles. Thus, the poles, meridian, and the geographical representation of space, are essential to Gilbert's description of variation.

A similar point can be made regarding another of Gilbert's magnetic movements: declination, "a descent of the magnetic pole beneath the horizon."[25] On a terrella, and on the earth, a magnetic needle only lies parallel to the sphere's surface at the (magnetic) equator. Closer to the poles, it will incline, or dip, towards the pole. At the pole, the needle will stand on end, perpendicular to the surface of the magnet. Notice, however, that Gilbert describes this motion as a "descent" "beneath the horizon," where the horizon is the plane tangential to the sphere.[26] The description again presupposes a sphere, so that the direction tangential to it is a null direction. Needles that lie tangential to the sphere exhibit no "descent" and, hence, no declination. The declination increases, however, as the needle moves "below" the tangent to the sphere, reaching maximum (the perpendicular) at the pole. Gilbert's description of declination, as of variation, demonstrates his use of a geographical representation of space.

---

[23] Gilbert (1958, 129, translation slightly altered). "Neq; etiam hi in tellure aut terrella vertendi tantum gratia existunt; sed etiam termini sunt dirigendi, & consistendi, tum versus destinatas mundi regiones; tum etiam inter se iustis conversionibus" (Gilbert 1600, 81).
[24] Gilbert (1958, 73). [25] Gilbert (1958, 73). [26] Gilbert (1958, 128).

Instantiations of the geographical representation of space

Gilbert's representation of space is actually an important component of his overall argument concerning the earth's motion. Gilbert asserts that the geographical representation of space is not an arbitrary descriptive framework chosen to generate descriptions. While astronomers and geographers use the geographical representation, with its meridians and poles, "to account for and observe the movements of the planets" or "delineate the fairness of the several regions" of the world, it is just a descriptive device for them. The meridians, parallels and poles are merely "imaginary lines." In the context of magnetism, however, these geometrical structures are physical features of the terrella:.

> In a different sense we accept those bounds and circles, for we have discovered many such, both in the terrella and in the earth; but these are determined by nature itself, and are not merely imaginary lines. Geographers make a division of the earth chiefly by defining the equator and the poles; and [in the terrella] these bounds are set and defined by nature. Meridians, too, indicate tracks from pole to pole, passing through fixed points in the equator; along such lines the magnetic force proceeds and gives direction.[27]

In geography, the geographical representation of space is imposed by the geographer, who "defines" its elements. In magnetism, the geographical framework is fixed by the nature of the magnet, which "sets" and "defines" its structure. These "lines," the meridians, the equator, the polar axis, etc., are determined by the nature of the terrella.

Gilbert's argument, then, amounts to a claim that the terrella, by virtue of its magnetic nature, *instantiates* the geographical representation of space. The geometric features of the framework are physical features of the spherical magnet, with real and observable effects in phenomena. A meridian, for example, is a geometric structure. It "indicates tracks from pole to pole." On the terrella, though, the meridians are instantiated by the magnetic force, which "proceeds" along them. Poles, meanwhile, are geometric points, but are also the foci of magnetic attraction, where the attractive power is strongest. Similarly, the equator is the line that separates the terrella into two halves, each "imbued with equal energy," and where attraction is weakest.[28] The parallels are loci of constant magnetic declination.[29] These "metes and bounds" are real features of the magnetic body. The representation used to describe magnetic phenomena is not just "imaginary," but in the very nature of the phenomena described. It is not imposed on the phenomena, but "discovered" in them.

---

[27] Gilbert (1958, 125).   [28] Gilbert (1958, 126).   [29] Gilbert (1958, 127).

For Gilbert, the close coordination of geometry and phenomena entails that the geographical framework is part of the phenomena. The terrella's "metes and bounds" are generated by its inherent magnetic nature, not by the observer trying to describe it. In this way, Gilbert slides over the distinction between coordinative framework and phenomena. He makes the framework used to generate the description part of the description.

This subtle slide results in a somewhat circular argument. Gilbert begins by assuming a certain geometry. He assumes a sphere and poles. When observing the terrella, he finds certain features that answer to these presupposed structures. Then he describes the terrella's features *as* the assumed structures. The conclusion that the terrella has real, objective poles relies, in part, on the descriptive assumption that the terrella has poles. This is not a necessary conclusion, of course. The foci of magnetic attraction are not geometric points, and nothing entails that they should be described as such. By extension, nothing requires that the parallel to the tangent be the "same" declination everywhere on a sphere. Others might find different representations that are, in their estimation, more satisfactory – though it is admittedly hard to imagine what the other representations might be.

Naturally, Gilbert's choice of descriptive framework does not come in a vacuum. As it turns out, the geographical representation of space *is* very appropriate to the terrella, and allows specific and detailed descriptions of its properties. Indeed, the terrella immediately suggests the geographical structure, as we have seen, and it is difficult to conceive another conceptual framework that could be substituted. Thus, Gilbert's conclusion that the geographical structure is an objective feature of the terrella can be weakened to the sound, almost equivalent claim that the physical features of the terrella can *best be described* on the basis of the geographical representation of space. The foci of the magnetic attraction are not poles, *per se*, but best described as poles. Lines of magnetic force, meanwhile, are not meridians, but best described as meridians. By contrast, a spherical representation of space, for example, does not provide as easy a way to describe the terrella's magnetic action. Since such a representation provides for the assumption of neither poles nor meridians, there would be no simple way to describe the foci or lines of magnetic force. In the end, as we shall see, this weakening will make little difference to Gilbert's argument.

De Magnete, Books III–V: magnetic motions

Book I of *De Magnete* established the common magnetic nature of the earth and terrella, which Gilbert promised to exhibit in "indubitable experiments." Book II begins the presentation of these "experiments." The first part introduces the five "magnetic motions" caused by the magnetic nature of the earth and terrella: coition, direction, variation, declination, and revolution.

The latter part of Book II examines coition, "an impulsion to magnetic union" "commonly called attraction."[30] Coition, Gilbert reasons, is a result of the joint nature of both attractor and attracted, rather than, as in the case of electric attraction, the action of the attractor alone.[31] He also presents numerous experiments demonstrating how magnetic power can be increased (by armoring the stone) or decreased (by corrosion or heating). The essential conclusion of this discussion, however, is that coition follows the inherent geometry of both earth and terrella. Coition respects magnetic poles, where it is strongest, and an equator, where it is weakest.[32] Also, in the terrella and the earth, the strength of magnetic action decreases in proportion to distance from the center of the sphere. This implies the "shape" of magnetic action is spherical. The terrella produces a magnetic "orb of virtue," whose center, the "center of force," coincides with the center of the magnet and whose action replicates the poles and lines of the terrella's surface.[33] Coition reveals the inherent shape of magnetic action.

Book III investigates the phenomenon Gilbert calls "direction," the movement of a magnet or needle to align its poles with those of the earth and the terrella. Here, Gilbert presents experiments demonstrating that magnetized needles will align with the meridians of a terrella. He also shows that magnetized needles (and even wrought iron, suitably worked) will align with the north and south poles of the earth, and how this movement can be used profitably for timekeeping, surveying, navigation, and so forth. Most important for Gilbert, though, is the fact that direction is manifested on both earth and terrella. This similarity constitutes empirical evidence for the affinity between earth and lodestone that is essential to Gilbert's argument.

For reasons I will come to, Gilbert assumed that the earth's magnetic axis coincides with its rotational axis. Of course, as we now know, this is not the case. As a result, compass needles will not perfectly align themselves with the rotational pole, along what Gilbert call the "true meridian," but along the magnetic meridian towards the magnetic pole:

---

[30] Gilbert (1958, 73).

[31] "Thus the magnetic coition is the act of the loadstone and of the iron, not of one of them alone: it is ... *conactus* (mutual action) rather than sympathy" (Gilbert 1958, 110). Gilbert argues that coition is caused by the natural desire for bodies with the same or similar natures to cohere. This is reminiscent of Copernicus's awkward explanation of gravitation. See Copernicus (1978, 18), and Chapter 2, above.

[32] Gilbert (1958, 115–19, 129–31, 151).   [33] Gilbert (1958, 119, 50–51).

Yet very oft it happens, afloat and ashore, that a magnetic needle does not look toward the true pole, but is drawn to a point in the horizon nigh to the meridian, and that there is a deflection not only of the needle and magnetized iron in general and of the mariner's compass, but also of a terrella ... for they often look with their poles toward points different from the meridian.[34]

As we have seen, Gilbert calls this deflection from the rotational meridian "variation."

Variation occurs on the earth, but not on the terrella. This dissimilarity calls Gilbert's analogy between earth and terrella into question. Book III of *De Magnete*, therefore, is dedicated to an argument that variation is merely a "perverted motion."[35] It is caused, Gilbert asserts, not by the true magnetic form of the earth, but by the irregularity of its surface – the "inequality among the earth's elevations."[36] Landmasses, projecting from the globe of the earth, form irregular concentrations of earthy, magnetic matter, disturbing the "direction" caused by the earth's true nature, resulting in variation. If similar protuberances are found or constructed on a lodestone, similar disturbances of "direction" are observed. Variation, then, is a "perversion" of the true action of the earth, caused by the transient world of "transformations" on its surface. If the earth were a smooth sphere, compass needles would all align with its true, immutable, magnetic – and rotational – poles.

Book V of *De Magnete* comes to "declination," the "descent of the magnetic pole beneath the horizon." Gilbert describes how, on a terrella, magnetized needles will "dip" toward the poles. Gilbert then describes experiments that demonstrate the same phenomenon on the earth. The demonstration of magnetic declination is supposed to clinch Gilbert's argument that the earth and the terrella are of one kind:

> We come at last to that fine experiment, that wonderful movement of magnetic bodies as they dip beneath the horizon in virtue of their natural verticity; after we have mastered this, the wondrous combination, harmony, and concordant interaction of the earth and the loadstone (or magnetized iron), being made manifest by our theory, stand revealed.[37]

Declination conclusively reveals the similarity between earth and lodestone. Magnetized needles on the earth decline according to latitude, just as they do on the terrella. Of course, Gilbert's theory is that this similarity is due to a shared magnetic nature. Thus, the harmony and concordance witnessed in the phenomenon of declination is a testament to the formal likeness of all magnets, including the earth and terrella.

---

[34] Gilbert (1958, 230).   [35] Gilbert (1958, 73).   [36] Gilbert (1958, 235).   [37] Gilbert (1958, 275).

Direction is seen in both earth and terrella. Variation, peculiar to the earth, is a spurious motion that may be dismissed. Most wonderful of all, declination is observed exactly on the earth as it is on the terrella. Hence,

> All the experiments that are made on the terrella, to show how magnetic bodies conform themselves to it, may – at least the principal and most striking of them – be shown on the body of the earth; to the earth, too, all magnetized bodies are associate.[38]

All the observed phenomena, so clearly expounded in the first five books of *De Magnete*, indicate that the earth and the terrella are of the same nature. All that is natural for the terrella is natural for the earth. The earth and terrella share a magnetic nature.

Notice that Gilbert's argument mainly concerns description, but the conclusion itself has explanatory import. The earth can be *described* in the same way as a spherical magnet is described, so it follows that the properties and powers of magnets are the properties and powers of the earth. Yet, since the earth can be described this way, one can go on to say that the earth moves *because* it is a magnet – it has a magnetic nature. This nature, moreover, causes the certain motions common to all magnets. This much is an explanation. Gilbert has not shown, though, why the earth is a magnet – why it is endowed with its peculiar nature – or why magnets exhibit the behaviors they do. This is left to the inscrutable wisdom of the Creator. Gilbert's explanation only reaches so far. The important move is to describe the earth and terrellae as members of a single class – magnets – over which ascriptions of features, including motions, can be generalized.[39] This includes the use of a geographical representation of space in both cases, as we will see.

De Magnete, Book VI: the earth's motions

Finally, in Book VI, Gilbert is ready to put the pieces of his argument together. Recall Gilbert's assertion that the terrella instantiates the geographical geometry. Meridians, poles, and equator are to be taken as real features of the terrella, determined by its nature. Since the earth is a terrella, and shares this nature, it also instantiates the geographical representation of space:

> And first, on the terrella the equinoctial circle, the meridians, parallels, the axis, the poles, are natural limits: similarly on the earth these exist as natural and not merely mathematical limits.[40]

[38] Gilbert (1958, 275).
[39] For an account of the explanatory shortcomings of Gilbert's theory, see Hesse (1960).
[40] Gilbert (1958, 313).

Just as poles, meridians, and an equator are real features of a terrella, they are real features of the earth. They are not merely "imaginary" or "mathematical" structures used to describe the earth, but elements of the inherent magnetic nature of the terrestrial globe.

That the earth has real poles is of critical importance for Gilbert's argument in favor of the earth's motion. The debate between Gilbert and his anti-Copernican opponents is whether the heavens or the earth rotates. Gilbert reduces this to a question of representational geometry. It is clear that the apparent movement of the sun, stars, and planets daily across the sky is a result of either a rotation of the entire heavens, or a rotation of the earth, "for in no third mode can the apparent revolutions be accounted for."[41] Now, "Bodies that by nature move with a motion circular, equable, and constant, have in their different parts various metes and bounds."[42] That is, bodies that move with a uniform rotation have certain identifiable features. In particular, they exhibit poles, points where the circular motion is minimal, and an equator, where the motion is maximal. From these, other "metes and bounds" can be derived, such as meridians and parallels. The body that exhibits poles, meridians, an equator, and so forth, must be the body in motion. If the earth really has these features, it is moving. Otherwise they belong to the rotating heavens.

Of course, and this is Gilbert's point, the earth has these characteristics. Gilbert's magnetic experiments were meant to prove that they are real features of the earth:

> Now the earth is not a chaos nor a chance medley mass, but through its astral property has limits agreeable to the circular motion, to wit, poles that are not merely mathematical expressions, an equator that is not a mere fiction, meridians, too, and parallels, and all these we find in the earth, permanent, fixed, and natural; they are demonstrated with many experiments in the magnetic philosophy.[43]

Magnetism has provided *independent* evidence for the existence of the geographic features of motion in the earth. The earth is a terrella. Like all terrellae, therefore, it instantiates the geographical representation of space. The earth has real poles, real meridians, and a real equator, each determined by its nature and demonstrable by its magnetic action, without reference to its motion. Thus, the earth is "fitted" – has the necessary geographic features – for diurnal rotation.[44]

---

[41] Gilbert (1958, 328).   [42] Gilbert (1958, 328).   [43] Gilbert (1958, 328).

[44] In effect, Gilbert has used magnetism to expand Copernicus's proposition that the earth is "naturally fitted" for circular motion because it is spherically shaped and circular motion is the natural motion for spheres. See Copernicus (1978, 8–12).

The geographic features ascribed to the heavens, meanwhile, have no real existence:

> But no revolutions of bodies, no movements of planets, show any sensible, natural poles in the firmament or in any *primum mobile*; neither does any argument prove their existence; they are the product of imagination.[45]

The firmament of fixed stars is homogeneous and isomorphic. It gives no observable evidence whatsoever for the existence of inherent, natural poles. The celestial poles are "the product of imagination," ascribed to the heavens as a result of their apparent motion, not because of their nature. The earth, on the other hand, possesses its particular motion as a result of it poles, "for nature has set in the earth definite poles and has established definite and not confused revolutions" around those poles. The earth, not the heavens, must be the moving body.[46]

I pointed out above that Gilbert's ascription of real poles to the terrella is somewhat misleading. A magnet exhibits foci of magnetic attraction. Gilbert *describes* these foci as "poles." Thus the "poles" are, at bottom, descriptions of phenomena, not phenomena themselves. However, Gilbert's argument goes through even if one assumes that the terrella does not possess physical poles, but only features best described as poles. As Gilbert himself points out in his presentation of his opponents' claims, it is not that a rotating body has poles – these are merely geometric points used to describe the features of the rotating body. A rotating body has real features – parts where its motion is minimal – that are best described as poles. Thus, if the earth is rotating, it should exhibit features best described as poles. Gilbert can then show, on the basis of magnetism, that this is the case. From this point, the argument follows. The earth's magnetic properties imply that it should be considered the body in motion.[47]

---

[45] Gilbert (1958, 328).

[46] Gilbert (1958, 338). For a fuller discussion of the metaphorical nature of Gilbert's argument see Dear (1995, ch. 6).

[47] The distinction between the phenomena and description does highlight, in a way not apparent in Gilbert's text, the accidental coincidence of the magnetic and rotational poles. For Gilbert's argument to go through, of course, he must assume the earth's magnetic axis coincides with its rotational axis. Yet, that the earth has a magnetic feature best described as a pole does not entail that the description "pole" also applies to a feature of its motion (or non-motion). By saying that the earth has an objective pole – without specifying whether it is magnetic or rotational – Gilbert can skirt the distinction without arguing that the two necessarily coincide. Observed "variation" raised the same problem empirically, since it indicates that magnetized needles on the earth respect a magnetic pole different from the earth's "true" rotational one. That is why Gilbert went to great lengths in Book IV to dismiss variation as a spurious, "perverted" motion.

Diurnal rotation: a blind alley

At this point, Gilbert's attempted magnetic explanation of the earth's motion runs into a blind alley. He wants to explain the diurnal rotation of the earth – Copernicus's first motion – on the basis of magnetic movements. If it can be shown that terrellae naturally revolve around their axes, Gilbert can argue that the earth's diurnal rotation is caused by its magnetic nature. The earth's magnetic nature would explain Copernicus's motion. Gilbert cannot, however, show that "revolution" – his term for rotation about the axis – is actually exhibited by spherical lodestones.

Gilbert has observed the rotation of terrellae, but this phenomenon does not support his conclusion that terrellae, and thus the earth, undergo revolution:

> That the earth is fitted for circular movement is proved by its parts, which, when separated from the whole, do not simply travel in a right line ... but rotate also. A loadstone placed in a wooden vessel is put in water so that it may float freely, rotate, and move about. If the [north-seeking] pole *B* of the loadstone be made to point, unnaturally, toward the south *F*, the terrella revolves round its center in a circular motion on the plane of the horizon toward the north *E*, where it comes to a rest.[48]

Here, a terrella indeed moves circularly around its center, but not around the axis between its poles, and not continually, as Gilbert would have the earth move. The motion described just realigns the terrella's poles with the earth's poles, i.e., along the meridian. It is the terrella's axis itself that rotates around an axis *perpendicular* to the magnetic axis. Once the terrella has reoriented itself in its "natural" configuration, the motion ceases. But this gives no evidence, in the terrella or the earth, for continuous "revolution" around the magnetic axis.

Indeed, Gilbert is forced to reject a report that spherical lodestones rotate. He simply cannot repeat the experiment:

> I omit what Petrus Peregrinus so stoutly affirms, that a terrella poised on its poles in the meridian moves circularly with a complete revolution in twenty-four hours. We have never chanced to see this: nay, we doubt if there is such movement.[49]

Such a motion, if observed, would be evidence that the earth naturally revolved around its axis. If it could be shown that terrellae revolve around their axes, then one could conclude that the earth, a giant terrella, exhibits the same motion. Gilbert, however, has "never chanced" to observe

---

[48] Gilbert (1958, 331). [49] Gilbert (1958, 332).

Peregrinus's rotation, even though, presumably, he has tried to replicate the result.

The motion of the terrella indicates only that it moves with a natural circular motion about its center, not that it revolves around its axis. This does imply, Gilbert argues, that the earth *can* move circularly.

> The natural movements of the whole and of the parts are alike: hence, since the parts move in a circle, the whole, too, hath the power of circular motion. . . . And this circular movement of the loadstone . . . shows that the whole earth is fitted, and by its own forces adapted for a diurnal circular motion.[50]

Since the motion of the whole earth will be like its parts, terrellae, the earth must, like terrellae, be capable of circular motion. This is a hollow conclusion, however. The behavior of the terrella shows that a magnetic nature can cause a circular motion, but it is the *wrong kind* of circular motion. It is not a continuous, diurnal rotation around the magnetic axis, but a short-lived rotation of the axis itself.

In the end, Gilbert's magnetic philosophy successfully describes the earth's magnetic nature. It can show that the earth has a magnetic axis and that it is "fitted" for circular motion. Yet it fails to support the desired conclusion: the earth's magnetic nature *causes* a daily rotation. Gilbert can set the earth upon its pole, but he cannot make it spin.

To complete his explanation of Copernicus's first motion, Gilbert appeals to causes beyond those demonstrated by his observation of magnets. He employs neoplatonic affinities, astral natures, and terrestrial animism to explain the motion of the earth. The earth rotates because of its "magnetic mind":

> And were not the earth to revolve with diurnal rotation, the sun would ever hang with its constant light over a given part, and, by long tarrying there, would scorch the earth, reduce it to powder, and dissipate its substance, and the uppermost surface of earth would receive grievous hurt: nothing of good would spring form earth, there would be no vegetation; it could not give life to the animate creation, and man would perish. In other parts all would be horror, and all things frozen stiff with intense cold. . . . And as the earth herself cannot endure so pitiable and so horrid a state of things on either side, with her astral magnetic mind she moves in a circle, to the end there may be, by unceasing change of light, a perpetual vicissitude, heat and cold, rise and decline, day and night, morn and even, noonday and deep night. So the earth seeks and seeks the sun again, turns from him, follows him, by her wondrous magnetical energy.[51]

[50] Gilbert (1958, 331–32).   [51] Gilbert (1958, 333–34).

The earth is animate, Gilbert argues, and seeks out the best preservation of itself. This entails a continuous diurnal rotation, forever towards the "benefit" of the heavenly bodies. For, if the earth did not rotate, it "would receive grievous hurt" from the sun on one side, and "all would be horror" on the other, a state of affairs "the earth herself cannot endure."

Altogether, then, the animate earth moves itself in harmony with the heavens to receive their most propitious influences:

> The motion of the whole earth, therefore, is primary, astral, circular about its poles . . . so that the globe by a definite rotation might move to the good, sun and stars inciting.[52]

Gilbert, finally, can explain the earth's diurnal rotation. The earth has a natural axis because it is a terrella – a spherical magnet. Poles are set out by its magnetic nature. It spins around this axis, however, because it is animate, and seeks out the harmony and benefit provided by the heavenly bodies. However, this explanation is no more supported by evidence than the Aristotelian appeals to quintessence and elemental natures that Gilbert rejects.[53]

The third motion: verticity and the Law of the Whole

We now can turn our attention, finally, to Gilbert's proposed explanation of Copernicus's "third motion," the supposed rotation of the earth's axis. Recall that Copernicus attributed a motion to the earth to account for the fact that the earth's rotational axis remains pointed at the same part of the heavens throughout the year. I have argued that Copernicus was led to describe the phenomenon as a motion because of his centered representation of space. Gilbert's geographical representation of space leads him to a quite different description. He will say that the earth's axis does *not* move.

---

[52] Gilbert (1958, 334–35).

[53] Note that this position places Gilbert in between several intellectual positions of his day. His argument relies on a Peripatetic notion of substantial form, but the form is active, like an alchemical principle. Gilbert's analytic approach to the substance of the magnet also evinces the thinking of the chemists. In addition, Gilbert appeals to astral intellects and influences, hearkening to neoplatonism and natural magic. All told, it is difficult to classify Gilbert with any of these groups, let alone as a "traditional" or "modern" thinker. He is a transitional figure, responding to the intellectual climate of his time, to whom labels do not easily apply. Gilbert intrigued contemporaries of all persuasions, but satisfied none. This has not stopped historians from trying to categorize Gilbert. Heilbron, for example, calls him a "moderate peripatetic" and a "plagiarist" prone to "Renaissance bombast" (1979, 169). Henry (2001) claims him for the magicians. Freudenthal (1983), meanwhile, puts him in the modern camp, but is more careful to note Gilbert's awkward position between Aristotelianism and neoplatonism. Zilsel (1941) names him the first experimental philosopher, who gained his insights from nascent capitalists more than any scholarly tradition. See also Burtt (1954, 162–67).

In so doing, however, he appeals to an important and novel feature of the representation of celestial space.

Gilbert has drawn an analogy between the earth and the terrella. Both have an essential magnetic nature, and both exhibit certain natural motions, such as direction, declination, coition, and (perhaps) revolution. Now, as we have seen, direction is the ability of a spherical magnet to align other magnets and magnetic materials to its meridians. Thus, magnetized needles will point to the poles, both on the terrella and on the earth. This is not all, however.

> Like the earth, the loadstone has the power of direction and of standing still at north and south; it has also a circular motion to the earth's position, whereby it adjusts itself to the earth's law [*quo se ad illius normam componit*].[54]

In addition to directing needles, a terrella will conform itself to the surrounding magnetic field – the "earth's law." That is, it will orient itself and remain in the north–south orientation dictated by the earth, such that the axes of terrella and earth lie in the same plane. Thus, a lodestone not only has the power to direct needles, but the power to move itself according to an external magnetic action. Gilbert labels this power of the lodestone "verticity."

Unlike "revolution," though, verticity is an observed phenomenon, caused by a magnetic nature. Recall the experiment with the terrella in a wooden bowl cited above. In that case, the magnet does indeed align itself with the earth's axis. Of course, Gilbert's argument all along has been that whatever movements are natural for a terrella are natural for the earth as well. Hence, the experiment supports Gilbert's ascription of verticity to the terrella and, therefore, the earth. As Gilbert explains, the earth itself has a verticity that aligns it with an external magnetic virtue, which he calls the "Law of the Whole":[55]

> For like as a loadstone ... does by its native verticity, according to the magnetic laws, conform its poles to the poles of the common mother, – so, were the earth to vary from her natural direction and from her position in the universe, or were her poles to be pulled toward the rising or the setting sun, or other points whatsoever in the visible firmament (were that possible), they would recur again by a magnetic movement to north and south, and halt at the same points where now they stand.[56]

---

[54] Gilbert (1600, 42; 1958, 67).

[55] "the loadstone possesses the actions peculiar to the globe, of attraction, polarity, revolution, of taking position in the universe according to the Law of the Whole [*totius normam*]" (Gilbert 1600, 41; 1958, 66).

[56] Gilbert (1958, 180).

Just as a terrella has the ability to conform itself to the "earth's law," the earth has the ability to conform itself to a cosmic magnetic field or Law of the Whole. Should the earth's axis ever be deflected, it will naturally return itself to its former orientation, pointing toward the same spot in the heavens:

> The whole earth would act in the same way, were the north pole turned aside from its true direction; for that pole would go back, in the circular motion of the whole, toward Cynosura [i.e., Ursa Minor].[57]

The earth, like the terrella, will naturally rotate about its center to "direct" its magnetic axes in the "true direction." In the absence of deflection, moreover, the magnetic power of the earth simply maintains the orientation of its axis, which remains ever parallel to itself, in the same "true" or "natural" direction.

But what is this Law of the Whole to which the earth adheres? A lodestone instantiates the geographical representation of space. Included in this descriptive framework are poles, which are instantiated as the foci of the magnetic force of the magnet. The poles, however, are not symmetric. They can be distinguished from one another by their activity. One seeks the earth's north pole, the other the south pole. Hence, the poles give the magnet itself an inherent direction or orientation – a way in which it is "pointed." This "pointing" is indicated along the line connecting the two poles – i.e., the axis, from "south" to "north." So, when the lodestone conforms its poles to the poles of the earth, it is bringing its own orientation into line with the "earth's law". It "points" itself along the meridian – north-seeking pole toward north pole, south-seeking toward south. The earth, like any other lodestone, also has this inherent linear direction indicated by its poles and the ability to align this internal direction to an external magnetic virtue. The lodestone aligns itself with the earth's orientation. The earth aligns itself with the orientation of the cosmos. The Law of the Whole is an extrapolation of the earth's orientation to the universe itself.

This extrapolation is interesting, however. Unlike Aristotle and Copernicus, Gilbert does not assume that the universe has a center.[58]

---

[57] Gilbert (1958, 331).

[58] Gilbert also eschews an assumed center in his account of terrestrial gravity. He vehemently rejects the Aristotelian view that heavy bodies seek a geometric point or place. Instead, he argues that bodies fall because they seek unity with like matter (a view similar to that of Copernicus). However, Gilbert is inconsistent regarding the salient features of matter that result in this desire for unity. Sometimes, he says that electrical activity, which has to do with moisture, brings bodies together. Elsewhere, he says it is magnetic mutual attraction that draws and keeps bodies together. In any case, centers, as geometric points, do not play any role. See Gilbert (1651, 116; 1958, 97, 142).

Directions in the cosmos are not referred to a central point. Notice that even if the earth were to "vary from her position," the poles "would recur again" and "halt at the same points where now they stand." At any arbitrary place in the universe, Gilbert is arguing, the orientation of the Law of the Whole is the same, toward the same points of the heavens. Here, the "same points" are not points in the field of the fixed stars, but points in the line of the earth's axis as it extends through the universe. Hence, the return to the "same points in the heavens" means that the orientation that the poles of the earth would assume (if it moved) is everywhere parallel. If the earth were to revolve around the sun, for example, the "lines of the axis of the earth [would be] parallel at equinoxes and solstices."[59] The orientation, therefore, must be rectilinear and self-parallel. Gilbert is referring the orientation to a presupposed straight line – the line connecting the earth's rotational poles, now extended to infinity. This is the null direction to which direction at all other positions is referred. Gilbert proposes something like an Epicurean space, with an inherent north–south orientation in place of Epicurus's up–down orientation. The Law of the Whole is a magnetic instantiation of the rectilinear, self-parallel orientation of space itself.

The direction of the earth's axis is described, moreover, on the basis of this orientation. Since the earth's axis is always directed along this orientation, and would remain so even if the earth moved, the direction of the earth's axis, so described, does not change. That is, the axis is described as stable and fixed. It does not move. Compare this to Copernicus's description on the basis of a radius to the center of his representation of space. As the earth moves, the direction of its axis, described in relation to the radius, changes. For Copernicus, then, the behavior of the axis is described as a motion. Gilbert's assumption of a cosmic orientation allows him to describe the phenomenon as a staying – a non-motion:

> This third motion introduced by Copernicus is not a motion at all [*non est motus omnino*]. The direction of the earth is stable, and if it were to go in a great circle, then it would constantly regard one part of the heavens.[60]

Even were the earth to revolve around the sun, its axis would stay in the same, self-parallel direction, specified by reference to the assumed orientation of the cosmos.[61]

---

[59] "Axis telluris lineae in aequinoctiis & solstitiis sunt parallelae" (Gilbert 1651, 166).

[60] "Tertius his motus a Copernico inductus, non est motus omnino, sed telluris est directio stabilis, dum in circulo magno fertur, dum unam partem coeli constanter respicit" (Gilbert 1651, 165).

[61] This discussion ignores the very slow precession of the earth's equinoxes, attributed by Copernicus to a small difference between the second and third motions and by Gilbert to a slow "wobble" of the "common mother" and, therefore, the earth's axis.

This yields Gilbert's explanation of the "third motion." The new concept of direction, and the resulting description of a "staying" instead of a motion, vastly simplifies Gilbert's explanatory project. To explain Copernicus's "third motion," one would have to appeal to an *active* cause – some power that brings about a change; in this case, the changing direction of the earth's axis. The description of this cause, moreover, would have to account for various features of the change. The purported cause would have to explain, for example, the speed and sense of the axis's rotation. On the other hand, Gilbert's description of the phenomenon as a non-motion allows him to explain it by appealing to a *static* cause – a cause that maintains a *stasis*. Gilbert does not need to say how his static cause operates. He does not need, for instance, to say how fast the axis would move under its influence. In other words, the cause required to explain the phenomenon is simpler when the phenomenon is described as a stasis rather than a motion. All Gilbert needs is a cause that *keeps* the axis pointed in the same direction.

In fact, Gilbert simply postulates that the spatial orientation he supposes in order to describe the behavior of the earth's axis has a physical instantiation. He claims there is a magnetic field that permeates the universe along its orientation. He calls this field the Law of the Whole or the "common mother."[62] Gilbert then argues that the earth itself is a large spherical magnet (whose magnetic and rotational axes coincide). Hence, the earth aligns its axis with the rectilinear orientation because of its innate magnetic power or "verticity." "By its native verticity," the earth can "conform its poles to the poles of the common mother" just as a magnetized needle aligns itself with the earth's magnetic field. The direction of the earth's axis is held constant by the earth's verticity and the Law of the Whole:

> But why the terrestrial globe should seem constantly to turn one of its poles toward those points and toward Cynosura, or why her poles should vary from the poles of the ecliptic by 23 deg. 29 min., with some variation not yet sufficiently studied by astronomers, – that depends on the magnetic energy.[63]

The "magnetic energy" of the Law of the Whole ensures the *stability* of the earth's poles, even if the earth moves "from her position in the universe." The orientation itself, as the Law of the Whole, keeps the axis pointed in a single, *unchanging* direction.

Of course, parallel pointings throughout space can only be described as a single direction in relation to an orientation of the whole of space. The Law

---

[62] Gilbert (1958, 66, 180).   [63] Gilbert (1958, 180).

of the Whole cannot be properly described or understood without assuming a rectilinear orientation. Once an orientation has been presupposed, it becomes possible to describe the Law of the Whole as a real magnetic virtue that follows it. And it is on the basis of this virtue that Gilbert explains the fixity of the earth's poles. Gilbert, in other words, has endowed the universe with an orientation. He has added a rectilinear orientation to his representation of cosmic space.

Interestingly, Gilbert's extrapolation of the geographical representation of the earth to a rectilinearly oriented space is not unlike the Mercator projection that had recently come into fashion among cartographers. As in the Mercator projection, Gilbert extends the poles of the representation to infinity. As a result, the meridians that converge on the pole on the earth/ terrella become parallel to one another throughout space. Consequently, any direction, say "northwest" or "south," is everywhere parallel to itself, equally deflected from the parallel orientation established by the extrapolation of the terrestrial axis. Of course, this was the most useful innovation in the Mercator projection, as directions could be represented as straight lines – known as "rhumb lines" – thereby facilitating course-plotting and navigation. By the same token, the Law of the Whole that keeps the earth pointed in the "same direction" keeps the earth's axis parallel to itself. One can speculate, moreover, that this connection to cartography was not coincidental. Gilbert was good friends with Edward Wright, the chief expositor of the mathematical basis for the Mercator projection, whose *Certaine Errors in Navigation* appeared in 1599. Indeed, Wright penned the preface to *De Magnete*.[64]

Conclusion

William Gilbert attempted to respond to part of the explanatory challenge posed by Copernicus's heliocentric description of the solar system. He tried to account for two of the three motions of the earth Copernicus had described but left unexplained. Gilbert carefully investigated and described the phenomena associated with magnets; spherical magnets, or terrella, in particular. He then drew an analogy between terrellae and the earth itself on the basis of the way they are described – i.e., using a geographical representation of space. He showed how the phenomena of one could be described in the same way as the phenomena of the other. On the basis of this similarity, Gilbert concluded that the earth *is* a magnet and suggested

---

[64] See Suter (1952, 376).

that its motions are *caused* by its magnetic nature. His attempts to show how a magnetic nature could cause the rotation of the earth, however, were unsuccessful.

Gilbert's argument is mainly descriptive. The point is that a geographical representation of space can be used to describe both magnets and the earth, so the two can be identified under a single theory of magnetism. The ultimate cause of magnetism, however, is ascribed to an unelucidated, Aristotelian form. Gilbert's descriptions, meanwhile, rely on a geographical representation of space quite different from the centered frameworks presupposed by Aristotle, Ptolemy, and Copernicus. Gilbert's magnetic spheres are described by referring to poles, not centers. The descriptive similarity at the crux of Gilbert's work hinges on his "discovery" of this geometric structure in magnets and the earth. That is, the argument relies on the fact that the geographical representation of space underwrites descriptions applicable to all spherical magnets, the earth included.

The geographical representation of space is also particularly important for Gilbert's treatment of Copernicus's "third motion" of the earth. The representation warrants Gilbert's appeal to the earth's axis and its "verticity." By extrapolating this geometric feature of the earth to the universe itself, Gilbert establishes a fixed, rectilinear orientation of space. On the basis of this orientation, he can then describe the behavior of the earth's axis as a "staying" rather than a motion. He can also appeal to a simple cause – the "law of the whole," which instantiates the orientation – to explain the phenomenon. Rather than confront the explanatory problem posed by the "third motion" directly, Gilbert shifted his descriptive framework, thereby greatly simplifying the explanatory task.

As we shall see in Chapter 4, when Kepler later found himself in a similar explanatory bind, he followed the same path out of the quandary. To make the explanatory task tractable, Kepler shifted the descriptive framework by adding a rectilinear orientation to his representation of space.[65]

---

[65] Gilbert also had a significant influence on the development of English astronomy, especially in the case of Christopher Wren. See Bennett (1975, 36).

CHAPTER 4

Respicere sinus: *Kepler, oriented space, and the ellipse*[1]

Introduction

In the *Mysterium Cosmographicum* of 1596, the twenty-five-year-old Johannes Kepler rashly banished straight lines from "the pattern of the universe." Straight lines "scarcely admit of order," Kepler wrote, since their homogeneity does not allow the specification of privileged locations by which one can construct a spatially ordered cosmos. Hence, God Himself could have no use for lines – only centers and spheres – in laying out the structure of this "complete, thoroughly ordered, and most splendid universe."[2] Twenty-five years later, Kepler reissued his *Mysterium* with additional notes and revisions. To the passage repudiating lines, he appended a note remarkable for its exclamatory tone:

> O, what a mistake! [*O male factum.*] Are we to reject them from the universe? ... For why should we eliminate lines from the archetype of the universe, seeing that God represented lines in his own work, that is, the motions of the planets?[3]

In the years between editions, Kepler learned that God had use for straight lines, after all. As Kepler had discovered, they were necessary to lay out the elliptical orbits of the planets. Straight lines were essential parts of the universe: they were elements in God's transcendental archetype of creation. The second edition's note is opaque, however. It does not indicate how the motions of the planets demonstrate God's need for straight lines. Why, then, did Kepler come to lament the rashness of his youth?

The answer lies deep in the details of Kepler's discovery of elliptical orbits in 1605. Unlike many of his more instrumentalist contemporaries, Kepler

---

[1] A version of this chapter was published as Miller (2008).
[2] Kepler (1981, 95–97). Kepler does admit finite straightness as the "distinguishing features" – i.e., the geometrical boundaries – of solid bodies. His argument is that the universe as a whole is inherently ordered by God and, therefore, laid out spherically about a single center.
[3] Kepler (1981, 102–03).

was driven to provide a complete theory of planetary motion. Rejecting the Ptolemaic compromise, he sought *both* an empirically adequate description of and a plausible physical explanation for the motion of a planet, particularly Mars, whose orbit Tycho Brahe had set Kepler to work on shortly before he died in 1601. Kepler, that is, sought to close both epistemic gaps I have discussed, thereby reconciling phenomena with descriptions and descriptions with explanations.

By 1605, Kepler had guessed that the Martian orbit was elliptical, but he thought that such an orbit was inexplicable. In particular, an ellipse required a planet to "respect the sines" (*respicere sinus*) – that is, move itself in directions that are everywhere parallel to themselves. In fact, the trouble was precisely analogous to the problem of the "third motion" of the earth: describing the planet's motion using a centered representation of space, "respecting the sines" required a continuous but varying rotation in order to keep a planet "pointed" parallel to itself. Using a centered representation of space, Kepler ascribed to the planet a motion that could not be plausibly explained. To Kepler, this meant that an elliptical orbit, though empirically adequate, was impossible.

At this juncture, though, Kepler was crucially inspired by William Gilbert's "magnetic philosophy," including Gilbert's use of a rectilinearly oriented space in order to solve the "third motion" problem. By abandoning his centered representation of space and adopting an oriented representation of space, Kepler was finally able to devise a mechanism by which an elliptical orbit could be explained. This successful conquest of the Martian orbit would be reported in the *Astronomia Nova*, published in 1609. Yet, this victory required an oriented representation of space, and thus the stipulation of a rectilinear line, *pace* the youthful Kepler's temerity. Without straight lines, not even God could construct the planets' elliptical orbits.

Kepler's discovery of the elliptical orbit represents an important step in the development of the modern representation of space, since it crucially depends on an oriented conception of direction. In particular, the explanatory mechanism at issue here accounts for the planet's motion toward and away from the sun, which would become, in the hands of Newton, gravitational attraction. By rectifying this effect, Kepler set the stage for Newton's use of a rectilinearly oriented framework in his own description of planetary orbits, as we shall see. The history of Kepler's reasoning demonstrates the close integration of changing descriptions with the explanatory development of the physical sciences. Conversely, recognizing the move toward an oriented representation of space reveals important details of Kepler's struggle to reconcile geometrical descriptions and physical explanations of the Martian orbit.

Several authors have discussed Kepler's attempts to reconcile geometrical hypotheses with physical causes, but they have not addressed the significance of an oriented representation of space in the actual process of Kepler's physical confirmation of the elliptical orbit.[4] To rectify this, this chapter depends heavily on a long letter Kepler wrote to David Fabricius, eventually dated 11 October 1605 and used as material for the *Astronomia Nova*, in which many passages from the letter appear almost verbatim.[5] The letter describes, in painstaking detail, the steps of Kepler's reasoning as he came upon the crucial realization of the elliptical orbit of Mars. The significance of this letter has been noted by several authors, but it has not been studied in extensive detail or completely translated.[6]

Two desiderata: descriptions and explanations

Throughout his extended attempt to discover the Martian orbit, Kepler sought two desiderata for his models of the planet's motion, familiar from our discussion of astronomical science above. First, an orbital model had to accurately *describe* phenomena. Second, Kepler required plausible physical *explanations* for his astronomical descriptions. A descriptive model must be produced by an intelligible physical mechanism, not a mere mathematical posit. A successful theory, Kepler thought, bridged both epistemic interfaces, from explanation to description and description to phenomena. However, something more needs to be said regarding what Kepler considered a successful reconciliation among these levels.

As for the empirical desideratum, Kepler sought a way to calculate planetary positions that agreed with what was actually observed in the sky, in the future, present, or past. This included deriving the longitude and latitude of a planet for a given time. Of course, none of Kepler's predecessors or contemporaries would have disputed that this was a central goal of mathematical astronomy. However, Kepler was one of the first astronomers to consider the *distance* of a planet as a phenomenon to be geometrically described. Distances in the heavens are measured by triangulation, that is, by the change in a planet's apparent position due to a known displacement of the observer's position. For instance, one might calculate the distance to a planet by observing the planet at the same position in its

---

[4] See Ruffner (1971), Goldstein and Hon (2005).   [5] Kepler (1937–, 15:240–80).
[6] See, for examples, Dreyer (1953, 402), Wilson (1968, 13–14), Koyré (1973, 259–61), Stephenson (1994, 107), Voelkel (2001, ch. 8).

orbit from different positions in the earth's orbit. Obviously, this requires one to assume that the earth is in motion – the Copernican hypothesis. As one of the first committed Copernicans, Kepler thought distances could be checked against observations, at least indirectly, so he thought a planetary model could not be considered an accurate description of phenomena if it did not predict proper distances. Thus, Kepler required that a hypothesis agree with observations in three respects: longitude, latitude, and distance.

By 1605 Kepler had guessed, almost by a blunt process of elimination, that the Martian orbit was elliptical with the sun at one focus. However, he had not yet conceived a geometrical model that could generate that ellipse. That is, he could not relate the planet's longitudinal motion around the sun to its change in distance from the sun. It also remained to relate the elliptical path to time, such that one could determine where on the elliptical orbit Mars could be found for a given time. All Kepler knew, that is, was the end product of Mars's motions, not how the orbit was produced.

Then, in early 1605, in the midst of testing yet another of his many geometrical models for the orbit of Mars, Kepler found that correct planetary distances were related to the versed sine of the eccentric anomaly.[7] The eccentric anomaly, meanwhile, could be derived by tabulation from the mean anomaly, the measure of time. In other words, Kepler could derive accurate distances for any given time. Now, Kepler's assumption of an elliptical orbit provided enough constraints to construct the orbit, since the geometric properties of an ellipse allowed Kepler to relate the distance to longitude. For a given time, Kepler could calculate the planet's distance from the sun, and from that distance, Kepler could calculate the planet's longitude. He could describe the motions of Mars.

The resulting elliptical model satisfied Kepler's first desideratum. It allowed the computation of observed longitudes "to the nail," and, while the values for distance and, consequently, latitude were "somewhat more lax," they were within observational error.[8] Subsequent observations might adjust his orbital parameters, but the ellipse was an accurate

---

[7] That is, its angular displacement from perihelion measured from the center of its orbit. This is a measure of the planet's longitudinal position (recall the discussion of anomalies in the treatment of Copernicus, above).

[8] "Computaui inde aequationes Eccentri in situbus acronychiis, officium faciunt ad unguem, de distantiis quominus idem dicam fecit earum inquirendarum Methodus paulò laxior, quae semper me circa 100 particulas in dubio relinquit, etiam cum optimae sunt obseruationes. Nosti enim optimas obseruationes uno minuto peccare posse. At unum minutum vitiat distantiam immaniter, si Planeta proprè [sun] vel [opposition to the sun] fuerit. Hoc tamen certum habeas; quam proximè verum venire" (Kepler 1937–, 15:249–50, bracketed insertions substitute for symbols unreproducable here).

description of the true planetary orbit. Kepler had achieved empirical adequacy.

As for explanations, Kepler rejected the Ptolemaic compromise that allowed mathematical astronomers to bracket physical explanations of celestial phenomena. Kepler's Protestant neoplatonism implied that, since man is created in God's image, human knowledge can approximate divine understanding and, via diligent effort, continually improve that approximation, just as straight lines can asymptotically approximate curves.[9] Therefore, God's design of the universe, including the causes of planetary motions, must be comprehensible, at least in the fullness of time. As a result, Kepler thought that physical reasoning could and should be an integral part of astronomy. He sought an astronomy "based upon causes"[10] that attempted to explain, as well as describe, the planetary orbits.

Kepler's estimation of explanatory success, however, was somewhat idiosyncratic. Kepler never presumed that a cause he proposed was necessarily *the* cause of the observed behavior. He believed that it is always within God's power to bring about the phenomena in a different way. Still, Kepler thought, God's action is amenable to human grasp, so the cause must be something accessible to reason *in principle*. Consequently, descriptive "hypotheses" that do not admit reasonable explanations cannot be realized. So, when Kepler suggested a physical explanation for a hypothesis, he sought to demonstrate only that the hypothesis is *compatible* with human reason, and thus within the realm of possible truth. Kepler only required that a hypothesis is physically *plausible* – that it could be explained in a humanly intelligible manner.[11] In general, Kepler's discussion of physical causes is in the hypothetical voice. He leaves aside the question of whether the proposed explanation *really* accounts for the phenomena.[12]

Nevertheless, this plausibility criterion suggests a test by which explanations might be judged satisfactory: Kepler supposes that the planets have

---

[9] Kepler (1981, 93). Kepler is here paraphrasing Nicholas of Cusa. See Aiton (1981, 91). For more regarding Kepler's epistemology and theology, see Caspar (1959, 376–84), Jardine (1979; 1984, ch. 7), Lindberg (1986), Field (1988), Kozhamthadam (1994), Martens (2000), Barker and Goldstein (2001).

[10] Kepler titled his book *Astronomia Nova ΑΙΤΙΟΛΟΓΗΤΟΣ seu physica coelestis, tradita commentariis de motibus stellae Martis ex observationibus G.V. Tychonis Brahe*; that is, *New Astronomy Based upon Causes, or Celestial Physics, Treated by Means of Commentaries on the Motions of the Martian Star, from the Observations of Tycho Brahe, Gentleman.*

[11] I say "plausible" rather than "possible" to emphasize the epistemic constraint on hypotheses. All hypotheses are "possible," but only those that admit reasonable explanation are "plausible." Note that Kepler's criterion for admissible hypotheses is not so different from Copernicus's reason for rejecting the Ptolemaic system, discussed in Chapter 2, above. Copernicus argued that Ptolemy's use of an equant did not admit of explanation on the basis of accepted physical principles, and was therefore implausible.

[12] Kepler wrote that all physical sciences include "a certain amount of conjecture" (1992, 47).

mental faculties similar to humans; that there are "planetary minds."[13] This is not to say that the planets actually do have minds (though this is not ruled out). Instead, Kepler uses minds as stand-ins for physical mechanisms he does not understand or has not yet worked out. Could an ellipse, Kepler asks, for example, have a humanly intelligible cause? Can it be comprehensibly constructed (other than by mere stipulation)? The easiest way to answer this is to suppose that the planet itself is rational. If the planetary mind has a method to "measure" its position and "deduce" an elliptical movement, then the resulting path can be rationally constructed. If this is the case, then the ellipse is a possible path for the planet. The unknown *real* cause of the motion will *a fortiori* be rationally comprehensible, as well.[14] Conversely, if a planetary mind *cannot* devise the path, the model itself becomes suspect.

In practice, Kepler's explanations of planetary motion were somewhat less mystical than the ascription of planetary minds. Since the *Mysterium*, in fact, Kepler had assumed that the motion of a planet could be explained by the effect of two forces. First, an *anima motrix* emanating from the sun carried the planets about the zodiac. This "extrinsic force" is something similar to both light and magnetism (Kepler's analogy changes over time) whose force decreases in some relation to distance. By 1605, Kepler had settled on a magnetic action emanating from the sun that decreased in direct proportion to distance from the sun. Since, at the time, Kepler generally assumed that force is proportional to speed, he concluded that there was a direct proportion between distance and the planet's "delay" in an arc of orbit. That is, the time a planet took to traverse equal (small) arcs of the orbit was proportional to the distance the (small) arc was from the sun and, therefore, to the (small) area of the circular orbit swept out.[15]

A planet's general revolution around the sun could be explained by this "magnetic" force. However, planets do not move at constant speed around the sun. Instead, they speed up and slow down as they approach and recede from the sun. Kepler attributed this change in speed to a second power, a *vis insita* inherent in the planet itself, which somehow regulates the planet's

---

[13] For example, in Kepler (1992, ch. 57; 1995, 52–53).

[14] Stephenson (1994, 3). Patrick Boner (2006; 2008) agrees that Kepler's supposition of terrestrial and celestial souls (*animae*) enables physical reasoning regarding distant or obscure phenomena by making them humanly intelligible, though Boner argues that the souls are an ineliminable part of Kepler's cosmos – they can be supplemented but not replaced by mechanistic explanations.

[15] Kepler (1981, 62–65; 1992, 372–75). By 1605, Kepler only possessed a preliminary version of the Area Law for which he is famous. It was not worked out in full generality until the *Epitome of Copernican Astronomy* (published 1618–21). See Aiton (1969, 1973), Barker and Goldstein (1994), Stephenson (1994, 161–65), Davis (2003).

distance from the sun.[16] Kepler assumed that the *vis insita* was something like a magnetic attraction and repulsion to the sun, which was supposed to be some sort of magnetic monopole. Thus, if the planet could "magnetically" move itself to the correct distance, the sun's "extrinsic" power would carry the planet around at the proper speed.

Ultimately, the elliptical orbit would satisfy both of Kepler's desiderata. Showing that the ellipse accurately described the Martian longitudes, distances, and latitudes was a long, difficult project. This descriptive project, though, was completed early in 1605. The explanatory project, however, presented its own, separate difficulties, which were not resolved for several months. Kepler struggled to figure out how the *anima motrix* and *vis insita* could bring about the elliptical orbit. I now turn to that story as it developed in the summer of 1605.

Note, meanwhile, that Kepler's desiderata conform to the model of scientific knowledge sketched above. For Kepler, an astronomical theory consists of both explanations and descriptions, and a satisfactory theory must be both explanatorily and empirically adequate. Of course, he was not alone in holding that a successful theory marries the empirical and the explanatory, bridging the interfaces between explanation, descriptions, and phenomena such that the latter are plausibly explained, though Kepler's measure of explanatory adequacy – plausibility tested by the limiting case of planetary minds – and his demand that empirical adequacy include distance measurements were perhaps unique. As we shall see, Kepler's work also supports the reciprocal iteration model of scientific change. The distinct epistemic levels slide across one another in Kepler's thought. When faced with problems at each level, he alternately shifts descriptions and explanations to achieve a coherent, explanatory theory of the phenomena: an astronomy "based on causes," "without hypotheses."[17]

The explanatory problem: "respecting the sines"

Despite the empirical success of the elliptical model, Kepler remained unsatisfied. To generate his descriptive model, he had set aside consideration of causes and worked directly from the geometric properties of the ellipse. Once he returned to thinking about causes, though, he found that the ellipse could not easily be accounted for by his *anima motrix* and *vis insita*. The key quantity of the elliptical model, as noted above, is the *sine* of

---

[16] Kepler (1992, 404–06).
[17] The phrase originates in Petrus Ramus, whom Kepler loosely interprets (Westman 1980, 128).

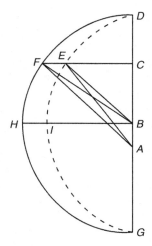

Figure 4.1 Elliptical orbit.[18]

the eccentric anomaly. The ellipse requires that the planet approach the sun according to this magnitude, which, in geometric terms, is the perpendicular distance from the planet to the apsidal line (i.e., the major axis of the ellipse). As Kepler would later explain, the size of the small "incursions" from a circumscribing eccentric orbit to the ellipse increase in proportion to this distance. Thus, in Figure 4.1, when the eccentric anomaly is angle *DBF*, the planet will be found at *E*, such that the perpendicular approach *FE* is to the greatest approach *HI* as the perpendicular *FC* is to the (unit) radius *BD*. The perpendicular *FC*, the sine of the eccentric anomaly, "measures" the approach *FE*.[19]

Moreover, the sine of the eccentric anomaly is also the key to locating the planet on the elliptical path. Once Kepler had discovered that the planet's distance from the sun varied as the sine of the eccentric anomaly, he assumed that the eccentric anomaly would actually measure the angle to the planet itself. Upon testing this assumption, however, he found that the orbit produced was not elliptical. Instead, the properties of the ellipse required the distance to be projected along the sine, that is, onto the perpendicular to the apsidal line dropped from the point on the eccentric circle corresponding to the eccentric anomaly. That is, in Figure 4.1, the "incursion" from *F* is directed along the sine *FC*, such that the planet is

[18] Kepler (1937–, 15:251).   [19] See Kepler (1992, ch. 60).

found at *E*. In other words, the planet had to move toward and away from the sun *as if* it were moving along the sine of the eccentric anomaly. The sine – the perpendicular to the apsidal line – determines both the size and the direction of the "incursions" that produce the ellipse.

It was not obvious, however, how a magnetic *vis insita* could bring about such a movement of the planet:

> But there is also something else that I find wanting in this hypothesis: because striving to the point of insanity I am unable to produce the natural cause why Mars, to which libration in the diameter is attributed with such great credibility (indeed, the thing was reducing so beautifully to magnetic virtues for us), should rather want to go in an ellipse or some path close to it. Nevertheless, I think magnetic virtues may not always respect the sines, but something somewhat different.[20]

If magnetic forces were responsible for the elliptical path, Kepler thinks, the planet should move in the direction of the source of the magnetic force, directly toward or away from the sun, at *A* in Figure 4.1. Thus, the planet should oscillate or "librate" in the diameter of an epicycle that is always directed to the sun, along *FA*. Yet this does not produce an ellipse,[21] which he knows to be the correct orbit. Kepler does not understand how "magnetic virtues" could be compatible with an elliptical orbit, since he does not see how the planet can both measure and move along perpendiculars to the apsidal line.[22] He cannot fathom how the planet can be made to "respect the sines."

In fact, the difficulty runs deeper than the incompatibility between orbital geometry and magnetic explanation. Even considering the planet as endowed with a mind (the limiting case of physical plausibility), it was not clear how it could find its way along the ellipse. Like most of his

---

[20] "Sed et aliud est quod desidero in hac hypothesi: nempe quod ad insaniam usque contendens causam naturalem confingere non possum, cur Mars cui tanta cum probabilitate libratio in diametro tribuebatur (res enim nobis ad virtutes magneticas pulchrè admodum recidebat) potius velit ire Ellipsin vel ei proximam uiam. Fortasse tamen puto uirtutes magneticas non omnino respicere sinus sed aliud aliquid" (Kepler 1937–, 15:251). See the corresponding passage in *Astronomia Nova*, Chapter 58 (Kepler 1992, 576). See also Voelkel (2001, 198).

[21] In fact, it generates the infamous *via buccosa*. The *via buccosa* is especially promising because the libration along the diameter of an epicycle is "measured" by the increase of the eccentric anomaly caused by the *anima motrix*. In other words, the "magnetic" *vis insita* moving the body toward and away from the sun is straightforwardly related to the "magnetic" *anima motrix* and everything "reduces so beautifully to magnetic virtues." Declaring himself a "wretch" (*miser*), Kepler reports the failure of this model to Fabricius (Kepler 1937–, 15:249). See also Kepler (1992, ch. 58).

[22] Kepler eventually resolved the need for the planet to move along the sine by redefining his astronomical terms. Since this part of the solution does not require an altered representation of space, I set it aside, though a similar problem arises again in relation to the direction of the planet's magnetic axis, as seen below. See Stephenson (1994, 126–30), Miller (2008, 61n21).

contemporaries and predecessors, Kepler adopted a centered representation of space in order to describe astronomical phenomena. In this framework, directions are specified and interpreted in relation to a stipulated center. Two spatial "pointings" (of objects, motions, etc.) are described as being in the same direction if they bear the same relation to the spatial center. In effect, this entails that a direction is conceived as a deflection from a radius to the center. Two rays, for instance, forming similar angles with radii to the center are described as "pointing in the same direction."

Recall Copernicus's "third motion" of the earth. This "motion" is a direct consequence of a centered way of representing direction. As the earth orbits the sun, its rotational axis stays roughly parallel to itself, always pointing toward the same region of the heavens near Polaris. Since the earth's axis is inclined to the ecliptic, this entails that the axis is tilted toward the sun at the summer solstice and tilted away from the sun at the winter solstice. Copernicus describes this behavior in relation to a stipulated center: the center of the earth's orbit, a point near the sun. Since the axis changes its relation to this point – sometimes tilting toward it, sometimes away – Copernicus asserts that the *direction* of the earth's axis is different at different times of the year. In other words, the earth's axis changes direction. It *moves*. Copernicus labels this change of direction the earth's "third motion." But this description of the phenomenon *as a change of direction* depends on the representation of space used to specify and compare directions.

The situation for Kepler is precisely analogous to Copernicus's "third motion." In order to "respect the sines," the planet has to measure magnitudes that are all parallel to each other, perpendicular to the apsidal line. But Kepler, like Copernicus, conceives of direction in relation to a spatial center, so the parallel magnitudes are actually described as being in different directions, since the perpendiculars to the apsidal line bear different relations to the center (in this case, the sun) at each point in the orbit. In other words, Kepler supposes that "respecting the sines" requires the planet to measure, as it descends from aphelion, magnitudes pointed in an infinity of different directions. If the planet were to keep a magnetic axis aligned with the "sines," Kepler says, it would have to "turn" at an unknown, varying rate that is maximal at quadrature and non-existent at the apsides.[23] He

---

[23] "Omnino sapit magneticam vim Eccentricitas, vt est in meis Commentariis: ut si globus Martis haberet axem magneticum, vno polo Solis appetentem, altero fugientem, eoque axe porrigeretur in longitudines medias, tunc quamdiu versatur in descendente semicirculo, maximè in longitudine media, porrigit polum appetentem versus Solem, itaque semper ad Solem accedit, sed maxime in longitudine media, nihil in apsidibus" (Kepler 1937–, 15:251).

considers this task impossibly difficult, even for a planetary mind. Neither Kepler, nor his supposed planetary mind, can recognize the perpendicular to the apsidal line *as a single, unchanging direction*. In a centered representation of space, from which lines have been banished, this direction is inconceivable.

Kepler does not see how his description of the elliptical orbit can be causally explicable. Kepler could conceive of no way, even if it has a mind, for a planet to "respect the sines" and move itself along an elliptical orbit. This meant, for Kepler, that the ellipse fails the test for physical plausibility and was irreconcilable with physical causes. Kepler does not see how an elliptical orbit, which he is convinced accurately describes the Martian orbit, could be *explained*. Yet, Kepler thought, if the orbit is inexplicable, it is *impossible*. Without a plausible explanation, the ellipse, which he knew to be empirically correct, would have to be rejected. He was driven "to the point of insanity" by the problem.

An explanatory mechanism: the magnetic balance

At this point in his work on Mars, Kepler had become convinced that the planet's orbit was elliptical, but he still sought a plausible physical mechanism that could account for it. Kepler had long thought that something like magnetism was responsible for moving the planets, but he could not understand how magnetism might "respect the sines" of the anomaly, as required by the ellipse. Frustrated, Kepler apparently consulted the authoritative contemporary treatment of magnetism, William Gilbert's *De Magnete*, published in 1600.[24]

Gilbert spurred Kepler's consideration of physical causes in two crucial respects. First, he corrected Kepler's method of representing magnetic action:

> Let us take the shape of the body of the planet to be the same as proposed above. I have said above that it is the same, whether the planet is considered as a globe or as a plain circle; now I say this as well, that it is the same whether it is considered as a plane circle or as a line. For it is certain from Gilbert the Englishman – and also in itself without his authority – that magnetic virtue extends in a straight line [*virtutem magneticam porrigi in rectum*]. So just as a globe is conceived to consist of infinite circular planes parallel to the eccentric, of all of which the disposition [*ratio*] is the same, so because of this rectilinear virtue the plane circle consists of an infinity of straight lines, of

---

[24] Kepler had acquired and read *De Magnete* upon its appearance in 1600. He discusses it in some detail in his *Apologia pro Tychone contra Ursum*, which was composed shortly thereafter (Jardine 1984, 146).

each of which the disposition is again the same. So the body of the planet can be considered as some straight line, since it does not obstruct any of the others, as I falsely maintained above.[25]

Earlier, Kepler had asssumed that the planet's magnetic attraction was proportional to its bulk. Therefore, he related the "strength" of magnetic action to volumes, areas, and circular angles. From Gilbert, though, Kepler has learned that magnetic virtue is fundamentally rectilinear – it "extends in a right line." Thus, though magnetic action propagates spherically through space, the action itself always respects the magnetic axis, the line extending through the magnet's poles. Consequently, Kepler need only consider its magnetic axis, a "right line," to study the inherent magnetic virtue of the planet.

As we have seen, Kepler supposed that the *vis insita* was a result of a magnetic interaction between the planet and the sun. After Gilbert's correction, Kepler could now consider the influence of the sun on two ends of a rectilinear axis to represent that interaction. This representation suggested the action of a magnetic "balance," whose motion is deter-mined by the different forces acting on the attracted and repelled ends of the axis:

> So [in Figure 4.2] let *AD* be the magnetic axis fleeing in *A*, approaching in *D*, representing one of the infinity of straight lines of virtue of the body of Mars. Now let *B* be the middle point of *AD*, with the Sun in *BI*. The reason why none of the said approaches or flights happens is because *A* and *D* are equal in action. Therefore, this is like equilibrium. See my *Optics*, chapter 1.[26]

The action of the sun on the magnetic axis of the planet is like the "equilibrium" found in balances. To understand the action of the *vis insita*, Kepler only needed to understand the action of a magnetic balance under the influence of a central magnetic power. Yet, Kepler had already consid-ered the behavior of balances under incident forces in his *Optics*, published

---

[25] "Sit nobis eadem figura coporis planetarii proposita quae supra. Dixi supra perinde esse, siue planeta consideretur vt globus, siue vt planum circuli; jam etiam hoc dico, perinde esse, siue vt planum circuli consideretur siue vt linea. Nam certam est ex Gilberto Anglo, et per se etiam sine eius authoritate, Virtutem magneticam porrigi in rectum. Quare vt globus fingitur constare ex infinitis circularibus planis, Eccentrico parallelis, quorum omnium eadem est ratio, ita circuli planum propter hanc virtutis rectitudinem, ex infinitis constat rectis, quarum rursum omnium eadem est ratio. Ergo planetae corpus ita considerari potest, vt quaelibet recta, cum nulla aliam impediat, vt supra falso confinxi" (Kepler 1937–, 15:253).

[26] "Sit ergo *AD* axis magneticus fugiens in *A*, appropinquans in *D*, repraesentans vnam ex infinitis rectis virtuosis corporis Martii. Sit autem *B* punctum medium inter *AD*, Sole in *BI*, dictum appropinqua-tionem vt fugam fieri nullam, causa est, quia *A* et *D* sunt in opere aequali. Ergo hoc est quasi aequipondium. Vide me *Optica* cap. I" (Kepler 1937–, 15:253–54).

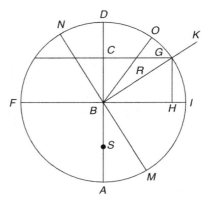

Figure 4.2 Measure of attractive force in the planetary body.[27]

in 1604. Thanks to Gilbert, Kepler realized he *already* had a mechanism that might explain how the *vis insita* "respects the sines."

The mechanism that leaped to Kepler's mind is found, in fact, in a passing remark in Chapter 1, Proposition 20, of the *Optics*, where Kepler seeks to prove that "Light that has approached the surface of a denser medium obliquely is refracted towards the perpendicular to the surface."[28] Throughout his proof, Kepler considers the action of light as a mechanical problem of impact or pressure. He compares light encountering a refracting surface to the percussive action of a "missile" striking a "panel" or to the continuous pressure exerted by a stream encountering an oar.[29] He then tries to determine how the panel or oar will move as a result of the impact. To do this, however, he draws an analogy between the panel or oar and the arms of a balance.

In the course of proving the proposition, Kepler considers the case of an oblique impact or pressure (see Figure 4.3).[30] This, he supposes, is akin to an equal-armed balance loaded with unequal weights, where the force of the

---

[27] Kepler (1937–, 15:252).   [28] Kepler (2000, 27).

[29] The example might have been inspired by Alhazen. See Smith (1987, 49). In the *Optics*, Kepler defines "violent motion" or "impulse" as an attribute of light. Therefore, he conceives the action of light as something similar to the action of hard bodies colliding. Reflection, for example, is not merely a turning back of a light ray, but a "repercussion" (*repercussus*). See Kepler (2000, 26, 34). The reference to optics is also significant because light, for Kepler, is both a geometrical and a natural phenomenon. Thus, if the sun's action could be compared to light, it might similarly be brought under mathematical description, and thus made comprehensible. For recent work on this issue, see Chen-Morris (2001), Gal and Chen-Morris (2005, 2012).

[30] Kepler (1604, 19–21; 2000, 33–34).

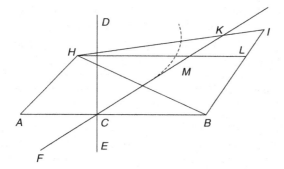

Figure 4.3 Optical percussion.[31]

impact or pressure is similar to the action of the support from which the balance hangs. In this situation, the ends of the balance resist the force of the support unequally. As a result, the balance will come to equilibrium tilted downward toward the heavier, more resistant, weight. In this position, the support makes an obtuse angle with the heavier weight. Again arguing by analogy, Kepler concludes that the end of the panel or oar making an obtuse angle with the path of the incident percussent will resist its action more, and therefore be moved further, than the end or oar making an acute angle. Hence, the panel or oars will be deflected toward the normal by the force of the impact or pressure.

Though it is not relevant to his argument in the *Optics*, Kepler makes a crucial observation at this point. Considering specifically the action of a stream on an obliquely positioned oar, Kepler says that, since the end of the oar at a greater angle to the oncoming water resists the impact more than the end at a lesser angle, it will be moved further. However, he continues, if the oar is "artificially held back in this position" and not allowed to turn, the "oar *AB* will at length be pushed forth to the shore," along its length toward the end moved further.[32] In other words, if the oar is kept parallel to itself, "in this position *AB*," by some "artificial" faculty resisting rotation, then the effect of the stream's pressure will be to move the oar in the direction of *B*, parallel to its length.[33]

In the *Optics*, Kepler did not try to deduce the distance the oar moves, since he was interested in the oar's deflection when it was not held "in

[31] Kepler (1604, 20; 1937–, 2:30).   [32] Kepler (2000, 34).
[33] This is apparently the source of the stream analogy that appears in Chapter 57 of the *Astronomia Nova*, though in that case, the oar is assumed to turn, rather than remain parallel.

position." The balance analogy, however, does provide a way to measure that motion, which Kepler adduces in his discussion of Mars's orbit:

> So now let the Sun be in *BCG* [in Figure 4.2]. And let the circle *DG* with center *B* and radius *BD* be drawn, and a [line] perpendicular to *DA* be drawn from *G*, the intersection of the circle with the line of the Sun. If therefore *GB* is the support and *AB*, *BD* the arms of a balance, as *DC* to *CA* will be the strength of angle *DBG* to the strength of *ABG*.[34]

Kepler considers the magnetic force of the sun in the same way as he considered the action of light on a refracting surface – as a balance problem. The impinging solar force (like the light "missile") is likened to the force exerted by the support of a balance (the line to the sun, *GB*), while its effect is determined by the "strengths" of resistance in the planet such that the more "resisting" end of the planet's magnetic axis will have a greater effect.

In fact, the quantification of the planet's own approach toward and away from the sun follows quite easily from the balance model:

> And so this flight is as much as *DC*, and the seeking as much as *AC*. Take from *AC* the equal of *DC*, which is *AS*. Therefore *SC* is the measure of the seeking, and *AD* the measure of the seeking at no angle. And as *AD* to *SC*, thus *BD* to *BC* or *GH*. Therefore the sine of the digression of the planet from apogee or perigee measures the speed of the approach.[35]

The planet's magnetic axis is supposed to be attracted to the sun at end *D* and repulsed at end *A*. Thus, the strength of the magnetic attraction is assumed to act at *D*, while the repulsion acts at *A*. Assuming that the position of the balance is "like equilibrium," Kepler has shown (in the *Optics*) that there is a point *C*, found by constructing a perpendicular to *AD* from *G*, such that *DC* is to *AC* as the repulsive action is to the attractive action. That is, the "flight is as much as *DC*, and the seeking as much as *AC*." The difference between the seeking and flight, then, will be measured by the difference between these distances, which is *SC*. Thus, *SC* is to the net attractive force as *AD* is to the maximum attractive force possible ("the seeking at no angle"). Halving both these quantities (which preserves the proportions), we find that the net attraction is measured by *BC* or *GH*, the sine of angle *IBG*. Thus, the "sine

---

[34] "Sit iam Sol in *BGK*. Et centro *B* spacio *BD* circulus *DG* delineatur, et ex *G*, sectione circuli cum linea Solis perpendicularis in *DA* ducatur. Si igitur *GB* sit trutina, et *AB*, *BD* brachia librae, erit vt *DC* ad *CA* sic fortitudo anguli *DBG* ad fortitudinem *ABG*" (Kepler 1937–, 15:254).

[35] "Itaque fuga hic tanta est, quanta *DC* appetentia tanta quanta *AC*. Aufer ab *AC* aequalem ipsi *DC*, quae sit *AS*. Ergo *SC* est hic modulus appetentiae, et *AD* mensura appententiae angulo nullo. Et vt *AD* ad *SC*, sic *BD* ad *BC* vel *GH*. Ergo sinus digressionis planetae ab apogaeo vel perigeo metitur celeritatem accedendi" (Kepler 1937–, 15:253–54). Throughout his work, Kepler uses "apogee" and "perigee" interchangeably for "aphelion" and "perihelion."

of the digression of the planet from apogee or perigee"[36] measures the force of attraction or repulsion. Since Kepler still thinks force is proportional to speed, the same sine measures "the speed of the approach."[37] A *vis insita* acting in accord with this magnetic force can therefore move the planet toward and away from the sun the distance necessary to produce the correct elliptical orbit. The planet's attraction and repulsion can "respect the sines."

Faced with an explanatory problem at the interface between explanation and description, Kepler altered his explanatory apparatus. He conceived a plausible mechanism by which a magnetic action can be made to "respect the sines." This resulted in a plausible explanation for the planet's motion in an ellipse. Thus, there was hope for the ellipse yet. All the mechanism required was that the planet's magnetic axis be somehow kept parallel to itself and perpendicular to the apsidal line throughout the orbit. As we have seen, though, this was not a trivial requirement. It was not clear how even a planetary mind might recognize this direction as a direction and keep its axis "in position" along it. Indeed, Kepler's inability to conceive of this direction as a direction is what drove him "to the point of insanity" in the first place. To solve this aspect of the problem, Kepler turned to the descriptive part of his astronomical theory. He eventually reconciled causes to phenomena not by inventing new causes, but by changing the way phenomena were described.

Oriented space

It was here that Gilbert exerted his second crucial influence on Kepler's thinking. In *De Magnete*, Gilbert tries to use magnetism to causally account for the motions of the earth described by Copernicus. In particular, he addresses the very problem that, as I have already noted, is analogous to Kepler's own: how to explain Copernicus's "third motion" of the earth – the change of direction of the earth's axis so that it remains parallel to itself.

To solve the problem, Gilbert introduced a new way of describing direction. He described direction in relation to a rectilinear spatial orientation instead of a spatial center. In this oriented space, directions are specified and interpreted as deflections from the stipulated orientation that is everywhere parallel to itself. Parallel "pointings" or rays, for instance, are

---

[36] Earlier, Kepler uses "digression of the planet from apogee" to signify the mean anomaly. Here, he means the eccentric anomaly.

[37] Note that this only applies to the instantaneous motion caused by the *vis insita*. Kepler had yet to realize that the accumulation of such motions, each proportional to the sine of the anomaly, would be proportional to the versed sine (i.e., cosine), as required by the ellipse. In yet another remarkable flash of intuition, Kepler would come to this conclusion shortly hereafter, but that is a subject for elsewhere. See Kepler (1937–, 15:255).

described as having the *same* direction since they will all have the same deflection from the orientation. Thus, for Gilbert, the direction in which the earth's axis points does not change. He says that even as the earth revolves around the sun, its axis stays pointed in the *same* direction. It does not change direction. It *stays*.

As we saw above, Gilbert's oriented representation of the earth's direction greatly simplified his explanatory task. Kepler realized that Gilbert's treatment of the "third motion" could simplify his own explanatory project. The problem he faced is similar to Gilbert's: how to explain why a planet's "direction" remains parallel to itself throughout an orbit, in this case perpendicular to the apsidal line. Kepler had thought that this entailed that the planet's direction continually changes, a motion he could not readily explain. But Gilbert had shown that – so long as one assumes a rectilinear spatial orientation – the earth's axis can be kept parallel to itself by a simple, static cause that merely keeps the axis pointed in the *same* direction. By introducing an oriented concept of direction, it becomes plausible to suppose that some faculty, be it magnetic or mental, can keep Mars's magnetic axis fixed "in position" perpendicular to the apsidal line. If this is the case, the planet's supposed mind can measure the magnetic virtue proportional to the sine of the eccentric anomaly, and move itself toward or away from the sun accordingly – exactly as required by the geometric construction of the ellipse. Adopting Gilbert's oriented way of representing direction solves Kepler's explanatory problem.[38] Kepler finally has a plausible mechanism by which the planet can "respect the sines." The ellipse becomes a physically possible orbit.

In the *Astronomia Nova*, Kepler explains this arrangement. He envisions a magnetic axis in the body of Mars, which is kept parallel either by a "retentive" force or an "animate faculty":[39]

> As before, let there be certain regions of the planetary body in which there is a magnetic force of direction along a line tending towards the Sun. However, contrary to the previous case, let it be an attribute, not of the nature of the body, but of an animate faculty of the sort that governs the

---

[38] Kepler explicitly credits Gilbert with the notion that magnetic axes remain parallel to themselves in the *Astronomia Nova*, ch. 57, and in the *Epitome*, 4.3.1 (Kepler 1992, 550–51; 1995, 95). In fact, Kepler was not alone in seeing the importance of Gilbert's thesis. There is a parallel discussion of Gilbert in Galileo (1967, 345–55, 410). Galileo endorses Gilbert's conclusion that the "third motion" is not a motion, but fails to comprehend the conceptual shift underlying that conclusion. This confusion leads to difficulties surrounding Galileo's argument for the motion of the earth based on the motion of sunspots. See Chapter 5, below.

[39] Kepler gives both explanations. See Kepler (1992, 553).

body of the planet from within, that as it is swept along by the Sun, it keeps that magnetic axis always directed at the same fixed stars. . . . The result will be a battle between the animate faculty and the magnetic faculty, and the animate will win. . . . On the basis of these presuppositions, the planet's mind will be able to intuit and perceive the strength of the angle from the wrestling match between the animate faculty, which is designed to keep the magnetic axis in line, and the magnetic power of directing it towards the Sun.[40]

The magnetic axis tends to point toward the sun. It is held in place, however, by the animate faculty, which counteracts the magnetic power. The magnetic power of direction is increased as the axis is more inclined to the sun, so the animate faculty will have to "struggle" more vigorously to keep the axis in line. Thus, by sensing this "struggle" (which is proportional to the sine of the eccentric anomaly), the planet can "intuit" the "strength" or force that measures the proper speed of its approach. In other words, the magnetic power of the planet becomes a measuring device by which the planet learns the proper action of its inherent *vis insita*:

> There was consequently a need for us to equip the mind with an animate faculty, as well as a magnetic one, and to contrive a battle between the two which would remind the mind of its duties, of which it could not have been reminded by the equality of either the times or the spaces traversed. So again we have asked nature to assist the mind.[41]

The natural, magnetic faculty assists the planetary mind to determine the sine of the eccentric anomaly (as opposed to the anomalies themselves – "the times and spaces traversed"). Once the mind knows this, it can (by measuring the apparent solar diameter) fulfill its "duty" to move itself to the proper distance to the sun.

Kepler admits that this magnetic/animate mechanism might seem bizarre to some readers:

> Moreover, I do not know whether I have given sufficient proof to the philosophical reader of this perceptive cognition of the Sun and the fixed stars, which I myself so easily accept, and bestow upon the planet's mind.[42]

Thus, Kepler does not believe he has proven that Mars possesses a mind, or even a magnetic axis as he has described. This, though, is not really his concern. The aim all along has been merely to establish a plausible physical cause, however far-fetched:

[40] Kepler (1992, 567).   [41] Kepler (1992, 569).   [42] Kepler (1992, 570).

I will be satisfied if this magnetic example demonstrates the general possibility of the proposed mechanism. Concerning its details, however, I have doubts.[43]

If Kepler can establish the "general possibility" of the mechanism, even by appealing to minds, he can cache the mechanism, and thus the elliptical orbit it produces, in the realm of the possible. In this, at least, he has succeeded.[44]

Conclusion: the need for rectilinearity

Kepler, finally, has satisfied all his desiderata. He has constructed the true, "physical" path of the Martian orbit. It is causally explicable and agrees with observations:

> Furthermore, at the same time you see both that that most earnestly desired union is now finally complete. ... Everything I sought has been accomplished; the causes of each eccentricity are given. You have an astronomy without hypotheses. [*Astronomiam habes sine hypothesibus.*] Of course it seems that up to now it had been a hypothesis when I said that Mars's eccentric is a perfect ellipse. But this was previously concluded from physical causes; it is not therefore a hypothesis in my Commentaries. It is indeed in the calculation, but it is also a true supposition of the true path of the planets, giving the distances and the equations.[45]

[43] Kepler (1992, 559). Kepler was disappointed to find, for instance, that the earth's axis is roughly *parallel* to its apsidal line, not perpendicular, as needed in the case of Mars, and that its direction slowly changes. Nevertheless, Kepler decided to "relinquish" these objections, emphasizing, meanwhile, the *conceptual* importance of Gilbert's treatment of the "third motion" over its factual content: "Nam in meis Commentariis relicta fuit haec obiectio: si planetae per directionem axis in easdem mundi plagas virtute magnetica eccentricitates conficiunt, Terra idem faciet. At Terrae axis is solum directus est qui porrigitur à [Cancer] in [Capricorn]. ... Illam vero obiectionem de Telluris axe in apsidum lineam inconstanter tamen porrecto superis discutiendam relinquamus" (Kepler 1937–, 15:254–56). Kepler also ignored the very important point that the anomaly in question here is the *eccentric* anomaly, which violates his rejection of physical references to empty points, such as the eccentric center. Thus, the anomaly should be the *equated* anomaly, which is measured to the body of the sun. In the *Astronomia Nova*, Kepler dismisses this difference as insignificant (Kepler 1992, 558; Stephenson 1994, 115–16). Later, in the *Epitome of Copernican Astronomy*, Kepler introduces another libration of the magnetic axis precisely equal to the optical equation – the difference of the two anomalies. Thus, the magnetic axis "measures" the eccentric anomaly even though it is physically affected according to the equated anomaly. See Stephenson (1994, 146–72), Kepler (1995, 99–106).

[44] In fact, Kepler emphasized the importance of the magnetic balance for planetary orbits throughout his career. He repeats the full explanation, including his "law of the balance," in the *Epitome*, Book V (Kepler 1995, 128–33). Also, one of the goddesses atop the Temple of Urania on Kepler's frontispiece of the *Rudolphine Tables* (1627) holds an unequally weighted balance with the sun at its fulcrum, which may also be a reference to this mechanism. The goddess is flanked by images of Magnetica, holding a compass and lodestone, and Geometria, displaying the elliptical orbit with its perpendiculars to the apsidal line. Though he had previously claimed otherwise, Owen Gingerich has told me he concurs in this speculation. See Gingerich (1992).

[45] Voelkel (2001, 199–200). "Simul autem vides, vel iam tandem perfectum esse illud exoptamissimum coniugium.... Omnia iacta sunt quae petiisti, causae sunt datae vtriusque Eccentricitatis,

When Kepler first proposed the ellipse, it was merely a hypothesis – a mathematical conceit. It was a good description of the orbit, and accurate planetary positions and distances could be calculated, but now plausible physical causes of the motion have been given, so the ellipse transcends mere empirical adequacy. It is the "true supposition of the true path," both descriptive and explicable. By reconciling phenomena, description, and explanation, Kepler has produced "astronomy without hypotheses."

Kepler could not have effected this "most earnestly desired union," though, without adopting, at least partially, an oriented representation of space. The accurate description of the Martian orbit required geometrical constructions that could not be described in reference to a single spatial center. In particular, the perpendicular to the apsidal line is not a unique direction that can be specified in relation to a presupposed center. As a result, Kepler could not conceive how the planet might "respect the sines." The solution only came when Kepler realized that magnetic action could be described on the basis of a "right line" – a rectilinear orientation of the cosmos. By adopting an oriented representation of space like Gilbert's, Kepler could *assume* the direction in space he needed. He could then describe a plausible magnetic or animate faculty on the basis of that direction, and use this faculty to explain the ellipse. The presupposition of an orientation allows the reconciliation of description and explanation. It allows the true discovery of the ellipse.

However, a rectilinear orientation was precisely the sort of thing that Kepler had banished from the universe in the first edition of the *Mysterium*. His long and trying struggle with the Martian orbit showed that the presupposition of a rectilinear orientation is necessary to establish and explain the true elliptical orbits of the planets. Thus, God himself could not have constructed this "complete, thoroughly ordered universe" without appeal to "right lines." Kepler was wrong to eschew lines in the *Mysterium*. Enlightened by his own "conquest of Mars," and his encounter with Gilbert's magnetic philosophy, Kepler candidly reported his "*male factum*" in the *Mysterium*'s second edition.

Astronomiam habes sine hypothesibus. Videtur quidem adhuc haec esse hypothesis dum dico Martis Eccentricum esse perfectam Ellipsin. At prius hoc ex causis physicis conclusum est, non est igitur hypothesis in meis Commentariis; est vero in calculo, sed vera suppositio veri itineris Planetarii: dantis distantias et aequationes" (Kepler 1937–, 15:261). See also Kepler's corresponding claim to have constructed an astronomy "without hypotheses" in the *Astronomia Nova* (Kepler 1992, 28).

Kepler's adoption of an oriented representation of space was always limited to part of his treatment of the *vis insita*. In general, Kepler's spatial framework remained centered, not oriented. He continued, for example, to privilege a geometric center, embodied by the sun. Indeed, the *anima motrix* moving the planets around their orbits is always, for Kepler, described on the basis of a centered framework. It emanates radially from the center and moves planets circularly about it. The ultimate effect of the *vis insita*, meanwhile, is always to move the planet along a radius to the sun.[46]

Nevertheless, Kepler's oriented representation of the animate faculty of the planet constituted an essential step in the emergence of oriented space in the early modern period. In Kepler's work, the motion of a planet is due to the combined action of the *anima motrix* and the *vis insita*. In time, these would become Newton's inertia and gravitation, respectively, which Newton similarly combined in an oriented framework. By bringing the *vis insita* into an oriented representation of space, Kepler set the stage for Newton's revolutionary synthesis. It awaited a rectified inertia to replace Kepler's *anima motrix*. This was the eventual contribution of Galileo and Descartes, whom I address next.

Notice, meanwhile, the negotiation of the two desiderata, descriptions and explanations, by which Kepler came to his crucial realization. As we have seen, Kepler worked both ends towards the middle. Though quite confusing at times, his method is a particularly clear demonstration of the reciprocal process of iteration between description and explanation. An empirically adequate description is considered false if it cannot be reconciled with a plausible explanation. Thus, upon discovering a geometrical construction of the elliptical orbit, Kepler considered what might cause it. This led him to the

---

[46] Even in the late *Epitome*, Kepler composes the rectilinear action of the *vis insita* with the spherically-conceived circular motion caused by the *anima motrix* in order to derive the motion of the planet. As Koyré notes, Caspar's reconstruction of Kepler's argument in the *Epitome* (Kepler 1937–, 7:598) is conceptually mistaken along precisely these lines: "Now, the concept of motion underlying Caspar's proof is quite different from that of Kepler; it implies the principle of inertia and the preponderance of the straight line over the circle. Consequently, the elements of motion – lateral and centripetal – which comprise the orbital motion are straight lines; and the elements of this latter motion are (infinitesimal) straight lines whose direction is that of the tangent to that point on the (curved) orbit occupied (for a moment) by the moving body. However, these elements are not at all straight lines in Kepler's view; those connected with libration undoubtedly are; but those connected with lateral motion are (infinitesimal) circular arcs. Even the infinitesimally short tangents play no part in his arguments" (Koyré 1973, 321). Davis (1992) convicts several others of a similar mistake.

magnetic balance mechanism. However, this mechanism could not be reconciled with descriptions generated in a centered representation of space, since "respecting the sines" requires an inexplicable "turning." As a result, Kepler alters the way descriptions are produced to effect the solution. The problem is finally solved – the "most earnestly desired union" achieved – when Kepler shifts his descriptive frame-work, i.e., his representation of space. Explanations are generated to save the descriptions. New descriptions are generated to save the explanations. This new description reconciles the phenomena to (plausible) explanations. It achieves, Kepler says, "the unexpected transfer of the whole of astronomy from fictitious circles to natural causes."[47]

---

[47] Kepler, *Rudolphine Tables*, quoted in Ferguson (2002, 346).

CHAPTER 5

Mille movimenti circolari: *from impetus to conserved curvilinear motion in Galileo*

The origins of inertial physics

As we have seen, Copernicus thought his geokinetic representation of the solar system was more consistent with Aristotelian explanatory principles of celestial motion than the Ptolemaic astronomy he sought to replace.[1] However, it was clear to most late Renaissance and early modern natural philosophers that the Copernican hypothesis was incompatible with Aristotelian principles of terrestrial motion. The existing physics predicted a slew of effects of a moving earth that were not observed. In particular, objected skeptics, if the earth is supposed to be spinning on its axis once a day, why are objects separated from the earth, such as thrown or falling bodies, not left behind as the earth spins beneath them? Copernicus himself, as noted above, did not respond in detail to these questions, and it was left to his successors to formulate a new terrestrial physics that could support the geokinetic description of the solar system. Copernicanism demanded new explanations that could account for the fact that the postulated motion of the earth is not readily observed.

One essential feature of the modern physics that emerged from this problematic was the principle of inertia: bodies in motion or rest conserve their state of motion or rest. This principle allowed Copernicans to explain that thrown or falling bodies are not left behind by the spinning earth because they conserve the motion imparted to them before their release, so they keep up with the earth's rotation. Famously, Galileo was a key figure in the introduction of the inertial principle. It has been well established, however, that Galileo's conservation principle was significantly different from the inertial principle that became part of modern physics. Galileo proposed the conservation of *circular* motion: horizontal motion around the earth's axis is conserved, so bodies tend to move uniformly at a constant distance from the earth's center – in a circle. This formed the foundation for arguments in favor of Copernicanism, since it is sufficient to explain why

---

[1] See Chapter 2.

the spinning earth does not leave objects behind. Yet Galilean conservation was ultimately supplanted by *rectilinear* inertia – the view that bodies conserve motion *along straight lines*.

The difference between the Galilean and the modern theory can be parsed according to the layered model of scientific knowledge I have proposed. What is at issue is not the explanatory principle itself. In Galileo's theory and in classical physics, motion is conserved – a body tends to persist in its state of motion or rest. Continuing motion or rest thus requires no explanation besides an earlier motion or rest. Only *changes* of motion or rest require explanation by additional force or action. The difference between Galilean and classical physics does not lie at the explanatory level. Instead, the theories differ in the descriptive frameworks that coordinate the explanatory principle with phenomena. The theories identify different phenomena as "conserved motions." For Galileo, circular motions are unchanging, while later theorists specify that only rectilinear motions are unchanging.

This much has been widely recognized, but merely noting that Galileo's conservation principle is coordinated with circular motions conceals a deeper ambiguity at the descriptive level. The theory implies that bodies conserve their motions, but the referent of "conserved motion" is not fully specified beyond its circularity. We can still ask what quantity the theory takes to be conserved. There are two possibilities. First, a body moving circularly could conserve its angular *rotation*, so that it subtends an equal central angle from moment to moment. On the other hand, a body might conserve its curvilinear *translation*, so that it subtends an equal curvilinear distance in each successive moment. The explanation of the motion remains the same; the phenomenon explained varies. Still, both versions of the theory constitute "conservation of circular motion": bodies moving circularly conserve their state of motion.

These two coordinations of Galileo's conservation principle are significantly different, and they entail different outcomes of the same initial conditions. Consider, for instance, a ball dropped from a tower on the earth, which is spinning rapidly eastward. If the falling ball conserves the angular rotation imparted by the tower before its release, it will continue to move horizontally at the rate of one rotation per day, even as it falls downward. Since this rotation is exactly shared by the tower and everything else on earth, the ball will fall at the foot of the tower, precisely below the point from which it was dropped. If, on the other hand, the falling ball conserves the curvilinear translation imparted by the tower, it will not fall exactly at the foot of the tower. The curvilinear translation of the ball at the top of the tower, further from the axis of the earth's rotation, is greater than the curvilinear translation of the ground beneath. Hence, if the curvilinear motion is conserved, the ball will outpace the ground beneath and fall (slightly) to the east, ahead of the foot of the tower. Thus, the theory of conserved circular motion can generate different predictions, depending on what phenomenon is *meant* by the circular "conserved motion." Different descriptive frameworks containing different coordinations generate different theories yielding different predictions.

The question therefore arises: What is Galileo's descriptive framework? That is, what is "conserved motion" for Galileo? Is it conserved angular rotation or conserved curvilinear translation? This is an important question in the history of physics. Rectilinear inertia is the conservation of a linear translation. The modern principle is therefore continuous with conserved curvilinear translation, but not with the conservation of angular rotation. In order for the conservation principle to be rectified, then, it first had to be made specifically curvilinear. Only then could it be "straightened out" into the modern theory. Examination of the descriptive frameworks associated with Galileo's conservation principle shows how his theory led to the modern one.

The establishment of modern inertial physics required two distinct developments, one at each epistemic level. First, conservation of motion was introduced as an explanatory principle that accounted for the continued motion of bodies, even in the absence of motive forces. In fact, this "essential core of the inertial concept"[2] was Galileo's most important physical innovation. It marked a departure from medieval and Renaissance theories of motion, which held that continued motion was the result of either an inherent natural tendency of bodies or an extrinsic action or force (an "impetus") continually acting on bodies. Ever since Pierre Duhem first linked Galileo to the medieval *doctores parisienses*, the origins of Galileo's conservation principle has exercised historians of science. The subtlety of the differences between Galileo's explanatory principle and those of his forebears serves to underscore the continuity of Galileo's theory with those of his predecessors (whoever those predecessors may be). The literature is now voluminous, tracing out the influences of a myriad of traditions – Aristotelian, Archimedean, and Platonic – from the ancient world to Galileo's immediate precursors. In what follows, I will skirt this already well-rehearsed discussion.[3]

---

[2] Drake (1970, 251; 1999, 143).
[3] See, for instance, Duhem (1913), Moody (1951), Clagett (1959, ch. 8), Hall (1965), Koyré (1966), Moody (1966), Weisheipl (1967), Drake and Drabkin (1969), Drake (1970), Finocchiaro (1980, ch. 4), Wallace (1981), Maier (1982, esp. 103–123), Clavelin (1983), Drake (1986, 167), Hooper (1998), Camerota and Helbing (2000), Roux (2006), Van Dyck (2006), Meli (2008).

The second development was the advent of an oriented representation of space that coordinated "conserved motion" with uniform rectilinear translation, considered as a simple motion everywhere similar to itself. Galileo did not accomplish this, but he did make great strides. In particular, he noticed the difference between angular rotation and curvilinear translation, and he eventually coordinated the conservation principle specifically with curvilinear translation. In fact, he even allowed that an oriented representation of space could be used as a small-scale approximation of a centered representation, thereby suggesting conserved rectilinear motion as an approximation of conserved curvilinear motion. It fell to Galileo's successors, especially Descartes (as we shall see shortly), simply to reverse the order of approximation and promote rectilinear conservation to the more fundamental position. The descriptive aspect of Galileo's work has not fallen under the scrutiny of scholars, and this chapter will take up the development of Galileo's descriptive apparatus.

The story begins with Galileo's early *De Motu* manuscripts, which adhere to Aristotelian explanatory principles, but alter the descriptive framework in which they are deployed. This, in turn, leads to an explanatory problem that Galileo remedies by introducing conservation of motion as a new explanatory principle. This brings us to the *Dialogue Concerning the Two Chief World Systems (Dialogo)*, where Galileo first recognizes the difference between curvilinear translation and angular rotation, though he tends to associate conserved motion with the latter. The coordination is finally reversed in the *Discourses and Mathematical Demonstrations Concerning Two New Sciences (Discorsi)*, where Galileo employs a theory of conserved curvilinear motion. The *Discorsi* also introduces the "Archimedean approximation," which suggests, just as an approximation, the coordination of the conservation principle with rectilinear translation via the introduction of an oriented representation of small-scale space. This last step leaves Galileo on the threshold of the modern principle, setting the stage for Descartes, Newton, and all that followed.

Galileo's antecedents

In the Aristotelian physics that had become standard in Scholastic natural philosophy, all local motions are either "natural" or "forced." That is, they are explained either by the inherent nature of the moving body itself, or by the action of some extrinsic agent or cause. These two explanatory principles were coordinated with the phenomena via a centered representation of space in which locations and directions are described in relation to a stipulated center. Thus, places are distinguished by their distance from the center and directions are distinguished by their relations to that center. The celestial spheres are assigned natural rotation around the center; that is, always in place as distinguished by distance from the center and always in the same direction identified as perpendicular to a radius to the center. The terrestrial elements, meanwhile, naturally seek their own proper places in the centered space: earth nearest the center, then water, air, and finally fire. Thus, terrestrial bodies naturally move up, away from the center, or down, toward the center. Since these three motions – around, up, and down – are the only "simple" motions in a centered space (i.e., they do not change direction with respect to the center),[4] they exhaust the natural motions of bodies, according to Aristotle. These, and only these, are explicable by a substance's inherent nature. All other motions are "forced" or "violent," and can be explained only by appeal to some additional, extrinsic cause. In this theory, the descriptive distinctions between motions up, down, around, and otherwise, are the only physically significant categories.

At least in some passages, Aristotle attributes forced motion to the action of the medium through which a body moves. In late antiquity and the medieval period, this explanation was supplanted by an "impetus" theory of motion. There were several variants of this view, but they all held that motion was the result of a quality – an *impetus* or *virtus impressa* – added to the moving body by that which originally set it in motion. The impetus produces the body's motion once it has been separated from the mover, and motion continues as long as the impetus remains in the body.

Aristotelian explanations drew no distinction between curvilinear translation and angular rotation. *Any* local motion, including spinning and turning, could be explained by natural motion or by impressed impetus. That is not to say, though, that the distinction was not at all present in any pre-Galilean descriptions of motions. Some late medieval and Renaissance natural philosophers employed a framework for the description of motions that implicitly differentiated between the two. In the fourteenth century, John of Holland, Albert of Saxony, and Nicole Oresme introduced descriptions that distinguished between "uniform" and "difform" (or "regular" and "irregular") motions. These terms had a very wide range of application. Motions could be "uniform" or "difform" with respect to time or with respect to the parts of the moving body. A rotating sphere, for instance, was said to move uniformly with respect to time in that it possesses the same motion, its constant angular rotation, from moment to moment. However,

---

[4] Setting aside some spirals.

the sphere moves difformly with respect to its parts in that the parts closer to the axis of rotation have smaller curvilinear translations than parts further away. Alternatively, a falling body moves uniformly with respect to its parts, since all parts move with the same rectilinear speed at any given moment, though difformly with respect to time, since the body accelerates.[5]

This was a sophisticated descriptive scheme. It recognized, among other things, that the curvilinear motion of the parts was different from the angular rotation of the whole sphere – one could be difform, while the other uniform. Albert of Saxony also noted that the top of a ship's mast undergoes a greater curvilinear translation than its hull on any voyage, since the mast is further from the earth's center, even though the angular motion is the same for all parts of the ship.[6] However, the difference between translation and rotation was merely implicit in these treatments; it was not itself the basis of a descriptive categorization. John of Holland, for instance, wrote that a body in uniform linear translation and a uniformly rotating sphere were interchangeable examples of uniform motion with respect to time. Moreover, none of these descriptive distinctions had any *physical* significance. For one thing, these schemata were employed in a kinematic context separate from any explanatory considerations. They were used merely to describe motions, without regard to their causes. Where causal explanations were applied, authors fell back on explanation of motions by appeal to nature and force, without distinguishing uniform from difform, let alone translation from rotation. So, while Galileo's predecessors possessed some recognition of the difference between angular rotation and curvilinear translation, they never specifically coordinated their explanations with one or the other. The explanation of motion in general, by nature or by force, applied indiscriminately to angular rotations and curvilinear translations.[7]

[5] In addition, the descriptions also extended to a second order, to describe the kind of acceleration of difform motion. A motion, therefore, could be either "uniformly difform" or "difformly difform." This terminology actually originated with the English Mertonians. However, the Mertonians took these as mathematical descriptions, and did not coordinate them with physical phenomena. See Wallace (1968, 386).

[6] Galileo would later quote this observation in the *Dialogo*, with the marginal note: "Ironic recitation of very puerile conclusions taken from certain encyclopedia" (*Sottiglieze assai insipide ironicamente dette, e cavate da certa enciclopedia*) (Galilei 1890–1909, 7:199; 1967, 173–74). See also Moody (1966, 34).

[7] The divergence of kinematic and dynamic contexts was partly due to the dispute between nominalist and realist philosophers The nominalists were primarily responsible for the distinctions between "uniform," "difform," and so on. However, they also held that local motion was just a body occupying a succession of places. It was not a real modification of a body, and thus required no causal explanation. Hence, the nominalists used their descriptive distinctions merely to characterize motion, and generally ignored the distinction between nature and force. Realists, on the other hand, did think that motion was a real quality added to bodies, like heat or moisture, and thus needed causal explanation, but they did not generally use the kinematic distinctions. See Wallace (1967, 1968), Murdoch and Sylla (1978).

Still, it is significant that the kinematic distinctions were repeated through the centuries, down to the work of Domingo de Soto in the sixteenth, which Galileo himself cited. The distinctions, meanwhile, were associated with a stock of archetypical exemplars. John of Holland himself used the examples of a falling stone and a rotating sphere, as well as Socrates walking. Albert and Oresme referred to falling bodies, sometimes in resisting media, and rotating wheels. Later authors added heavenly spheres, millstones, potters' wheels, tops, thrown lances, towed ships, and other more complicated cases. Galileo would also appeal to some of the same examples.[8]

De Motu

Galileo, in his early *De Motu* manuscripts,[9] generally adheres to Aristotelian explanatory principles. He maintains, most importantly, the two explanations of terrestrial motion: bodies move either by their nature or by the imposition of some impetus. Also as in Aristotelian physics, these causal principles are associated with a centered ordering of space. The universe is structured around a stipulated center, places and directions are distinguished in relation to that center, and bodies seek out their "natural" places in the spatial order of places. Galileo, speculating about the creation of the universe, describes how the elements were placed in a previously empty space according to their form:

[8] Wallace (1968). John Buridan's use of a top (*trocus*), smith's wheel (*mola fabri*), thrown lance, and towed ship is well known. See his *Questions on the Eight Books of the Physics of Aristotle* in Clagett (1959, 532–38). The distinction also arose in astronomy, where Erasmus Rheinhold noted that the physicists' "regular motions" could be coordinated with either angular rotation or curvilinear translation, since they are equivalent: "Writers of physics in fact define regular motion to be that which covers equal spaces in equal times. But astronomers, because they consider celestial motions to be circular hold the following definition: Regular motion is that which describes in equal times either equal angles with respect to its center or equal arcs on the circumference of the circle. For equal angles at the center intercept equal arcs on the circle's circumferences and, on the other hand, equal arcs imply equal angles at the center, just as is demonstrated in Book III, Chapters 26 and 27 of [Euclid's] *Elements*" (*Commentary on* Theoricae novae planetarum [1542], quoted in Westman 1980, 113).

[9] These manuscripts were penned by Galileo around 1591, when he was a professor at Pisa. They consist of a dialogue and a treatise on local motion and falling bodies, along with notes and emendations. Eventually, Galileo collected them into a file he apparently labelled "*De motu antiquiora scripta mea*," or "My older writings on motion," and retained them, though he never brought them to press except insofar as they form the basis of other work. The manuscripts are preserved in the Biblioteca Nazionale Centrale in Florence as MS 71, available online at http://echo.mpiwg-berlin.mpg.de/content/scientific_revolution/galileo/photographicdocumentation. Favaro published them in Volume I of the *Edizione Nazionale* as "*De motu*" (Galilei 1890–1909, 1:243–419). For translations, see Galilei (1960b), Galilei and Fredette (2000). For a summary of arguments about the composition and relative dating of these materials, see Wallace (1990), Giusti (1998), Fredette (2001).

If, for example, we suppose that nature, at the time of the construction of the universe, divided all the common matter of the elements into four equal parts, and then assigned to the form of the earth its own matter [i.e., earth], and likewise to the form of air *its* own matter [i.e., air], and that the form of the earth caused its matter to be compressed in a very narrow space, while the form of the air permitted the placing of its matter in a very ample space, would it not be reasonable for nature to assign a larger space to air, and a smaller space to earth? But in a sphere the spaces become narrower as we approach the center, and larger as we recede from the center.[10]

Primordial space has a spherical structure. Locations and directions are distinguished by reference to a stipulated center. Thus, intuitively speaking, this space is "narrower" nearer the center. A portion of space with unit radial height and unit solid angle will have a greater volume further from the center. The appropriate place for denser elements, then, is in the denser, "narrower" space, nearer the center. The "heavier" elements, earth and water, are placed by nature nearer the center and the "lighter" elements, air and fire, are placed further away.[11]

Regarding terrestrial phenomena, Galileo also preserves the coordinations between the explanatory principles and the vertical motions identified as those toward or away from the stipulated center. In early *De Motu* essays, Galileo wrote that both the motion of "heavy" bodies downward and the motion of "light" bodies upward was "natural," exactly as Aristotle held:

For, since heavy bodies have, by reason of their heaviness, the property of remaining at rest under lighter bodies – inasmuch as they are heavy, they have been placed by nature under the lighter – they will also have the property, imposed by nature, that, when they are situated above lighter bodies, they will move down below these lighter bodies, lest the lighter remain at rest under the heavier, contrary to the arrangement of nature. And, in the same way, light bodies will move upward by their lightness, whenever they are under heavier bodies.[12]

That is, motion both up and down is a result of an inherent tendency in bodies to seek their natural ordering around the spatial center. In later

[10] Galilei (1890–1909, 1:253; 1960b, 15).
[11] A similar discussion appears in the dialogue version of the *De Motu* treatise. There, Galileo comments that the "argument is not to be considered a conclusive reason for this disposition of the elements, still it has in it some appearance of truth" (Galilei 1890–1909, 1:374–75; Drake and Drabkin 1969, 339). Kepler similarly argues that the density of bodies near the sun is consonant with the "certain form of narrowness" of "the very places which are near the center" (Kepler 1995, 40).
[12] Galilei (1890–1909, 1:253–54; 1960b, 16).

re-workings of the manuscript, Galileo came to define gravity and levity relatively, not absolutely, in terms of density.[13] That is, Galileo came to believe that *all* bodies naturally tend toward the center. "Lighter" or "less heavy" (i.e., rarer) bodies are extruded upward by denser media, while "heavier" (i.e., denser) bodies are able to force aside rarer media and move downward. In sum, all motion toward the center is natural, caused by the intrinsic tendency toward the center all bodies possess. Motion away from the center is (in the Aristotelian sense) "forced," caused by the extruding action of a denser medium.

Galileo's account thus preserves the rudiments of Aristotelian physics for vertical motions, but *De Motu* embarks on a more significant departure from Aristotle with regard to motions that do not alter a terrestrial body's place – i.e., its distance from the center. Whereas Aristotle and his successors had said *any* non-vertical terrestrial motion was "forced," Galileo carves out a new descriptive category for place-preserving motions. He calls them "neutral" or "indifferent" motions. Such motions have no effect on the arrangement of the universe around its center. Neutral motion therefore does not alter the ordering of denser or rarer bodies, so nature offers neither encouragement nor resistance; they are "neither natural nor forced." Nature is "indifferent" to place-preserving motion.[14]

It must be stressed that Galileo is *only* adjusting the descriptive framework associated with his explanatory principles. He withdraws the coordination between force/impetus and terrestrial motion in place (as identified in the centered representation of space). He does not, however, offer a new explanation for these motions. This is an explanatory problem: Galileo describes "neutral" motions, but he cannot make them fit with the explanatory principles on hand. A body may start to move in place by nature or force, but neither nature nor force causes the continuation of neutral motion.

Neutral motion *per se* has no explanation, and this leads to a problematic understanding of the phenomena. Galileo cannot give predictions, for instance, about what will happen once a neutral motion begins:

> [I]f at the center of the universe there were a sphere that rotated neither naturally nor by force, the question is asked whether, after receiving a start of motion from an external mover, it would move perpetually or not. For if its motion is not contrary to nature, it seems that it should move perpetually;

---

[13] Galilei (1890–1909, 1:341–66; 1960b, 115–16). See also Moody (1951, 1966), Drake and Drabkin (1969, 37–41, 196), Hooper (1998), Wallace (1998), Drake (1999, 210–11).

[14] For earlier adumbrations of this theory in Oresme and Cardano, see Clagett (1959, 602–03, 681–82), Drake and Drabkin (1969, 28–29), Büttner (2008, 46–48).

but if its motion is not according to nature, it seems that it should finally come to rest.[15]

Galileo holds that impetus is contrary to nature, which therefore resists forced motion. A forced motion, then, quickly dissipates, decelerates, and ceases.[16] Natural motions, meanwhile, are self-generated and continuous. In fact, Galileo says, they are accelerated, as more and more motion is generated by the natural heaviness of a body. Thus, on the one hand, a neutral motion is not contrary to nature, so it seems a body should remain in motion. On the other hand, the motion is not itself natural, so the body should not continue moving. Galileo cannot say, then, whether the neutral motion will continue "perpetually." In the end, Galileo does not answer his own question, except to say that neutral motions "suggest the quality of the forced rather than of the natural" in that they eventually are halted by the action of "accidental" causes like friction and air resistance.[17]

This inconclusive discussion, however, suggests its own resolution. Eventually, Galileo will introduce a conservation principle to explain "neutral" motions. Neutral motions persist, Galileo will say, because bodies conserve the state of motion in which they are placed. Since there is no reason for a neutral motion to accelerate or cease, it simply remains constant. Only a change in neutral motion needs explanation by nature or force. In other words, Galileo will add a conservation principle to his theory of motion in order to resolve the explanatory difficulty raised by his introduction of the new descriptive term. "Neutral" motion will become "conserved" motion.[18] Hence, it will be useful to linger over the question of just what "neutral motion" refers to. What counts as a "neutral motion"?

---

[15] Galilei (1890–1909, 1:305; 1960b, 73).

[16] Galilei (1890–1909, 1:310–11; 1960b, 79–80). Early in his career, Galileo held that impetus dissipated spontaneously on its own. This was a traditional view held by Simplicius, John Philoponus, Ibn Sīnā (Avicenna), Franciscus de Marchia, Francesco Buonamico (Galileo's professor at Pisa), and others. Later, he appears to have moved in the direction of an impetus that persists until removed by external forces, and thus closer to a conservation principle. This also was a traditional view, held by Buridan, Oresme, Giovanni Battista Benedetti, Niccolò Tartaglia, and others. See Clagett (1959, ch. 8), Moody (1951, 1966).

[17] Galilei (1890–1909, 1:307; 1960b, 76).

[18] I do not find, as some authors do, a "pre-inertial principle" in the *De Motu* manuscripts themselves, or even in *Le Mecchaniche* (ca. 1600). Galileo says only that an ideal sphere on a frictionless horizontal surface would move under the influence of the slightest force (Galilei 1890–1909, 2:180; 1960a, 171). This is consistent with Aristotelian dynamics, and it does not constitute a conservation principle, since Galileo does not say that the motion will continue should the slightest force be removed.

Neutral motion

Galileo offers two phenomena as archetypes of "neutral motion" in *De Motu*. The first arises during a consideration of balls moving on inclined planes. Here, Galileo attempts to relate the speed of the balls' descent to the planes' angle of inclination. He assumes, because of its natural tendency downward toward the center, that a heavy ball resists motion up an incline, and spontaneously rolls down. Furthermore, the speed of descent depends on how much the body "weighs" on the plane, which depends in turn on the inclination, such that a ball moves faster down a more inclined plane. The details of this derivation need not concern us, but a corollary to the derivation is significant. What, Galileo asks, happens to a ball on a plane that is perfectly level, i.e., exactly parallel to the horizon and inclined neither up nor down? Galileo asserts that the motion along a horizontal surface is "neither natural nor forced." It is, in fact, a case of neutral motion, and the motion can be generated by any force whatsoever:

> A body subject to no external resistance on a plane sloping no matter how little below the horizon will move down [the plane] in natural motion, without the application of any external force. This can be seen in the case of water. And the same body on a plane sloping upward, no matter how little, above the horizon, does not move up [the plane] except by force. And so the conclusion remains that on the horizontal plane itself the motion of the body is neither natural nor forced.[19]

Setting friction and other "external resistance" aside, a body moving along a horizontal surface exhibits "neutral motion" that is "neither natural nor forced."

The horizontal surface is not a flat plane, however. A flat plane is not everywhere equidistant to the center, so motion along it does not maintain a body's place:

> [A] plane cannot actually be parallel to the horizon, since the surface of the earth is spherical, and a plane cannot be parallel to such a surface. Hence, since [in the aforesaid experiment] the plane touches the sphere in only one point, if we move away from that point, we shall have to be moving up.[20]

Motion along a flat horizontal plane necessarily changes distance to the center; as one moves away from the normal to the center, one moves "up." A truly horizontal surface is actually a sphere, everywhere equidistant from the center of gravitation. Thus, a ball moving neither up nor down, with a motion that is "neither natural nor forced," moves along a spherical surface.

[19] Galilei (1890–1909, 1:299; 1960b, 66).   [20] Galilei (1890–1909, 1:301; 1960b, 68).

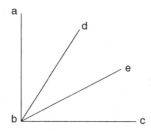

Figure 5.1 Inclined planes in *De Motu*.[21]

That is, it moves in a circle around an axis through the center. "Neutral motion" is *circular* motion.

Notice, though, that this discussion conceives "motion" as a linear translation. Bodies are considered to be moving along inclined planes and horizontal surfaces. All of the inclined planes are described as having linear *lengths*, and the motion of the ball along them subtends those lengths. Consider how Galileo poses the problem:

> Let there be a line *ab* [in Figure 5.1] directed toward the center of the universe and thus perpendicular to a plane parallel to the horizon. And let line *bc* lie in that plane parallel to the horizon. Now from point *b* let any number of lines be drawn making acute angles with line *bc*, e.g., lines *bd* and *be*. The problem, then, is why a body moving down descends most quickly on line *ab*; and on line *bd* more quickly than on *be*, but more slowly than on *ba*; and on *be* more slowly than on *bd*.[22]

Here, "motion" refers to linear translations along *bd*, *be*, *ba*, etc., and moving "faster" simply means covering a greater linear distance in an equal amount of time. It follows that the motion of the ball on the horizontal is also a linear translation, since it is merely the transition between motion up and motion down an inclined plane, and is therefore continuous with those linear translations. Thus, Galileo considers the neutral, circular motion of a ball on a spherical, horizontal surface as a linear translation. "Neutral motion" is a curvilinear quantity in this case.

A ball rolling on a horizontal surface was a novel example of motion, not included among the kinematic archetypes of Galileo's predecessors. However, Galileo supplements that case with another example, familiar from medieval physics. Galileo argues that a homogeneous sphere rotating

---

[21] Galilei (1890–1909, 1:296).   [22] Galilei (1890–1909, 1:296–97; 1960b, 63–64).

around its own axis is another archetype of "neutral motion."[23] So long as the center of gravity of the sphere does not move relative to the center of the universe, Galileo holds that such a motion does not disturb the "arrangement of nature" and therefore is "neither natural nor forced":

> Now if the body is of homogeneous parts, e.g., a marble sphere, rotating on an axis, such motion will be neither natural nor forced. For the center of gravity of the sphere neither approaches nor recedes from the center of the universe, and the weight of the parts of the sphere that are moving up is equal to the weight of the parts that are moving down, so that the sphere is always in equilibrium.[24]

The sphere as a whole remains in place, at a constant distance from the center. Each *part* of the sphere moving toward the center is counterbalanced by an equal part moving away from the center, so the rotation does not change the overall ordering of heavy and light bodies. As before, nature offers neither encouragement nor resistance, and the motion is "neutral." In this case, however, the "neutral motion" conserved is the rotation of the whole sphere. It is not the linear translations of the various parts, which themselves vary by distance from the axis of rotation, and may indeed be individually resisted or encouraged by the nature of the parts considered separately. Nor is it the linear translation of the sphere as a whole, for there is none. In this part of *De Motu*, the "neutral motion" is an *angular* quantity.

"Neutral motion" that does not change the ordering of heavy and light bodies around the spatial center is "neither natural nor forced." But the "neutral motion" can be *either* a curvilinear translation, as in the case of a ball on a horizontal surface, *or* an angular rotation, as in the case of a rotating homogeneous sphere. Galileo says both motions are instances of one kind: *circular* motion *simpliciter*. Both have the same (lack of) explanation. Indeed, the discussion of spheres rotating neither by nature nor by force is intended to reinforce the notion that bodies on horizontal surfaces move neither by nature nor by force, as well. The rotating sphere, that is, is meant to show that the rolling ball will continue moving neither by nature nor by force.[25] In keeping, as we have seen, with earlier theories of motion,

---

[23] Büttner (2008) argues that Galileo had in mind the flywheels used by contemporary engineers.

[24] Galilei (1890–1909, 1:306–07; 1960b, 75). Galileo also considers a homogeneous sphere rotating around the center of the universe, a heterogeneous sphere rotating around the center, and a heterogeneous sphere rotating around some other center. Only the last case is not neutral, but "sometimes natural and sometimes forced," as the sphere's center of gravity falls and rises (Galilei 1890–1909, 1:304–07; 1960b, 72–76).

[25] This is clear from the structure of *De Motu*. The fourteenth chapter discusses motion along an inclined plane, with the conclusion that motion on a horizontal plane is neither natural nor forced.

Galileo does not clearly recognize the physical divergence between these cases and does not clearly distinguish these motions into separate descriptive categories.

Dialogo

Much of what was proposed in *De Motu* is reiterated in Galileo's *magnum opus*, the *Dialogue Concerning the Two Chief World Systems*, written some three decades after *De Motu* and published in 1632. However, by the time Galileo wrote the *Dialogo*, there were two important developments in his thought. The first is his adoption of a conservation principle to explain continuing neutral motions. I need not belabor this point, except to note its appearance in Galileo's work in the first years of the seventeenth century.[26] Certainly it was well established by the time of the *Sunspot Letters*, published in 1613. There, Galileo explicitly associates the conservation of motion with "indifferent motion" that does not change a body's place with respect to the center:

> For I seem to observe that natural bodies have a natural inclination to some motion – heavy ones, for example, tend downward – and they exercise this motion through an intrinsic principle and without need of a particular external mover, as long as they are not impeded by some obstacle. To some other motions they have resistance – those same heavy bodies, for instance, to upward motion – and therefore will never move in this way except when thrust violently by an external mover. Finally, they are indifferent to some movements – as are the same heavy bodies to horizontal motion – to which they have neither inclination, because it is not toward the center of the Earth, nor aversion, because it is not away from the same center. And therefore, with all the external impediments removed, a heavy body on the spherical surface concentric to the Earth will be indifferent to rest and to movement toward any part of the horizon, and it will remain in the state in which it has been put; that is, if it has been put in a state of rest it will remain in it, and if it has been put in motion, toward the west, for example, it will remain in the same motion.[27]

The fifteenth chapter establishes that rectilinear motions, like those on a plane, are comparable to circular motions, since they "have a ratio to each other" (Galilei 1890–1909, 1:302; 1960b, 70). Finally, the sixteenth chapter introduces spinning spheres as another example of circular motion that is neither natural nor forced, comparable, by the content of the intermediate chapter, to the motion of bodies on planes. (Jochen Büttner pressed me on this point.)

[26] Drake (1978, 82). Isaac Beeckman and Pierre Gassendi also formulated conservation principles at about the same time (Pav 1966; Gabbey 1971, 16; Roux 2006, 471). In a 1607 letter, Castelli also attributes to Galileo the principle that "movement is necessary to begin motion, but to continue it, it is enough not to have resistance [*contrasto*]" (Galilei 1890–1909, 10:170).

[27] Galilei (1890–1909, 5:134), Galilei and Scheiner (2010, 125, translation slightly altered).

This passage concisely summarizes Galileo's physics in the period before the *Dialogo*. Motions are due to a body's inherent nature, an impressed impetus from some extrinsic source, or the conservation of a state of motion. The latter explanation is associated with motions around the center; that is, the very "neutral motions" of *De Motu*. Bodies conserve motions that do not alter their place with respect to the center.[28]

The second development is that Galileo had become a convinced Copernican, perhaps as early as 1597, but certainly by the publication of the *Sidereus Nuncius* in 1610.[29] As a result, he was forced to grapple with the empirical and explanatory problems that afflicted the Copernican hypothesis, particularly the lack of empirical proof of the earth's motion. In fact, the very purpose of the *Dialogo* is to offer a staunch defense of the geokinetic hypothesis and to answer some of these objections. Galileo's pro-Copernican arguments are mainly directed along two fronts. On the positive side, he seeks to establish that the earth's annual and diurnal motions are naturally suited to the earth as a celestial body. On the negative side, Galileo seeks to explain why most "experiments practicable upon the earth are insufficient measures for proving its mobility, since they are indifferently adaptable to an earth in motion or at rest,"[30] thereby obviating the common objection that the earth's motion cannot be observed. The conservation principle itself is most important for the latter project, as we shall see. However, the former project inclines Galileo toward a conception of conserved motion as an angular quantity, so I turn to that discussion first.

As Galileo explains, nature can only assign circular motions to the celestial bodies, because only circular motions preserve the order of the universe. "I admit," says Salviati, the character speaking for Galileo, "that the world is . . . most perfect. And I add that as such it is of necessity most orderly, having its parts disposed in the highest and most perfect order amongst themselves."[31] The various physical bodies in the universe are all located in their proper places. Consequently, nature can only allow motions that do not disturb the ordering of the universe:

[28] At this point, Galileo still has not distinguished curvilinear translation from angular rotation. The argument that the curvilinear translation of a body on the earth is conserved is actually part of an argument that the angular rotation of the *sun* is conserved, "indifferent" motion, thus repeating the interchange in *De Motu* (Galilei 1890–1909, 5:134–35; Galilei and Scheiner 2010, 125).

[29] Famously, Galileo had privately declared himself a Copernican in a 1597 letter to Kepler (Galilei 1890–1909, 10:68), though there is some debate about the extent of Galileo's Copernicanism before 1610. See Gingerich and Van Helden (2011), Gingerich (2013).

[30] Galilei (1890–1909, 7:30; 1967, 6). The text reads "all the experiments" (*tutte l'esperienze*), but Galileo does think that the tides demonstrate the motion of the earth, as seen in Day 4 of the *Dialogo*.

[31] Galilei (1890–1909, 7:43; 1967, 19).

I therefore conclude that only circular motion can naturally suit bodies which are integral parts of the universe as constituted in the best arrangement, and the most which can be said for straight motion is that it is assigned by nature to its bodies (and their parts) whenever these are to be found outside their proper places, arranged badly, and are therefore in need of being restored to their natural state by the shortest path. From which it seems to me one may reasonably conclude that for the maintenance of perfect order among the parts of the universe it is necessary to say that movable bodies are movable only circularly; if there are any that do not move circularly, these are necessarily immovable, nothing but rest and circular motion being suitable to the preservation of order.[32]

It is assumed that all "integral parts of the universe" are already and always in their suitable, natural places. Circular motion keeps a body *in place*, or continually returns it there. In Aristotelian terms, the origin of a circular motion – its *terminus a quo* – is identical to the end toward which it develops – its *terminus ad quem*. In this sense, then, nothing actually changes, and the arrangement of nature is maintained. Nature, if it causes a celestial body to move at all, will only cause circular motion. The earth may be at rest, as the Aristotelians hold, but if Galileo and the Copernicans are right and the earth moves, it moves naturally in circles.[33]

Notably, Galileo departs from *De Motu* in that he does not stipulate a *unique* center of the spatial ordering of the parts of the universe. Bodies are arranged with respect to one another, not with respect to a spatial center. Thus, natural, circular motions, including those of the earth, are not presumed to be concentric:

> Moreover, it appears that Aristotle implies that only one circular motion exists in the world, and consequently only one center to which the motions

---

[32] Galilei (1890–1909, 7:56; 1967, 32). See also Galilei (1890–1909, 7:43; 1967, 19): "This principle being established then, it may be immediately concluded that if all integral bodies in the world are by nature movable, it is impossible that their motions should be straight, or anything else but circular; and the reason is very plain and obvious. For whatever moves straight changes place and, continuing to move, goes ever farther from its starting point and from every place through which it successively passes. If that were the motion which naturally suited it, then at the beginning it was not in its proper place. So then the parts of the world were not disposed in perfect order. But we are assuming them to be perfectly in order; and in that case, it is impossible that it should be their nature to change place, and consequently to move in a straight line." Note the similarity to Kepler's youthful rejection of straight lines, discussed in Chapter 4, above.

[33] In the *Sunspot Letters*, Galileo had argued as much for the sun: "Now the Sun, a body of spherical shape, suspended and balanced around its own center, cannot fail to move along with the motion of its ambient because it has neither an intrinsic aversion nor an external impediment to such a rotation. It cannot have an internal aversion, seeing that by such a rotation the whole does not move from its place, nor do the parts change places among themselves or alter in any way their natural constitution, so that as regards the constitution of the whole in relation to its parts such a movement is as though it did not exist" (Galilei 1890–1909, 5:135; Galilei and Scheiner 2010, 125).

of upward and downward exclusively refer. All of which seems to indicate that he was pulling cards out of his sleeve, and trying to accommodate the architecture to the building instead of modeling the building after the precepts of architecture. For if I should say that in the real universe there are thousands of circular motions [*mille movimenti circolari*], and consequently thousands of centers, there would also be thousands of motions upward and downward.[34]

Aristotle, Galileo says, assumed that, because terrestrial objects are seen to move away from or toward the center of the earth, *all* bodies whatsoever move away from, toward, or around that center. Yet this is to illegitimately turn a local consequence into a universal principle. That terrestrial motions are centered on the earth does not rule out the possibility of motions respecting other centers. Galileo has just shown that each natural motion is circular, and each natural motion thereby defines its own center. There may be, then, "thousands of centers" about which bodies naturally move, and there may be no single center about which all bodies and their motions are ordered.

"Now let us have the grace to abandon the argument," Galileo writes,

that their [i.e., heavy bodies'] natural instinct is to go not toward the center of the earth, but toward the center of the universe; for we do not know where that may be, or whether it exists at all. Even if it exists, it is but an imaginary point; a nothing, without any quality.[35]

It is perfectly reasonable to suppose that terrestrial bodies order their motions around the center of the earth, while the earth itself and the other planets circle the sun. Yet, insofar as any motion is circular, it maintains the ordering of nature, regardless of the location of its center. Galileo thus argues his way into the Ptolemaic compromise between Aristotelian explanations and astronomical descriptions involving eccentrics, epicycles, and so on.[36] Nature is said to cause the heavenly bodies to move in circles, as Aristotle held, whether or not the motions are concentric, which Aristotle insisted upon.

Moreover, the circular motion of the earth through the heavens would not interfere with the natural motion of terrestrial bodies. Echoing Copernicus, Galileo holds that the celestial bodies, including the earth, each have a natural tendency to seek their own kind. The natural place of a terrestrial part is therefore with the rest of the terrestrial whole. Terrestrial bodies naturally seek their common center, and likewise for the other celestial bodies:

---

[34] Galilei (1890–1909, 7:40; 1967, 16).   [35] Galilei (1890–1909, 7:61; 1967, 37).
[36] See Chapter 2, above.

> [I]f it should be said that the parts of the earth do not move so as to go toward
> the center of the universe, but so as to unite with the whole earth (and that
> consequently they have a natural tendency toward the center of the terrestrial
> globe, by which tendency they cooperate to form and preserve it), then what
> other "whole" and what other "center" would you find for the universe, to
> which the entire terrestrial globe would seek to return if removed therefrom,
> so that the rationale of the whole might still be like that of the parts?[37]

The proper place of a *part* of a celestial body is around the center of that
body. So parts of the body, sharing in some way its nature, will spontaneously move toward the center of the body should they be accidentally
separated from it. Therefore, all terrestrial bodies naturally seek the terrestrial center, even though this may not be the center of the universe.[38]

Galileo also argues that terrestrial bodies will spontaneously order
themselves around the terrestrial center according to density or rarity, as
in *De Motu*. The proper place of a terrestrial body, then, is determined by
its density and distinguished by its distance from the center. Moreover,
the natural tendency of terrestrial parts to return to their proper places in the
terrestrial ordering is rectilinear – directed directly toward or away from
the terrestrial center:

> And as to motion by a straight line, let it be granted to us that nature makes
> use of this to restore particles of earth, water, air, fire, and every integral
> mundane body to their whole, when any of them find themselves separated
> and transported into some improper place – unless this restoration can also
> be made by finding some more appropriate circular motion.[39]

All terrestrial elements, as parts of the terrestrial whole, tend toward the
terrestrial center, but denser elements naturally fall through rarer media,
and rarer elements are extruded upwards by heavier media. Therefore, when
a "mundane" object is improperly placed in the ordering by density, it
naturally finds its proper distance to the center, following a straight line
directly toward or away from the center (or a circular motion that – as we

---

[37] Galilei (1890–1909, 7:58; 1967, 33–34).

[38] Compare this to Copernicus's explanation of gravity as the "natural desire" of terrestrial bodies "to
gather as a unity . . . in the form of a globe" (Copernicus 1978, 18) and to Gilbert's similar explanation
of gravity as "coition" (Gilbert 1958, 110), discussed in Chapters 2 and 3, above. Galileo was a close
reader of Gilbert, and he repeats Gilbert's conclusion that the "third motion" of the earth is "not a real
thing, but a mere appearance" (Galilei 1890–1909, 7:425–26; 1967, 399–400). However, Galileo did
not comprehend the centerless, oriented representation of space that grounds this description. As a
result he says that, if the *sun* orbits the earth, the fact that its axis stays parallel to itself – an exact
analogue of the earth's "third motion" – *is* a motion. Similarly, he says that the fact that the moon
stays facing the earth is *not* a motion, even though Gilbert's framework requires it be described as one
(Galilei 1890–1909, 7:90, 381; 1967, 65, 354). See also Gingerich (2003).

[39] Galilei (1890–1909, 7:70; 1967, 45).

shall see shortly – combines the rectilinear tendency with the diurnal rotation of the earth). This explains, of course, why heavy bodies fall toward the center of the earth and lighter bodies rise away from it.[40]

Note, though, that terrestrial bodies all tend toward the center of the earth even while the earth, considered as a celestial body, might move circularly through the heavens:

> Now since Aristotle argues generation and corruption from the contrariety of straight motions, let us grant such motions to the parts, which alone change and decay. But to the whole globe and sphere of the elements will be ascribed either circular motion or perpetual continuance in its proper place – the only tendencies fitted for the perpetuation and maintenance of perfect order.[41]

Even as the earth itself might be moving circularly around its own axis or around the sun, its parts, terrestrial bodies, will move toward or away from its center. All these motions, Galileo holds, are caused by the inherent nature of the moving bodies: the earth's celestial nature as an "integral part of the universe"; and the "mundane" bodies' terrestrial nature as parts of the earth. Galileo concludes that circular motion is suited to the earth, and this would not interfere with the natural motion of its parts toward or away from its center.

Incidentally, notice that Galileo is here suggesting a multiply centered representation of space. Descriptions of motion as "up," "down," or "around" refer to motions away from, toward, or around *some* center, but the center by which these descriptions are coordinated with phenomena can vary, depending on the situation described.[42] The single center that grounded the Aristotelian ordering of nature and physical explanations has disappeared. Now, the ordering of nature and the physical phenomena determine the center by which a phenomenon is described. Each local situation has its own stipulated reference point. "Down" on the earth refers to the direction toward the center of the earth, but "down" in the solar system refers to the direction toward the sun. Thus, Galileo, like Copernicus, has no answer to the Averroist question: Where is *the* center? For Galileo, as for Copernicus, spatial descriptions are not univocal for all phenomena. The referents of spatial terms can only be specified locally, not universally.

---

[40] Galileo does not think that the ultimate *cause* of the inherent "gravity" of bodies is explicable, beyond the mere fact of the tendency toward the earth. He refrains from speculating about essential natures (Galilei 1890–1909, 7:260–61; 1967, 234). See also Galilei and Scheiner (2010, 255). (Thanks to Filip Buyse and Dan Garber for stressing this point.)

[41] Galilei (1890–1909, 7:70; 1967, 46).

[42] See Moody (1951, 168–69), Shea (1972, 118–19), Westfall (1972, 187), Shapere (1974, 87–90), Finocchiaro (1980, 349–53).

Galileo's discussion of natural motions suggests that the "natural motion" of a celestial body is an angular quantity. The essential feature of this natural motion is that it does not disturb the ordering among the parts of the universe, which it is to say that it is motion *in place*. Such motion is circular precisely because motion in a circle does not disturb the overall arrangement of integral bodies with respect to one another. As with the marble sphere in *De Motu*, the circular motion of a whole body necessarily maintains the ordering among the parts of the universe, wherever the center of the ordering might be, if there is one. As for the diurnal motion, the rotation of the entire globe around its own center preserves its place in the universe. The "integral part" of the universe that is "by nature moveable" is the terrestrial globe as a whole, and the "motion" that pertains to the entire globe is its angular rotation, not the various curvilinear translations of its various parts. The "natural," diurnal motion thus refers to the angular quantity. Galileo also seems to suppose that the same analysis can be extended to the earth's annual movement around the sun, which he also takes to be circular and *ipso facto* order-preserving. This, too, is apparently conceived as an angular rotation, by analogy to the diurnal motion, though the analogy itself is not argued for.

Notice also that the version of the theory of conserved motion one employs depends, in part, on one's presumption of a spatial center. For Galileo, motion is conserved because it does not alter a body's *place* in the arrangement of the universe, where places are distinguished by distance from some center. Curvilinear motion is place-preserving when it is horizontal – i.e., everywhere equidistant to the center. But this means that, in order to say that a particular curvilinear motion is place-preserving, one must *already assume* where the center of the spatial ordering is. To explain that a certain curvilinear motion is conserved requires the prior determination of a center around which nature is arranged.

By contrast, angular rotations of corporate bodies are always *in place*, regardless of what the place is, since they keep the body in (or return it to) its location with respect to everything else in the universe. Rotations can be said to be place-preserving even if the center of the spatial ordering is unknown, or even non-existent. Some *parts* of the rotating body might be changing place – moving toward or away from a center – though the body as a whole is not. Of course, a rotation, as a circular motion, defines a (local) center, but this is contingent on the motion, not the other way around. Thus, one need *not* already assume where the center is to say that a rotation is place-preserving and conserved. Curvilinear conservation can be employed as an explanation only if one assumes the location of the center, while rotational conservation does not require such an assumption. As we have seen, Galileo's Copernicanism leads him to explicit ignorance about the location of *the* center of the universe. It is merely an "imaginary point," if it exists at all, he says. The motions of the celestial and terrestrial bodies, meanwhile, define "thousands" of local centers. Yet this commits him to the conservation of angular rotation, since the centers are consequences of the conserved motions, not *vice versa*. Referring to angular rotation allows Galileo to figuratively "model the building after the precepts of architecture," not the other way around.

Conserved motion

The inclination to consider circular motion as an angular quantity carries over into the defensive part of Galileo's project, where he seeks to explain why the earth's motions, and the diurnal motion in particular, are not readily observed. Generally, Galileo's arguments rest on an explanatory principle of conserved motion. He says that, impediments aside, a body will conserve its motion, even when separated from the original source of motion. Therefore, projectiles, falling bodies, and the like will conserve the circular motion they possessed before they were set loose from their connection to the earth. Since the observer shares this motion, and only relative motions are observable, the observer will not observe the shared diurnal rotation. But as we have just seen, the "diurnal motion" refers, for Galileo, to an angular rotation, at least in his argument that a rotation is suited to the earth. So we should expect that the "motion" a body conserves is an angular rotation. Galileo's conservation principle should be coordinated with an angular quantity.

Galileo employs this version of the conservation theory in the *Dialogo*, though his usage is far from consistent. Consider, for instance, the famous discussion of a stone falling from a tower in Day 2. This is the culmination of a long argument responding to a standard objection to the motion of the earth, put in the voice of Simplicio (the character representing the Aristotelian position), that a stone dropped from a tower should be left behind, far to the west, by the eastward rotation of the earth.[43] Of course, this is not observed – the stone lands at the foot of the tower – which Simplicio takes as an empirical refutation of the Copernican hypothesis. Galileo, as Salviati, explains that one should not expect the stone to be left behind, even on a moving earth. Before the stone is released, he says, it

[43] See Galilei (1890–1909, 7:150–51; 1967, 125–26).

shares the "diurnal rotation" of the earth, the tower, and everything else. After the stone is released, the "indelibly impressed" circular movement is conserved, even while the stone acquires a new motion directed toward the center of the earth.[44] However, "we never see anything but the simple downward [motion], since this other circular one, common to the earth, the tower and ourselves, remains imperceptible and as if non-existent. Only that of the stone, not shared by us, remains perceptible."[45] Together, the conservation of motion and the imperceptibility of shared motion result in the lack of observable effect of the earth's motion.

In the course of this discussion, Galileo does analogize the horizontal motion of the stone with a ball on a smooth horizontal surface. Without inclination up or down, he says, the ball will move "perpetually" once set in motion. Though this is not quite the same as the inclined plane demonstration of conserved motion, since Galileo does not mention the *lengths* through which the ball moves, it does hint that the ball's conserved motion (and, by analogy, the stone's) is a curvilinear quantity.[46] This suggestion is belied, however, by Galileo's elaboration of the tower-drop itself, which clearly indicates that the "motion" conserved by the falling body is an angular rotation. He draws a figure (see Figure 5.2) to illustrate the path of the stone falling from a tower (*CB*) toward the center of the earth (*A*), and concludes "the semicircle *CIA* is described, along which I think it very probable that a stone dropped from the top of the tower *C* will move, with a motion composed of the general circular movement and its own straight one."[47] But the conserved "circular movement" of the stone carries it through equal *angles* in each moment:

> For if equal sections *CF*, *FG*, *GH*, *HL*, are marked on the circumference *CD*, and straight lines are drawn to the center *A* from the points *F*, *G*, *H*, and *L*, the parts of these intercepted between the two circles *CD* and *BI* represent always the same tower *CB* carried by the earth's globe toward *DI*. And the points where these lines are cut by the arc of the semicircle *CIA* are the places at which the falling stone will be found at the various times.[48]

In other words, the conserved "circular movement" carries the stone through the equal angles *CAF*, *FAG*, *GAH*, etc., in each successive moment,

---

[44] It might appear that the "natural propensity" of the stone is *not* an example of the conservation of motion, since it seems that the stone tends toward motion and would resume moving if temporarily obstructed. The state of motion or rest itself is not conserved. However, the case Galileo uses to demonstrate the conservation of the stone's rotation once released from the tower is the fall of a stone dropped from the mast of a moving ship, which emphasizes the motion "impressed" upon a moving body is conserved (Galilei 1890–1909, 7:141–76; 1967, 141–50).

[45] Galilei (1890–1909, 7:189; 1967, 163).   [46] Galilei (1890–1909, 7:171–74; 1967, 145–48).

[47] Galilei (1890–1909, 7:191; 1967, 165).   [48] Galilei (1890–1909, 7:191; 1967, 165).

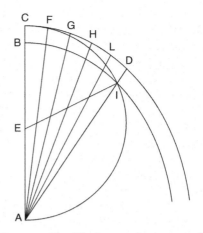

Figure 5.2 The fall of a stone from a tower.[49]

denoted by the "equal sections" on the circumference. The tower also moves at the same angular rate – one rotation per day – and the stone falls exactly at its foot, directly below the point from which it was released. Note, in contrast, that the curvilinear motion of the stone is *not* conserved. As the stone approaches the center of rotation (*A*), its curvilinear translation in each moment decreases. Galileo is here committed to the conservation of an *angular* quantity.

The tower-drop example is far from the last word on this subject, however, and there remains significant ambiguity surrounding the phenomenal significance of Galileo's conservation principle. For instance, Day 1 repeats *De Motu*'s argument for conserved motion based on motions on inclined planes, with the conclusion that motion on a horizontal surface will be conserved, stated in nearly the same language as before:

> Hence a plane may be given so small an inclination that to acquire in it the assigned degree of velocity, a body must first move a very great distance and take a very long time. In the horizontal plane no velocity whatever would ever be naturally acquired, since the body in this position will never move. But motion in a horizontal line which is tilted neither up nor down is circular motion about the center; therefore circular motion is never acquired naturally without straight motion to precede it; but, being once acquired, it will continue perpetually with uniform velocity.[50]

[49] Galilei (1890–1909, 7:191; 1967, 165).   [50] Galilei (1890–1909, 7:52–53; 1967, 28).

Once again, motion on a horizontal surface, all impediments removed, encounters no reason to increase or to decrease, so it is conserved. Also as before, the conserved motion is circular, around an axis through the terrestrial center. However, the motion is again continuous with motions up and down infinitesimally inclined planes, and there is explicit mention of the "very great distance" through which a body must move to acquire any given finite velocity. Here, the "conserved motion" is a curvilinear translation.

Galileo's oscillations regarding the referential meaning of his conservation principle come to a head in two remarkable passages where Galileo disagrees *with himself.* The first of these discussions is a consideration of a cannonball dropped from the distance of the moon, a case analogous to the tower-drop experiment. As before, if one assumes that the earth is rotating eastward about its axis once a day, the ground under the falling cannonball will move a considerable distance to the east in the time the ball takes to fall, so it seems the ball should land far to the *west* of the point over which it was dropped, left behind by the earth's rapid rotation. Galileo must explain why this is not the case, since falling bodies are seen to land where one would expect them to if the earth does not move – below the point from which they are dropped. As Simplicio poses the challenge, "It seems to me a remarkable thing in any case that in coming from the moon's orbit, distant by such a huge interval, the ball should have a natural tendency to keep itself always over the same point of the earth which it stood over at its departure, rather than to fall behind in such a very long way."[51]

Galileo, as Salviati, responds:

> The effect might be remarkable or it might be not at all remarkable, but natural and ordinary, depending upon what had gone on before. If . . . the ball had possessed the twenty-four-hour circular motion while it remained in the moon's orbit, together with the earth and everything else contained within that orbit, then that same virtue which made it go around before it descended would continue to make it do so during its descent too.[52]

That is, the cannonball conserves the twenty-four-hour circular rotation it shares with the earth even while it falls. So it is *not* remarkable that "the ball should have a natural tendency to keep itself always over the same point" and fall on the place beneath. This suffices as a response to Simplicio's Aristotelian objection. Note that, thus far, the motion conserved is the circular *rotation* of the earth. The falling ball conserves the "twenty-four-hour circular motion" shared by the earth and everything on it. To this point, the moon-drop is exactly similar to the tower-drop.

But Salviati is not finished. He continues with a striking observation:

> And far from failing to follow the motion of the earth and necessarily falling behind, it would even go ahead of it, seeing that in its approach toward the earth the rotational motion would have to be made in ever smaller circles, so that if the same speed were conserved in it which it had within the orbit, it ought to run ahead of the whirling of the earth, as I said.[53]

All of a sudden, Saliviati switches tack and offers a novel prediction. If the cannonball conserves its original motion, it will *not* "keep itself always over the same point." It will run ahead of the earth's rotation and land to the *east* of the point over which it was dropped. To reach this conclusion, Galileo has changed the referent of the "motion" conserved. It is no longer the angular rotation of the earth and everything else. Rather, it is the curvilinear translation the ball has in its orbit at the distance of the moon. Since the cannonball is further from the axis of the earth's rotation before it is dropped, it is moving along a greater curvilinear magnitude than any point beneath, which moves along a smaller circumference. Once dropped, it conserves this greater *curvilinear* quantity, and outpaces the ground beneath, landing to the east.[54] The conservation of angular *rotation* does not lead to this result. If *rotation* is conserved, we would expect no deflection at all, which is what Galileo suggests in the first part of the passage. The passage deploys *both* versions of the theory of conserved motion.

A similar oscillation appears in a discussion of cannons firing along a meridian, another experiment cited as evidence against the rotation of the earth. As Salviati recapitulates the Aristotelian argument:

> Not only this, but shots to the south or north likewise confirm the stability of the earth; for they would never hit the mark that one had aimed at, but

---

[53] Galilei (1890–1909, 7:259–60; 1967, 233, translation slightly altered).

[54] This passage is the first prediction of the eastward deflection of falling bodies due to the rotation of the earth. The phenomenon was not observed until 1679, when Isaac Newton, following similar logic, predicted the eastward drift of falling bodies. Moreover, he designed an experiment to demonstrate this effect that he thought would "argue ye diurnall motion of ye earth." Robert Hooke later carried out the experiment, the success of which he judged a conclusive "Demonstration of the Diurnall motion of the earth as you [Newton] have very happily intimated" (Turnbull 1960, 302, 313). See Chapter 7, below. The deflection, like that of the cannon shot discussed below, is today subsumed under a class of phenomena known as *Coriolis effects*. These are "uncaused" deflections brought about by inertial, and therefore rectilinear, motion in a rotating reference frame. The deflections result from the rotation of the frame itself, rather than any physical forces operating on the moving body. The effect was formalized by Gaspard Gustave de Coriolis in 1835. See Dugas (1941), Acloque (1982, 15–33), Tabarroni (1983), Dugas (1988, 374–80), Finocchiaro (2001, 501–02), Persson (2005).

would always slant toward the west because of the travel that would be made toward the east by the target, carried by the earth while the ball was in the air.[55]

According to Aristotelian principles, Salviati says, the projectile should move in the line along which it was aimed. While the ball is airborne, however, the earth's continuing rotation will carry the target a considerable distance eastward. Thus, the shot will miss to the west. An Aristotelian would conclude that an artilleryman's ability to hit a target simply by aiming at it is evidence against the rotation of the earth.

Galileo has Salviati address this issue of marksmanship and aim by way of a discussion of bird hunting. Salviati reports that hunters are able to hit their targets simply by keeping a moving bird in their sights, as if the bird were motionless:

> They [the hunters] work in exactly the same way as if shooting at a stationary bird; that is, they fix their sights on a flying bird and follow it by moving the fowling piece, keeping the sights always on it until firing; and thus they hit it just as they would a motionless one. So the turning motion made by the fowling piece in following the flight of the bird with the sights, though slow, must be communicated to the ball also; and this is combined with the other motion, from the firing.[56]

Salviati imagines a hunter turning on his heel to match the bird's progress across the range. He argues that this rotation is imparted to the bullet, which then conserves this rotation after the gun is fired. Together, the two motions – one from the firing toward the bird, the second matching its angular motion across the range – result in the bullet striking the target.

Salviati then argues that this is precisely analogous to a cannon firing along the meridian on a moving earth. He notes that in this case, the cannon is always aimed at the mark. Thus, just as the marksman hits the bird by maintaining his aim, the cannon also hits the target:

> Upon this depends the proper answer to that other argument, about shooting with the cannon . . . It must be answered that the sighting changes in no way. . . . And if the sights are so maintained, the shot always travels true, as is obvious from what has been said previously [about the hunters].[57]

As in the hunters' sport, the gun, shot, and target all share the same angular rotation before firing, in this case caused by the rotation of the earth. This angular rotation is then conserved after the cannon is fired. Thus, as long as the cannon is initially aimed at the target, the shot will land true.

---

[55] Galilei (1890–1909, 7:153; 1967, 127, translation slightly altered).
[56] Galilei (1890–1909, 7:204; 1967, 178).   [57] Galilei (1890–1909, 7:204; 1967, 178–79).

Salviati takes the conservation principle to imply the conservation of angular rotation. In both hunting and artillery fire, the only motion that the gun, shot, and target share is an angular rotation – "the turning motion" in the former case, and the twenty-four-hour diurnal rotation in the latter. The shots land true if this rotation is conserved. Salviati concludes, confuting the Aristotelian argument he presented earlier, that an artilleryman's ability to hit his target simply by aiming at it is not evidence against the motion of the earth, after all.

At this point of the *Dialogue*, though, the third character, Sagredo, interrupts:

> Just a minute please, Salviati, while I bring up something which occurs to me about these hunters and the flying birds. . . . It seems to me to follow from this that the small motion conferred upon the shot by the turning of the barrel cannot multiply itself in the air up to the speed of the bird's flight . . . in such a way that it always stays aimed at the bird. Rather, it seems to me that the bullet would necessarily be anticipated and left behind.[58]

According to Sagredo, curvilinear translation, not rotation, is conserved. Before being fired, the bullet has a much smaller curvilinear motion than the bird, since it is closer to the axis of rotation. Once in flight, then, the shot conserves this smaller curvilinear quantity. The bullet "cannot multiply itself . . . up to the speed of the bird" and will miss behind. As for cannons firing along the meridian, Sagredo notes that the initial linear speeds of ball and target are only equal if both are located at the same latitude on the surface of the earth, "Although the cannon will sometimes be placed closer to the pole than the target and its motion will consequently be somewhat slower, being made along a smaller circle." That is, higher latitudes are closer to the axis of rotation than the equator, so a shot from nearer the pole has a smaller eastward translation than the target closer to the equator. And just as with the birds, the ball will conserve its smaller curvilinear motion and miss behind – to the *west*. Sagredo says that the effect is "insensible because of the small distance from the cannon to the mark," but he acknowledges the existence of a deflection, based on the conservation of a curvilinear quantity.[59]

It is not Galileo's usual practice to put important arguments, let alone experimental predictions, in the mouth of Sagredo, who is supposed to be an intelligent but impartial auditor of the discussion. Salviati, Galileo's usual mouthpiece, does endorse Sagredo's reasoning, but he never retracts his own alternative explanation. Galileo explicitly recognizes that the two

[58] Galilei (1890–1909, 7:205; 1967, 179).   [59] Galilei (1890–1909, 7:205; 1967, 179).

coordinations of his conservation principle lead to different conclusions about the outcome of a physical situation, so it seems he should choose which theory, and thus which prediction, is the right one. But Galileo never says which of his characters is right. He simply moves on to other topics. In essence, Galileo disagrees with himself. He holds that there is conserved motion, and that it is circular. Projectiles and falling bodies conserve their motions. But the referent of "conserved motion" oscillates between angular rotation and curvilinear translation, even though Galileo explicitly realizes these coordinations imply different effects.[60]

In the end, there is no clear answer to the question of whether Galileo's conservation principle is coordinated with angular rotations or curvilinear translations in the *Dialogo*. This ambiguity should not be surprising, since the difference between these coordinations results only in "insensible" changes in the outcome of experiments, which therefore remain "indifferently adaptable to an earth in motion or at rest." Galileo, that is, does not have to take a firm position in order to defend the Copernican hypothesis. The reader is confronted with another one of those instances in which Galileo's considered authorial intent must be synthesized from the somewhat competing positions of his characters. My subjective impression is that the text reveals a preference for the *rotational* version of the theory. For one thing, the rotational version of the cannon firing along the meridian is put in the mouth of Salviati, Galileo's regular mouthpiece. Moreover, if there is an "official" account of the fall of heavy bodies, it is the explanation of the tower-drop experiment, which receives the clearest and most extensive treatment. The account of the tower-drop, however, relies almost exclusively on the conservation of an angular quantity. Finally, and most importantly, the rotational version of the theory comports best with Galileo's arguments that diurnal (and annual) rotations are suited to the earth, since it does not rely on the prior stipulation of a single spatial center in order to delineate the "horizontal." Conservation of angular motion thus fits well with Copernicanism, which makes the stipulation of a spatial center problematic, and the support of Copernicanism is ultimately the point of the

---

[60] In another instance, not discussed here, Galileo even goes so far as to *calculate* the effect due to the deflection. Galileo deduces the effect of the earth's rotation on the range of a cannonball fired along the parallel, i.e., east and west, and finds that a westward shot would fall about one inch shorter than an eastward one. He finds that the effect is insignificant, not because it does not occur – he insists that "each one of these variations [in the ranges] contains one of one inch caused by the motion of the earth [*cagianato dal moto della Terra*]" – but because to make the effect observable, one would have to find "a method of shooting with such precision [*tanto esatta*] at a mark that you never miss by a hairsbreadth" (Galilei 1890–1909, 7:208; 1967, 182). The physical set up is somewhat contrived in this case, however (Galileo ignores the effect of gravity, for example), so it is not clear what conclusions can be drawn. For more analysis see Finocchiaro (1980, 399–403), Galilei (1997, 147n.).

book. Whatever the case, the important fact remains: even if Galileo does not express a preference for one version of his conservation theory, he makes an explicit descriptive distinction between angular rotations and curvilinear translations, and he realizes that coordinating his conservation principle specifically with one or the other is physically significant.[61]

Discorsi

In the time between the *Dialogo* and the publication of the *Discorsi* in 1638, Galileo's motivations had drastically changed. In the first place, Galileo had realized that his account of the tower-drop experiment was obviously mistaken. Pierre de Fermat, for one, showed that the combination of a rotation and an accelerated descent should be a kind of spiral, not the semicircle Galileo had described. Galileo's account also had the implausible consequence that the gravitational acceleration varied widely with altitude, such that, if they could, all falling bodies would reach the center of the earth in the same amount of time (six hours), regardless of the height from which they were dropped. Galileo accepted the validity of these criticisms. In a 1637 letter responding to Fermat, Galileo dismissed his tower-drop discussion as an "audacious jocularity" (*iocularis quaedam audacia*) offered "in jest" (*per scherzo*).[62] Galileo thus discarded the "official" account of falling bodies that depended on conserved angular rotation. In fact, the same letter goes on to offer an account of projectile motion essentially identical to the

---

[61] Notably, Galileo does mention conserved *rectilinear* motions in the *Dialogo*. In the case of a rock thrown from a notched stick, Galileo says the "impressed impetus … is undoubtedly in a straight line" (Galilei 1890–1909, 7:218; 1967, 191). The example then leads to a broader discussion of the centrifugal motion of heavy bodies on the surface of the earth (Galilei 1890–1909, 7:219–42; 1967, 193–218). Galileo asserts that bodies whirled by the motion of the earth tend to continue moving along straight lines tangential to the earth, just as the rock flies off tangentially to the motion of the notched stick. This seems to express, if for an instant, a theory of conserved *rectilinear* motion. There are several ways to accommodate this apparent counterexample. First, one can simply assert that it is just a rare exception to an otherwise general rule (rather than a rare assertion of Galileo's true principle, as some authors claim), perhaps resulting from the confusion of the "violent" motion of the stick with the "natural" diurnal motion of terrestrial bodies. Second, the argument is counterfactual. The conclusion of the discussion is that if a body were to move off along a tangent, this would be a *change* of the body's motion – the component of its motion toward the center would have to disappear. Galileo admits rectilinear, tangential motion only for the sake of argument, and ends up reinforcing his original claim that bodies naturally conserve their circular motion around the earth. For similar interpretations see Shea (1972, ch. 6), Shapere (1974, 109–17), Franklin (1976, 81), Roux (2006, 460–61). For contrary views see McMullin (1967, 29), Drake (1970, 267), Finocchiaro in Galilei (1997, 171–212), Hooper (1998, 168–70). See also Koyré (1967).

[62] Galilei (1890–1909, 17:89). See Drake's note in Galilei (1967, 476–77), Koyré (1955), Drake (1978, 376–81).

treatment published later in the *Discorsi*, which relies solely on the conservation of curvilinear translation.

Secondly, Galileo, and Copernicanism with him, had been condemned as
theologically suspicious in 1633. Galileo could no longer breathe a word of the
earth's motion, and he makes no suggestion of it in the *Discorsi*. By the
same token, though, the verdict resolved the conundrum of the spatial center.
The *Discorsi* only discusses terrestrial phenomena, so the terrestrial center is
the only center to which descriptions refer. Hence, Galileo returns to the
singly-centered representation of space of *De Motu*, and he abandons
the conserved angular rotation that suited his need to allow for "thousands
of centers." Of course, describing terrestrial phenomena in relation to the
terrestrial center does not preclude the possibility of other centers by which
celestial phenomena might be described, but Galileo is perforce silent on this
topic. Moreover, the constrained intellectual ambit also brought Galileo's
demand for argumentative certainty to the fore. Galileo's purpose in the
Discorsi is to create new *sciences*, rigorous and certain understanding of
phenomena immune from the cavils of Aristotelians and the Church. The
key, for Galileo, is to make his new sciences mathematical, so that the rigor of
mathematical proof will extend to his physical demonstrations.[63]
Conservation of angular rotation is inconvenient for this end, as we shall see.

In the *Discorsi*'s second "new science," the "science of local motion,"
Galileo's conservation principle is coordinated with horizontal motion
around the center toward which terrestrial bodies tend. Notably, the
principle is exclusively justified by the arguments related to inclined planes:

> The better to explain this, let the line *AB* [in Figure 5.3] be assumed to be
> erected vertically on the horizontal *AC*, and then let it be tilted at different
> inclinations with respect to the horizontal, as at *AD*, *AE*, *AF*, etc. I say that
> the impetus of the heavy body for descending is maximal and total along the
> vertical *BA*, is less than that along *DA*, still less along *EA*, successively
> diminishes along the more inclined *FA*, and is finally completely extin-
> guished on the horizontal *CA*, where the moveable is found to be indifferent
> to motion and to rest, and has in itself no inclination to move in any
> direction, nor yet any resistance to being moved. ... Whence, on the
> horizontal, which here means a surface [everywhere] equidistant from the
> said [common] center, and therefore quite devoid of tilt, the impetus or
> momentum of the moveable will be null.[64]

---

[63] Galileo famously claimed that "Philosophy is written in this grand book, the universe ... written in
the language of mathematics ... without which it is humanly impossible to understand a single word
of it" (Galilei 1957, 237–38). For an extended overview of the context of Galileo's view of mathematics
in natural science, see Feldhay (1998).

[64] Galilei (1890–1909, 8:215; 1989, 172).

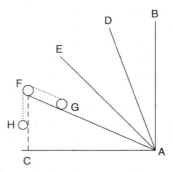

Figure 5.3 Motion on inclined planes in *Discorsi*.[65]

As in *De Motu* and the *Dialogo*, a body is indifferent to horizontal motion that does not change its place, distinguished by distance to the "common center." Neither nature nor force acts to change the motion, so a body will conserve its state of horizontal motion. As noted earlier, though, this explication of conserved motion refers to a curvilinear translation, not to an angular rotation, since the conserved motion is continuous with the linear translations along inclined planes. Conserved angular rotation, on the other hand, does not appear in the *Discorsi*.[66]

The conservation principle is plainly coordinated with curvilinear translations in the famous derivation of the parabolic trajectory of projectiles, with which the new "science of local motion" culminates. Galileo's archetypical case is a body moving off the edge of a table. Just as in the *Dialogo*, the resulting motion is derived from a natural acceleration downward and a conserved horizontal motion.

> Imagine a horizontal line or plane *ab* [in Figure 5.4] situated on high, upon which the moveable is carried from *a* to *b* in equable motion, but at *b* lacks support from the plane, whereupon there supervenes in the same moveable, from its own heaviness, a natural motion downward along the vertical *bn*. Beyond the plane *ab* imagine the line *be*, lying straight on, as if it were the flow or measure of time, on which there are noted any equal parts of time *bc, cd, de*.[67]

[65] Galilei (1890–1909, 8:215).
[66] The difference between angular rotations and linear translations does appear in the treatment of the *rota Aristotelis* in the First Day (Galilei 1890–1909, 8:93–96; 1989, 55–57). However, this context does not involve the conservation of motion. (Alison Laywine helpfully pointed this out.)
[67] Galilei (1890–1909, 8:272; 1989, 221).

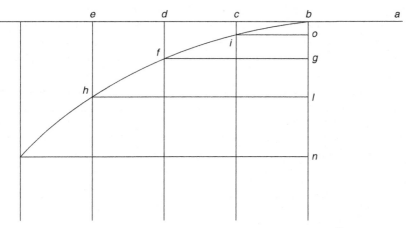

Figure 5.4 The parabolic trajectory of a projectile in *Discorsi*.[68]

On the table, the ball moves uniformly from *a* to *b*. Once the body leaves the table, this "equable motion" is conserved, which is to say that the proportion between distance and time remains constant. Thus, as the distance *ab* is to the time taken to move from *a* to *b*, so will the equal distances *bc*, *cd*, and *de* be proportional to equal times. The conserved horizontal motion is then combined with an accelerated descent in the vertical, producing a parabolic trajectory. The horizontal distances, however, are all linear magnitudes. The conserved "equable motion" is a linear translation.

Remarkably, the conservation principle here is actually coordinated with a *recti*linear quantity: *be* is a *straight* line. In fact, Galileo has, for the moment at least, introduced a centerless, oriented representation of space where directions are specified in relation to an orientation, not in relation to a center. A direction is specified as a constant deflection from the vertical orientation of the space described. The direction in which heavy bodies tend – i.e., "down" – is everywhere parallel to the orientation, and the "horizontal" is everywhere perpendicular to the orientation. Hence, a motion always in the "same direction" is everywhere parallel to itself, maintaining a constant deflection from the orientation, even when combined with a second, oblique motion. The parallel segments *io*, *fg*, *hl*, etc., each represent the accumulated translation due to a single, conserved motion, always in the same horizontal

[68] Galilei (1890–1909, 8:272).

direction. Furthermore, since a "direction" is everywhere parallel to itself, if the body were not subject to the agency of nature or force, it would stay along a self-parallel trajectory: a straight line. In this representation of space, then, conserved motion is motion along a straight line, with an equal linear translation in each moment.[69]

However, as the exposition progresses, it becomes clear that Galileo does not take this representation of space as fundamental. Instead, he employs it as an *approximation* of fundamentally centered space. The explanatory and descriptive levels do not fit with one another: the physical principles meant to explain the phenomenon cannot be coordinated with the description of it. As Galileo has the character Simplicio object:

> [W]e assume the [initial] plane to be horizontal, which would be neither rising nor falling, and to be a straight line – as if every part of such a line could be at the same distance from the center, which is not true. For as we move away from its midpoint toward its extremities, this [line] departs ever farther from the center [of the earth], and hence it is always rising. One consequence of this is that it is impossible that the motion is perpetuated, or even remains equable through any distance; rather, it would be always growing weaker.[70]

Conserved motion is coordinated with motion *in place*, at a constant distance to the center and neither up nor down. Motion along a straight line necessarily moves a body either closer to or further from the center; if the body moves along a rectilinear line, starting from the normal to the center, the body will necessarily move away from the center. According to the centered coordination of conserved motion, a body will not be naturally indifferent to this motion. The rectilinear motion will be naturally resisted and diminish. Only circular motion around the center keeps a body "in place." Only circular motion is conserved.

Galileo admits that the assumption of the oriented framework used in his demonstration is false. Salviati responds to Simplicio that the "conclusions demonstrated in the abstract are altered in the concrete, and are so falsified that horizontal [motion] is not equable; nor does natural acceleration occur [exactly] in the ratio assumed; nor is the line of the projectile parabolic, and so on."[71] Strictly speaking, a projectile does not move in a parabola, since the conservation principle does not apply to motion along a straight line.

Still, says Galileo, the conserved rectilinear motion in the demonstration of the parabolic trajectory can be understood as an approximation of conserved circular motion:

---

[69] See Naylor (1980).   [70] Galilei (1890–1909, 8:274; 1989, 223).
[71] Galilei (1890–1909, 8:274; 1989, 223).

But on the other hand, I ask you not to reject in our Author what other very great men have assumed, despite its falsity. The authority of Archimedes alone should satisfy everyone; in his book *On Plane Equilibrium* [*Mecaniche*], as in the first book of his *Quadrature of the Parabola*, he takes it as a true principle that the arm of a balance or steelyard lies in a straight line equidistant at all points from the common center of heavy things, and that the cords to which [balance-]weights are attached hang parallel to one another. These liberties are pardoned to him by some for the reason that in using our instruments, the distances we employ are so small in comparison with the great distance to the center of our terrestrial globe that we could treat one minute of a degree at the equator as if it were a straight line, and two verticals hanging from its extremities as if they were parallel.[72]

This "Archimedean approximation"[73] allows a direct substitution of the oriented representation of space for the centered at the descriptive level of the theory. So long as the phenomenon described is relatively small and far from the center, and the vertical orientation roughly coincides with the "vertical" of centered space,[74] one can simply substitute the oriented coordinations of spatial terms for the centered coordinations. So "horizontal," which strictly refers to a spherical surface equidistant to the stipulated center of a centered representation of space, can refer to a (small) flat planar surface in an oriented representation of space.

Galileo assumes that any difference in the "proofs," descriptions, and explanations resulting from these different coordinations will be negligibly small. The small-scale oriented representation of space is a legitimate framework for the description and explanation of phenomena, insofar as it approximates large-scale centered space. The approximate truth of the derivation is warranted by the "insensible" difference between the referents of spatial terms in the different descriptive frameworks. Thus, the parabolic trajectory, though derived from the fallacious assumption of conserved rectilinear motion, is "insensibly" different from the true path, generated by conserved curvilinear motion.[75]

Galileo's coordination of the conservation principle with linear quantities satisfies his desire for mathematical rigor. Galileo could not use an angular

---

[72] Galilei (1890–1909, 8:274–75; 1989, 223–24).   [73] The term is my own. See Miller (2011a).

[74] Even in the oriented approximation, Galileo's representation of space is not isotropic. This is related to Galileo's general inability to free himself from conceiving vertical fall as the model of accelerated motion. See Westfall (1966, 89), Renn (2004, esp. 264), Roux (2006, esp. 459).

[75] "ben potranno solo insensibilmente alterar quella figura parabolica" (Galilei 1890–1909, 8:275; 1989, 224). Galileo leaves these "insensible" changes unanalyzed. He argues that they would be easily overwhelmed by air resistance, anyway. Nevertheless, he does say that these changes are "impossible to remove" and that his argument would fail were the projectile to fall to the center of the earth, where the Archimedean approximation breaks down. In fact, the true path (ignoring air resistance) is elliptical, as Newton later demonstrated.

rotation as the conserved quantity. The failure of the *Dialogo* tower-drop construction would have already made him wary of this approach. Moreover, linear translations and angular rotations are geometrically incommensurate. If horizontal motion is considered as an angular rotation, while vertical motion is considered as a linear translation, the two motions would be heterogeneous magnitudes. They would bear no relation to each other, so the resulting path could not be reduced to a geometric proportion.[76] There would be no *science* of projectile motion. The path could be drawn by a pointwise plotting, provided the angular rotation and the linear translation were independently known for each point. Yet the curve could not be assimilated to a conic section, and the one motion could not be directly calculated from the other. (So, for instance, an unknown range for a given cannon elevation could not be calculated from a known range for a known elevation.)

The rectilinear approximation of a curvilinear motion is also appropriate to the *Discorsi*'s mathematizing ends. Galileo had used it before, even as early as *De Motu*,[77] for the simple reason that he simply did not have the geometrical wherewithal to handle curving horizontal motion and a convergent vertical direction of fall (in fact, this requires the yet-to-be-invented calculus). In order to perform geometrical manipulations and assimilate the path to a conic section, Galileo had to assume that the components of the motion were always perpendicular to one another, just as Archimedes had done. The rectilinear approximation of a curvilinear motion makes Galileo's new science, by his own lights, scientific. Notice again, though, that Galileo's "Archimedean approximation" only succeeds if inertially conserved "circular motion" refers to a curvilinear translation. A curvilinear magnitude is continuous with a rectilinear magnitude as curvature diminishes. An angular quantity, by contrast, is heterogeneous to a linear translation, and goes to zero with the curvature (since the radius goes to infinity). Galileo's conservation principle is coordinated with a *curvilinear* quantity.

Fundamentally, Galileo remains committed, as he had been in *De Motu*, to the centered representation of space. Conserving the "same" horizontal motion still means conserving a circular motion around the center. Galileo's theory of conserved motion is, as always, a theory of conserved *circular* motion. The intimation of an oriented representation of space and, consequently, conserved rectilinear motion is restricted to a small-scale approximation. Yet the *Discorsi* specifically coordinates the conservation principle

---

[76] The path produced by a point moving along a uniformly rotating radius is, in fact, an example of what Descartes calls a "mechanical curve," in distinction to geometrical curves (Descartes 2001, 191).

[77] Galilei (1890–1909, 1:300; 1960b, 67).

with curvilinear magnitudes. The explanatory principle, that is, now unequivocally and exclusively explains curvilinear translations.

Conclusion

Galileo stepped to the threshold of modern inertial theory, but did not cross it. Galileo did adopt the "essential core of the inertial concept," the explanatory principle that bodies continue their motion unless acted upon, and completed the shift to the explanatory apparatus of modern inertial physics. However, in Koyré's apt phrase, Galileo never escaped *l'hantise de la circularité*.[78] The centered representation of space always remained fundamental, and spatial descriptions were always applied in relation to some stipulated center. A conserved motion, being a motion that does not disturb the arrangement of nature in its places, must keep a body in place, at a fixed distance from the center and a fixed direction relative to it. Consequently, conserved motion, for Galileo, was always circular. We can now see, though, that Galileo's conserved motion was not *simply* circular; nor was his descriptive framework the same as his Aristotelian predecessors'. Galileo drew an important distinction within the genus of "circular motion," and he ultimately coordinated his conservation principle specifically with curvilinear translations, distinct from angular rotations. From Galileo on, conserved motion referred particularly to linear quantities. He even signaled the way forward by using an oriented representation of space as an approximation of the centered framework, thereby introducing the conservation of rectilinear motion as a valid approximation of the curvilinear theory of conserved motion. His successors would reverse that approximation.

Finally, note that the development of Galileo's theory of motion can be seen as another case of reciprocal iteration. The story began with an Aristotelian theory that coordinated the explanatory principles, nature and force, with phenomena via a centered representation of space. Specifically, this theory aligned the motions of terrestrial bodies toward and away from the center with nature, and force with every other local motion. Galileo thought that motions that do not disturb the ordering of nature give no reason for inclination or resistance. They did not fit properly with explanations by nature or force. He therefore adjusted the descriptive part of the theory, breaking the Aristotelian coordination linking these motions and force and adding the category "neutral motion" to describe

---

[78] Koyré (1966, 187, 263). See also Panofsky (1956).

terrestrial motions at a constant distance from the center. This move, however, left an explanatory anomaly, since neutral motions were now unexplained. Galileo thus adopted a new explanatory principle, conservation of motion, to account for them. The descriptive level was then again amended. Galileo distinguished curvilinear and rotational motions as distinct categories, though in the *Dialogo*, Galileo's Copernicanism motivated a preference for conserved rotations. The demand for mathematical rigor in the *Discorsi* motivated the final, definitive move to a curvilinear theory and the "Archimedean approximation." Descriptive change led to an explanatory change, which led to a descriptive change.

CHAPTER 6

Directions sont entre elles paralleles:
Descartes and his critics on oriented space and the parallelogram rule

Inertia and the composition of motion

We saw in Chapter 5 how Galileo introduced a precursor to the modern theory of inertia. He adopted a conservation principle according to which motion is conserved, and only changes of motion need to be explained. However, Galileo ultimately coordinated unchanging, conserved motion with horizontal, curvilinear translations around an axis through the center of the earth. This coordination was framed in a centered representation of space, where directions are specified in relation to a stipulated center, so that motion remains in the "same direction" by remaining perpendicular to the center – i.e., to the vertical. In this descriptive framework, the "motion" conserved is circular. However, Galileo did propose an oriented framework by which small-scale phenomena could be approximately described. This "Archimedean approximation" represents motions using an oriented representation of space in which directions are specified in relation to a vertical orientation. Consequently, a conserved horizontal motion remains parallel to itself, even when combined with an accelerated vertical motion. The conservation principle combined with this approximation is a theory of conserved *rectilinear* motion: unchanging motion is uniform rectilinear translation.

As near as this might seem to the modern theory, the approximation imposes severe limitations. Above all, it remains an approximation. Thus, the theory of conserved rectilinear motion is neither fundamental nor universal. Galileo takes the large-scale, centered representation of space to be the proper framework for the description of phenomena. Fundamentally, conserved motion is not parallel to itself throughout space. Strictly speaking, conserved motion is really circular for Galileo – it maintains its deflection from a stipulated spatial center. At the same time, the orientation of the approximation is not arbitrary. The vertical of the smaller framework must coincide with the radial direction of the larger framework. As a result, the approximation does not represent space as isotropic. Motion is only conserved in one direction, the horizontal. Other motions disturb the order of nature and are therefore naturally encouraged or resisted, which is to say accelerated or retarded. In the modern theory, by contrast, uniform motion in any direction is conserved. So, how did the "Archimedean approximation" get promoted to the foundations of physics and freed from these limitations? How was the conservation principle brought into association with a universal and fundamental oriented representation of space? How, that is, was inertia finally rectified?

There is a second, related question to be asked. As noted in Chapter 1 and revisited in Chapter 7, below, Newton's physical theory includes the parallelogram composition of motions, upon which the first proposition of the *Principia* depends. The parallelogram composition is a descriptive framework for the representation of physical magnitudes, such as motions or forces. It stipulates that a motion (etc.) is equivalent to – the "same thing" as – the combination of other motions. Specifically, the motion represented by the diagonal of a parallelogram is equivalent to the combination of the two motions represented by its sides. In modern terms, a motion is identical to its vector decomposition, and, conversely, the combined effect of two motions is identified with the motion indicated by their vector addition.

These descriptive identifications involve several presuppositions. First, they presume that the physical magnitude in question, such as motion, is a directed quantity, and can therefore be represented as a directed length – that is, as a vector. Second, they rely on the notion that the vector calculus of parallelogram constructions faithfully represents the physical phenomena. The descriptions presuppose, that is, that the physical phenomena can be described mathematically, such that the result of a physical interaction is represented by the result of a geometrical construction. I can ask, therefore, when and how this descriptive framework was accepted by physical theorists in the period leading up to Newton.

The mathematical representation of directed magnitudes by itself was well known by the early modern period. In fact, parallelogram compositions were used to represent physical magnitudes even in ancient times. The parallelogram composition of motions is elaborated, for instance, in the pseudo-Aristotelian *Mechanica*.[1] It is also implicit in Simon Stevin's sixteenth-century proof of the law of inclined planes, though the rule is

[1] *Mechanica* 23 (Aristotle 1984, 2:1311–12). See Vilain (2008, 151), Lange (2011, 381).

not stated explicitly, and it is not applied to motions.[2] Nevertheless, though known in other contexts, the parallelogram rule was not employed in early modern kinematics before Descartes.

This is perhaps because the use of a parallelogram composition is intimately related to an oriented representation of space. The construction presumes that the "direction" of a physical magnitude remains the same if and only if it remains parallel to itself at different locations in space, constantly deflected from some orientation. Hence, the parallel pairs of sides of a parallelogram each represent one and the same directed magnitude insofar as they are parallel and equal to one another. In the combination of two motions, the parallelogram composition supposes that the direction of each motion remains parallel to itself, even when combined with the other, oblique motion. Our two questions are thus connected. The adoption of an oriented representation of space allowed parallelogram compositions, and use of the parallelogram rule signals the acceptance of an oriented representation of space.

This chapter offers answers to both questions. In what follows, Descartes will play a starring, if somewhat complicated role. In particular, his early work on optics suggested a fundamental oriented representation of space for the description of physical phenomena. This early suggestion was then expanded in association with his mature metaphysics and epistemology. As we shall see, though, Descartes's own elaboration of his descriptive framework was not without its own limitations and difficulties. For one thing, Descartes never explicitly offers parallelogram compositions as the proper representation of conjoined motions. This is true despite the fact that some of his optical arguments tacitly depend on such compositions. For another thing, once Descartes began to generalize his early work into a grand system of natural philosophy, he moved away from the oriented representation of space. In his mature work, Descartes represents large-scale phenomena using a centered representation of space; as in Galileo, the oriented framework is only applicable in the small-scale. Thus, while the oriented framework was present in Descartes's early work on optics, it cannot be taken to be a general feature of his physical theory.

Nevertheless, the oriented representation of space implicit in Descartes's early optics was noticed by his critics, most importantly Pierre de Fermat. Remarking on Descartes's discussion, Fermat made the implicit oriented representation of space explicit. He also formalized the parallelogram composition of motions. These developments were then picked up by Fermat's

---

[2] See Proposition 19 of the *Elements of the Art of Weighing* (Stevin 1586, 40–42; 1955, 1:174–79).

readers, such as Gilles Personne de Roberval, and were thereby incorporated into state-of-the-art physical theory, laying the foundation for Newton.

Descartes's trajectory

In 1618, Descartes was a cadet at the military engineering academy in Breda, where a chance meeting brought him into contact with a local schoolmaster, Isaac Beeckman. Over the late fall and winter of 1618–19, and in correspondence afterward into the early 1620s, Beeckman mentored Descartes, setting him mathematical and physical problems, thereby kindling the interest in mathematical science that laid the foundation for his philosophical career. Beeckman and Descartes apparently discussed several topics, including harmonics, hydrostatics, and falling bodies. Descartes's primary interests, however, seem to have been geometry and optics.[3] For it is in these two subjects that Descartes made truly novel discoveries. In optics, he discovered the sine law of refraction and solved the problem of the anaclastic curve – the shape of a lens able to focus incoming light on a single point. In geometry, he struck upon the use of geometrical compasses to solve problems involving mean proportionals, a key difficulty.

Descartes's obvious pride in these achievements led him to consider how they, in particular, and the methods that led to them, in general, could be expanded into a systematic epistemology and metaphysics. Descartes first embarked on this *mathesis universalis* in the abortive *Rules for the Direction of the Mind*, written around 1626. This was followed by an attempt "to explain all the phenomena of nature; that is to say, all of physics"[4] in the *World* (part of which Descartes called the *Treatise on Light*), begun around 1629 but abandoned in 1633. Then came the statement of a systematic epistemology in the *Discourse on Method*, published in 1637 and accompanied by scientific treatises on optics, meteorology, and geometry, partly drawn from the pre-1626 work and meant to illustrate the fruitfulness of the epistemological method. These initial attempts were then re-worked and expanded in Descartes's mature publications: *Meditations on First Philosophy* (published 1641), *Principles of Philosophy* (1644), and *Passions of the Soul* (1649). Thus, Descartes's philosophical career can be seen as a continual development of his very early theories about light and magnitude. Let us, then, ask what Descartes's early physical theories, especially his optics, contained. What were his explanatory principles

---

[3] Perhaps harmonics should also be included among Descartes's foremost interests during this period. However, unlike in optics and geometry, his early interest did not persist.
[4] Descartes (1897–1913, 1:70).

and, more importantly, his descriptive framework, including his representation of space?

At the explanatory level, Descartes's physics was remarkably austere. Descartes, following Beeckman, conceived of the natural world as an ensemble of hard, moving corpuscles, interacting solely by collisions. All natural phenomena, therefore, could ultimately be explained by the mechanics of hard bodies. But the mechanical behavior of hard bodies could, in turn, be accounted for by a single conservation principle: in any closed system, the quantity of motion is conserved. Thus, a body moving freely will remain in motion, and collisions redistribute motions such that the total quantity remains constant. The only dynamic principle is the tendency or "force" by which bodies conserve their modal states.[5]

This aspect of Descartes's physical theory has been well-documented, and I need not belabor the point, except to note its consistency throughout Descartes's career. In one of his assignments in late 1618, Beeckman expressed to Descartes the principle that "in a vacuum, what is once moved is always moved" (*semel movetur, semper movetur, in vacuo*),[6] versions of which Beeckman had expressed since 1612.[7] Descartes used the principle in his solution to Beeckman's problem,[8] and thereafter adopted it as the central feature of his own theories of motion. It appears in a 1629 letter to Mersenne: "Firstly I suppose that the movement which is once impressed in some body remains there perpetually, if it is not removed by some other cause; which is to say that *in a vacuum, what once begins to move, is always moved with equal speed.*"[9] Then again in the *World*: "The first [law of nature] is that each individual part of matter continues always to be in the same state so long as collision with others does not force it to change that state."[10]

Once Descartes began developing his mature philosophical system, the conservation principle became a central tenet of his metaphysics of corporeal substance, insofar as the conservation of bodies in their modal states – archetypically their states of motion – is taken to be a direct consequence of God's simple and immutable nature. Ultimately, God is the only genuine causal power in the physical world, and all motion is a consequence of God's creative

---

[5] See *Principles* II.43 (Descartes 1983, 63): "We must however notice carefully at this time what the force of each body to act against another or to resist the action of that other consists: namely, in the single fact that each thing strives, as far as is in its power, to remain in the same state, in accordance with the first law stated above."

[6] Beeckman (1939–1953, 1:263).   [7] Beeckman (1939–1953, 1:10).   [8] Descartes (1897–1913, 10:78).

[9] "Premierement ie suppose que le mouvemant qui est une fois imprimé en quelque cors y demeure perpetuellement, s'il n'en est osté par quelque autre cause, c'est a dire que quod in vacuo semel incoepit moueri, semper & aequali celeritate moueutr" (Descartes 1897–1913, 1:71–72).

[10] Descartes (1897–1913, 11:38; 1985–1991, 1:93).

act. Divine simplicity and immutability in turn entail the conservation principle. As God brings each moment of the universe into being, the simplest action, and thus the one God actually takes since His immutability precludes spontaneous change, is to re-create (or sustain) each closed system in its prior state, so far as possible. Hence, in the *Principles*, all the "laws of nature," including the conservation of motion, follow "from the same immutability of God."[11]

With a paucity of explanatory principles at hand, the task of Cartesian physics was to eventually reduce all observed phenomena to the mechanics of hard bodies, and thence to the conservation principle. Cartesian physics was therefore primarily kinematical. It was a matter of working out the descriptive coordinations by which the conservation principle accounts for the phenomena. The *Principles*' "laws of nature," for instance, include descriptive principles that determine what aspects of a phenomenon count as the conserved quantities in a closed system. The "first law of nature" dictates a general conservation of modal state when a body is left undisturbed, but it also specifies that "motion" is the archetype of such a conserved mode: "each and every thing, in so far as it can, always continues in the same state; and thus what is once in motion always continues to move." The second law, to which I will return below, dictates that directions are also conserved, so "all movement is, of itself, along straight lines." And the third and final law, with its associated collision rules, says how the total motion is conserved as particular motions are redistributed during interactions between particles.[12]

As much as the explanatory foundation of Descartes's physics remained austere, its descriptive coordination with phenomena became ever more messy and convoluted. Descartes sought to explain a vast diversity of phenomena – from planetary orbits to animal physiology. This range of phenomena, however, required a myriad of descriptive accounts, positing a multitude of intermediary entities. Thus, magnetism was described as the action of screw-shaped particles,[13] color became the spin of corpuscles,[14] and so on.[15]

---

[11] *Principles* II.37–40 (Descartes 1983, 59–61).   [12] *Principles* II.37–40 (Descartes 1983, 59–61).

[13] *Principles* IV.133–182 (Descartes 1983, 242–72).   [14] Descartes (2001, 337–38).

[15] Similarly, Beeckman's conception of the "motion" conserved was almost too catholic to be of much use. He associated his conservation principle with motions of all kinds, circular and straight (Beeckman 1939–1953, 1:253). In its earliest appearance in his *Journal*, the conservation principle is used to explain the continual rotation of the heavenly spheres, which Beeckman says does not require the sustaining action of intelligences or God. It is subsequently applied to fluid vortices (Beeckman 1939–1953, 1:167), the "third motion" of the earth (Beeckman 1939–1953, 1:253), and other cases, all before Beeckman suggests it to Descartes in connection with falling bodies (Beeckman 1939–1953, 1:263). Incidentally, Beeckman at one point notes the different curvilinear speeds of the parts of a body rotating around a center due to their varying distance to the center, thus distinguishing curvilinear translations from angular rotations. He goes on to apply the conservation principle to the former in order to explain why such a body does not continue rotating once released from its pivot. The difference between the conserved curvilinear motions, Beeckman says, introduces a torque that converts the circular motion into a rectilinear one

The descriptive flexibility, however, led to significant ambiguities and even inconsistencies in Descartes's descriptive apparatus. As a result, it is never quite clear what the conservation principle actually applies to – that is, what magnitude or magnitudes are conserved. Descartes provides no definitive list of the genuine "modes" that are conserved. One cannot, for instance, definitively determine whether conserved "motion" is translation or rotation; while the collision rules speak only of translations, the *Meteorology* speaks of corpuscular rotation as another, presumably conserved, modal state.[16] Thus, I do not intend to suggest that Descartes's descriptive scheme was as well considered as, say, Galileo's. Descartes's contemporaries and modern commentators alike have struggled to make consistent sense of his physical theories, especially in light of his broader metaphysical system.[17]

However, I can circumvent this tangle by focusing attention on a more limited domain: Descartes's work on reflection and refraction, described in the *Optics*, which he wrote early in his career, probably before 1626,[18] and published as one of the *Essays* accompanying the *Discourse on Method* in 1637. As we shall see, it was this work, and the criticism it produced, that led to the use of an oriented representation of space in the descriptive framework of physical science.

Descartes's *Optics*

The first thing to do is to draw the connection between Descartes's conservation principle and his account of light phenomena. At the outset of the *Optics*, Descartes explains that he considers light to be "a certain movement or action"[19] of bodies. Specifically, light is a pressure in the subtle fluid consisting of the smallest particles of corporeal substance, which surround the larger particles of grosser bodies. Since the universe is a plenum, moreover, the luminous particles are everywhere, even passing within the microscopic interstices in dense materials, such as glass. When we see, then, our

(Beeckman 1939–1953, 1:254). As for the "third motion," Beeckman, like Gilbert, tries to show that it is not a motion (*tertium motum omninò abolet*). He does so, however, by arguing that each point of the earth's diurnal axis rotates annually around its own center. For instance, the north pole has a different orbital center than the south pole. Thus, in abolishing the "third motion," he infinitely multiplies the second motion (Beeckman 1939–1953, 1:253).

[16] Descartes (2001, 336–39).

[17] See, e.g., Shea (1991), Garber (1992a), Gaukroger (2002), Hattab (2007), Schmaltz (2008), Machamer and McGuire (2009).

[18] The *Rules* seems to adumbrate the sine law of refraction reported in the *Optics*. In fact, I would claim that Descartes's success with the anaclastic led him to attempt a systematization of his method in order to apply it to other lines of inquiry, which is the project of the *Rules*. In other words, the work reported in the *Optics* and *Geometry* directly inspired the *Rules*. Whether this is actually the case does not materially affect the present discussion, though. See Descartes (1985–1991, 1:28–29, 3:35–36).

[19] Descartes (2001, 67).

eyes are in fact feeling the pressure in the luminous fluid caused by the presence of bright objects. Descartes here uses the analogy of a stick used to feel terrain. Just as the stick transmits the contours of objects to our hands, the subtle fluid transmits the visual properties of objects to our eyes.[20]

For Descartes, then, light ultimately consists of the pushing of one body on another. But this is each body's "action or inclination to move," checked by the press of bodies in the surrounding plenum. As Descartes puts it:

> [I]t is necessary to distinguish between movement, and the action or inclination to move. . . . And in the same way considering that it is not so much the movement as the action of luminous bodies that must be taken for their light, you must judge that the rays of this light are nothing else but the lines along which this action tends.[21]

Light is a tendency toward motion, and when we describe the behavior of light, such as representing its rays as lines, we are in fact describing the nascent motions of the particles of subtle matter.

The distinction between the inclination to motion and motion itself raises a difficulty: do explanations of motion apply to the inclination to motion, as well? Is the conservation principle an explanation of the behavior of light? Descartes says yes: "For it is very easy to believe that the action or the inclination to move which I have said must be taken for light, must follow in this the same laws as does movement."[22] Later, Descartes will add that "easy to believe" (*bien-aisé à croire*) in fact means that it is "so clear and so evident" that it needs no demonstration; a necessary, not probable truth.[23] In other words, whatever principles account for the motion of bodies will account for the tendency to motion, as well. Consequently, analogies to the behavior of bodies actually in motion, such as a tennis ball struck by a racket against different surfaces, are regulative – light must behave in the same way. The primary "law" of motion, in fact the only "law" of motion Descartes has yet stated, is the conservation principle: once moved, always moving. The *inclination* to motion is subject to the same conservation principle. Only changes in inclination to motion need to be explained.

There are, however, complications that need to be noted at this point. Descartes's principle is not as straightforward as it might seem. In the first place, Descartes explicitly coordinates "conserved motion" only with the scalar total speed of a body. The inclination to move in one *direction* or another is determined by another quantity, which Descartes calls "determination." Thus, when considering a tennis ball struck by a racket, which is analogous to light,

---

[20] See also Rule 12 (Descartes 1985–1991, 1:40–42).   [21] Descartes (2001, 70).
[22] Descartes (2001, 70).   [23] Descartes (1897–1913, 1:450–51).

> It is only necessary to note that the power, whatever it be, which causes the movement of this ball to continue is different from that which determines it to move in one direction rather than in another, as is quite easy to know from the fact that it is the force with which the racket has impelled it upon which its movement depends, and that this same force could have been able to make it move in any other direction as easily as toward *B*; whereas it is the position of this racket which determines it to tend toward *B*.[24]

The conserved "power" to move a body is "different" from whatever directs the motion toward one place or another. The conservation principle, then, is coordinated only with the total movement of a body, not its direction. It is conservation of *movement*, not of motion. Changes of speed need further explanation, according to the law, but it implies nothing at all about how changes of direction are to be explained.

On the one hand, Descartes has good reasons to draw the distinction between movement and determination. First, and here one can see the need for descriptive flexibility noted above, whatever might be true in the analogous tennis ball case, light itself is not an actual motion, but a tendency to motion. Therefore, light can have a determination without having a movement.[25] Second, Descartes's analysis of the motion of the tennis ball – and thus of the tendency of light – depends on a decomposition of components in different directions. Determination, Descartes says, can be so decomposed:

> Moreover, it must be noted that the determination to move toward a certain direction, as well as movement and any other sort of quantity generally, can be divided among all the parts of which we can imagine that it is composed; and we can easily imagine that that part of the ball which is moved from *A* toward *B* [in Figure 6.1] is composed of two others, one of which causes it to descend from the line *AF* toward the line *CE* and the other at the same time makes it go from the left *AC* toward the right *FE*; so that the two, joined together, conduct it to *B* along the straight line *AB*.[26]

Determination is a *directed* quantity. Here, the diagonal determination from *A* to *B* is divided into the vertical and horizontal determinations from *AF* to *CE* and from *AC* to *FE*. Note that, in this passage, Descartes ignores the scalar magnitudes (i.e., lengths) of the components, noting only their directions.[27] As Descartes notes, movement can also be divided, but it

---

[24] Descartes (2001, 75–76).
[25] Note that this implies that determination is not simply a qualification of motion. It is not a mode of a mode. For this position, see Garber (1992a, 188), Gaukroger (2002, 116).
[26] Descartes (2001, 76). For parallel discussions of these passages, see Sabra (1981, chs. 3–4), Smith (1987), McLaughlin (2000).
[27] The decomposition of *AB* should in fact be from *AH* to *CB* and from *AC* to *HB*.

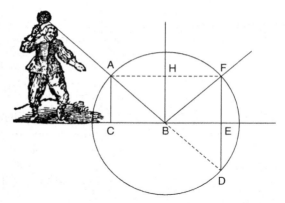

Figure 6.1 Descartes's analysis of reflection.[28]

is a *scalar* quantity, so total speeds can be only *arithmetically* added or subtracted. Movement alone cannot determine direction.

On the other hand, the distinction between movement and determination leaves significant gaps in Descartes's account, which his contemporaries were quick to note, as we shall see. Most generally, Descartes does not clarify how the total determination is related to the total movement or, in the case of light, to the total inclination to movement. One might suppose (and, in fact, Descartes tacitly does so) that the scalar quantity of the total determination must be proportional to the total movement or inclination to movement. That is, the total determination to move measures the "power" that actually moves or would move a body, if not constrained by the plenum. But Descartes explicitly denies this. He says that the "power, whatever it be" that causes movement is completely independent of that which causes determination. So it is not clear that the two have any relationship whatsoever. As a result, it is not clear how the laws of motion, including the conservation principle for movement, are to be applied to determination, if at all. Whereas the conservation principle generates a prediction of a body's speed at subsequent times given an initial speed, Descartes does not *explicitly* provide a comparable rule for determination. Given a body's initial determination to move in one direction, or even one component of that determination, one cannot, apparently, say what will happen to that quantity thereafter.[29] By the same token, Descartes does not provide a *rule* for composing or decomposing determinations. All Descartes

---

[28] Descartes (1897–1913, 6:93).   [29] See Smith (1987, 28), Garber (1992a, 192), Osler (2008, 132).

says is that we may divide a determination "among all the parts of which we can imagine that it is composed." There is no explicit method by which parts are to be added to find the whole.

Despite the lack of explicit answers to these questions in the *Optics*, Descartes's analyses of light suggest certain tacit positions. Take, for instance, the case of reflection. As noted above, light is analogized to the case of a moving tennis ball, in this case struck against the ground. For the purposes of this idealization, the ball is supposed to be perfectly elastic and the ground perfectly hard, flat, and smooth. Thus, in the above diagram (Figure 6.1), the ball is supposed to approach the ground along the line *AB*, with a total speed proportional to the length of *AB*. Since the ball is perfectly elastic, this speed is retained after the ball bounces, so the ball's speed after reflection will be proportional to the length of *AB*, which is to say that the motion will be represented by a segment from *B*, the point of reflection, to the circle *AFD*, with radius *AB*:

> In order to discover, then, precisely in what direction this ball must return, let us describe a circle from the center *B* which passes through the point *A*, and let us say that in as much time as the ball will take to move from *A* to *B*, it must infallibly return from *B* to a certain point on the circumference of this circle, inasmuch as all the points which are the same distance away from *B* as *A* is, are to be found on this circumference, and inasmuch as we assume the movement of this ball to be always of a constant speed.[30]

The conservation of movement entails that the total speed of the ball before and after reflection is the same. Thus, in equal instants of arbitrary length before and after reflection, the ball will be found at equal distances from the point of reflection, on the circle *AFD*.

The *direction* of the ball's motion, meanwhile, depends on the incident *determination* to move along *AB*. This, as we have seen, can be decomposed into two parts, the determination to move from *AH* to *CB*, normal to the surface, and the determination to move from *AC* to *HB*, parallel to the surface. Only the former, Descartes says, is affected by the interaction with the ground. The latter is perfectly conserved, since the ground cannot resist it. Thus, the parallel component of the ball's determination to move along *AB*, that is the determination to move from *AC* to *HB*, will also be present upon reflection. We can therefore draw a line, *FE*, such that the distances *CB* and *BE* are equal. The determination that carried the ball from *AC* to *HB* before reflection will carry it from *HB* to *FE* thereafter:

---

[30] Descartes (2001, 76–77).

Then in order to know precisely to which of all the points of this circumference it must return, let us draw three straight lines *AC*, *HB*, and *FE* perpendicular to *CE*, in such a way that there is neither more nor less distance between *AC* and *HB* than between *HB* and *FE*; and let us say that in as much time as the ball took to advance toward the right side from *A* (one of the points of the line *AC*) to *B* (one of those of the line *HB*), it must also advance from the line *HB* to some point on the line *FE*; for any point of this line *FE* is as far removed from *HB* in this direction as is any other, and as far as are those of the line *AC*; and also the ball is as much determined to advance toward that side as it had been hithertofore.[31]

The conservation of the ball's movement entails that it will be found along the circle *AFD*. The conservation of the ball's parallel determination entails that it will be found along the line *FE*. The intersection (presuming the ball does not penetrate the surface) is the point *F*. So, Descartes concludes, the motion of the ball after reflection will be represented by the line *BF*. Converting the analogy back into the case of light yields the law of reflection:

And so you can easily see how reflection occurs, namely according to an angle which is always equal to the one we call the angle of incidence; in the same way that if a ray, coming from point *A*, falls to point *B* on the surface of the flat mirror *CBE*, it is reflected toward *F* in such a manner that the angle of reflection *FBE* is neither greater nor smaller than that of the angle of incidence *ABC*.[32]

The angle of incidence equals the angle of reflection.

Notice that this derivation requires several presuppositions not made explicit in the text. First and foremost, direction is described in relation to an orientation of the space provided by the reflecting surface, not in relation to a center. As a result, parallel directions are identified. The parallel component of the determination is conserved precisely insofar as it is always directed parallel to the reflecting surface, "to the right," and the parallel segments *AC* and *HB*, represent motion in the "same direction." In other words, Descartes uses an oriented representation of space to describe direction. Directions are identified if and only if they are parallel. The "same" determination is directed everywhere along parallels.

---

[31] Descartes (2001, 77).

[32] Descartes (2001, 77). More precisely, the horizontal component of the incident determination is *AB cos ABC*. This is equal to the horizontal component of the reflected determination *BF cos FBE*. But *AB* is equal to *BF*, since the total movement is conserved. Thus, *cos ABC* equals *cos FBE*, so *ABC* equals *FBE*. Peculiarly, Descartes measures the angles of incidence and reflection from the surface, not the normal, as became standard. They should be *HBA* and *HBF*, but these can be obtained from *ABC* and *FBE* by subtraction from right angles. In the treatment of refraction that follows, Descartes measures the incident and refracted angles from the normal.

This oriented descriptive framework also supports a parallelogram composition of determinations, which Descartes presupposes in his derivations. Descartes divides the total determination to move along *AB* into the components normal and parallel to the surface. Conversely, the composition of the determinations represented by the sides of the rectangle *AHBC* is the diagonal, *AB*. This is true because the parallel component of the ball's motion before reflection carries it from *AC* to *HB*, even when combined with the normal component carrying it from *AH* to *CB*, and *vice versa*. In the absence of the oblique motion, the body would have continued along *AH*, in a straight line.

Furthermore, despite his protestations to the contrary, Descartes presumes that the total determination is proportional to the total movement (or tendency to movement). The initial movement and the total initial determination are both represented by the same line segment, *AB*. Moreover, the derivation supposes that the parallel component of determination contributes part of the total *movement*, the length *BF*, after reflection. The location of the point *F* is then found by solving for the normal contribution to the known total movement by vector subtraction. But the normal and parallel components are *determinations*, not movements, which do not have directions. So the calculation is only coherent if the scalar magnitude of the total determination is proportional to the total movement.[33] The "power" that causes movement varies in proportion to the "power" that directs it. By contrast, if the scalar magnitude of the total determination is not proportional to the total movement, the normal component before and after reflection is unconstrained, and *F* could be anywhere along the line *FE*.[34]

All of these presuppositions together constitute a statement of a descriptive framework containing all the rudiments of the modern theory. Movement taken together with a determination is a *motion* – a speed in a direction – which is a vector quantity. Thus, the explicit conservation of movement, which says that a body's speed remains uniform, linked to the conservation of direction yields the conservation of motion. As the description includes an oriented representation of space, this implies the conservation of uniform rectilinear motion – a modern principle of inertia. Moreover, the oriented representation of space supports parallelogram

---

[33] In formal terms, Descartes finds the location of the point *F* by solving for the vector component $\overrightarrow{EF}$ such that $|\overrightarrow{EF} + \overrightarrow{BE}| \sim |AB|$. But $|\overrightarrow{EF} + \overrightarrow{BE}|$ is the scalar magnitude of a determination, while $|AB|$ is a (scalar) movement.

[34] That determinations have magnitudes is made even clearer by Descartes's derivation of the sine law of refraction later in the *Optics*, discussed below. On this point, see Garber (1992a, 188–93).

compositions of motions. Inertia has been rectified, at least in this part of the *Optics*. At the very least, centers have fallen away from the theory of motion, and they play no role in the description and explanation of bodily-cum-optical interactions. It remains to be seen how general we can take Descartes's implicit theory to be.

Descartes on oriented space: physical considerations

There are indications elsewhere in Descartes's corpus that aspects of the explanatory principles and descriptive frameworks in the *Optics* are meant to be generally held. Early in his career, Descartes lacked interest in the causes of gravitation and in planetary motions.[35] He did not deal, therefore, with centers of force to which a centered representation of space naturally applies. Moreover, his early work in optics and geometry itself would have disposed Descartes toward an oriented representation of space.

In Descartes's time, light was considered from two points of view.[36] On the one hand, it was thought of as a spherical phenomenon. Light spreads out in all directions from a central source, so that the projection of a luminous point forms a sphere around it. Kepler, for example, wrote that all luminous things (those that "share in light") "imitate the sun," which occupies the "middle place ... and the center" and "pour[s] itself forth equably into the whole orb."[37] On this view, light is described as a series of spheres expanding from the luminous source at the center of the projected "orb." On the other hand, it was universally acknowledged that the individual parts of light or "rays" propagate rectilinearly, unless they encounter refractive or reflective surfaces. After noting the spherical shape of the luminous projection, Kepler goes on to say that the "nature of light is to move in straight lines, as long as it is not at all affected by the interposition of surfaces."[38] Light is here thought of as a collection of straight lines propagating from a source. The infinitude of rays spreading from the source in all directions constitutes a centered "orb" of light. Considered

---

[35] Beeckman did set Descartes problems about the kinematics of free fall, but he and Descartes seem not to have discussed the causes of gravitation. Descartes's attempts to explain gravitation begin with the vortical account in the *World*.

[36] This dual consideration of light follows a long tradition. See Dijksterhuis (1961, 150), Lindberg (1976, 1986), Smith (1987).

[37] Kepler (2000, 19–20). Descartes called Kepler his "first teacher in optics" (Descartes 1897–1913, 2:86). Schuster (2000) sketches a possible path from Kepler's optical proofs, discussed above in Chapter 4, to Descartes's own work.

[38] Kepler (2000, 34).

individually, though, the behavior of the rays indicates a rectilinear framework in which the "direction" of a ray is always parallel to itself. Hence, the behavior of light could suggest both centered and oriented representations of space, depending on whether light was considered as a single spherical projection or as a multitude of linear ones.[39]

For Descartes, as for his predecessors, the action of light spreads out spherically from all points of a luminous source. Descartes's focus, however, was not on optics in general, but on problems in catoptrics and dioptrics – the behavior of reflected and refracted light rays. This brought his attention to bear on individual rays, which, it was assumed, acted along straight lines: "rays should always be imagined to be exactly straight, when they go through only one transparent body which is uniform throughout."[40] Individual "rays" follow straight lines, and their subsequent behavior does not depend on the location of the light source. This particular interest suggests an oriented representation of space. In particular, the "direction" of a light ray is given by the straight line itself, not any relation to any center. This representation of light is thus isotropic. Any straight line, in any direction, represents a light ray. Descartes simply stipulates that a straight line, even as drawn on a page, is a ray and that geometric manipulations of straight lines represent the actual behaviors of rays of light. As we have seen, the *Optics* goes on to use such geometrical arguments to describe optical phenomena.[41]

Descartes's early work in geometry also suggested the priority of straight lines, if not an oriented space, *per se*. As he explained to Beeckman in 1619, Descartes sought "a completely new science by which all questions in general may be solved that can be proposed about any kind of quantity, continuous as well as discrete."[42] That is, Descartes aimed at a geometrical method that could solve any quantitative problem whatsoever. He acknowledged that this task was "incredibly ambitious," but claimed that he had "through the dark confusion . . . seen some kind of light."[43] The "light" he had seen, Descartes continued, was the use of his "new compasses," which he described in the

---

[39] As we have seen, Kepler stresses the former view in his astronomical work. He compares the *anima motrix* that emanates from the sun and moves the planets around their orbits to the action of light. Both propagate spherically from the central body, i.e., the sun, and diminish in intensity as distance increases. Moreover, in both cases the purported forces or actions are described in relation to a spherical framework. A center is presupposed – the sun – as is the indistinguishability of locations at equal distances from the center. The sphericity of the *anima motrix* is part of the explanation of its ability to move the planets circularly around the sun.

[40] Descartes (2001, 70).

[41] Shea (1991) argues that this "diagrammatic" form of argument is fundamental to all of Cartesian science. See also Maull (1980, esp. 262–63), Ribe (1997), Friedman (2008, 75).

[42] Descartes (1897–1913, 10:156–57), Bos (2001, 232).

[43] Descartes (1897–1913, 10:157–58), Bos (2001, 232).

Geometry and the unpublished *Cogitationes Privatae*. These compasses consisted of several straight pieces hinged together or sliding across one another. They could be used to find any number of mean proportionals between given quantities represented as line segments, and it was well known that the discovery of mean proportionals was the key to many outstanding mathematical problems.[44] The compasses operated by constructing curves that satisfied the proportionalities sought in the problem under investigation. They did so by ensuring that the position of each rectilinear part of the compass retained the proper relation to the other parts as the compass was manipulated. The necessary curve was then generated by the intersection of two of these rectilinear parts. In other words, the curve was constructed by the motion of points along presupposed straight lines. The mechanical connections of the compass ensured the commensurability of these motions.[45]

The intent here is not to limn the details of Descartes's early work on geometry. It suffices to note that Descartes's geometry requires the *presupposition* of straight lines, in the form of the parts of his "new compasses," in order to construct curves. Thus, rectilinearity is postulated prior to any particular problem or situation and then used to *construct* the necessary curves. Descartes's geometry, like his optics, requires the assumption of straight lines, without reference to centers, in order to represent (in this case, mathematical) phenomena. Curves are generated on the presupposition of straight lines.

The important point is that Descartes's oriented representation of space, however it actually came about, did so in a practical and applied context. In

---

[44] In fact, in 1593, François Viète had shown that all "solid," third-degree problems in geometry could be solved by the construction of two mean proportionals or the trisection of an angle. Descartes expected (not unreasonably, though he had no proof) that problems of higher degrees, which included nearly all existing unresolved mathematical puzzles, could be solved by the construction of additional mean proportionals. If any third-degree problem could be solved by constructing two mean proportionals, then perhaps all fourth-degree problems could be solved by the construction of three mean proportionals, and so on. The compasses could be used to construct these additional mean proportionals. In other words, Descartes's compasses presented the possibility of solving most, if not all, existing mathematical puzzles. They held out the promise of a "completely new science." See Bos (2001, 243), Mancosu (2008). Descartes's awareness of Viète's work prior to 1631, when he began drafting the *Geometry*, is a matter of scholarly debate. See Shea (1991, 44–45, 48), Gaukroger (1995, 124–34), Sasaki (2003), Manders (2006), Rabouin (2010). In any case, it is clear that Descartes was at least partly inspired to treat the "whole of knowledge" by his geometric successes (Beeckman 1939–1953, 3:95).

[45] The compass could not generate "mechanical" curves, generated by two or more distinct and incommensurate motions. Problems requiring such curves could not be solved using Descartes's method. In his letter to Beeckman, Descartes called such curves "imaginary only" and he excluded them from the scope of the *Geometry*. For examples of mechanical and geometrical curves and the operation of Descartes's compass, see Bos (1981), Mancosu (1996, ch. 3), Bos (2001, 231–53), Domski (2009, 2013).

his early work, Descartes was trying to solve very specific descriptive and explanatory problems in narrow subject matters. His choice to privilege lines over points and spheres proved appropriate or convenient to the problems at hand. Indeed, the choice led to remarkable success: the discovery of the anaclastic curve and analytic geometry. The oriented representation of optical phenomena and geometric curves allowed fruitful descriptions and explanations. This initial descriptive and explanatory success led Descartes to adhere to an oriented framework in his later, broader work.

Descartes on oriented space: metaphysical considerations

It is possible to trace out this subsequent development of the oriented representation of space in Descartes's later work, as he expanded his optics and geometry into a broader philosophical system.[46] For instance, in the *Rules for the Direction of the Mind*, Descartes develops an account of sensory experience and knowledge. Central to this account is the distinction between "simple" and "complicated" ideas. Simple ideas are those that can be known immediately and directly, without further elucidation or investigation by the intellect. Complicated ideas are known if they can be reduced to the simple ideas out of which they are composed. What is significant is that motion is listed as an example of a simple idea.[47] This entails that it is something perceived immediately by the intellect. It is not something recognized in relation to anything else, or via some further cognitive analysis. Indeed, in the following discussion, Descartes famously ridicules the Aristotelian definition of motion ("the actuality of a potential being, in so far as it is potential") for unintelligibly attempting to define the basic and indefinable.[48] At the same time, though, Descartes says that "straight" is an "absolute" notion with a "pure and simple nature" that can likewise be known directly and without relation to anything else.[49] This is in explicit contrast to "oblique," which is listed among "relative" notions to be further reduced. Thus, "straight" is something that can be directly and

---

[46] For more on this process of expansion, see Lenoir (1979), Galuzzi (1980, 39–40), Maull (1980), Gaukroger (1995, esp. ch. 4), Clarke (1996), Ribe (1997).

[47] Descartes (1985–1991, 1:44).

[48] Descartes (1985–1991, 1:49). The criticism is repeated in the later *World* (Descartes 1998, 26).

[49] Descartes (1985–1991, 1:21). In the *Rules*, the "absolute" notions are the ultimate categorical connections by which ideas are connected to one another. That is, in any process of reasoning about some problem, the absolute is the "simplest and easiest" connection between premises and conclusion by which the problem is solved.

immediately recognized by the intellect. It does not require composition of more basic perceptions or ideas.[50]

Descartes's view seems to be that recognition of straight motion can be accomplished in an instant, while curved motion can only be recognized as such by its departure from straight motion in subsequent instants. That is, curved motion can only be understood by a comparison of perceptions in different instants. It requires a further cognitive process beyond immediate perceptual recognition. For Descartes, then, simple motion is straight motion.[51]

This interpretation is confirmed by what Descartes writes in the *World*, where the mechanics and optics of his earlier work began to take on some of the metaphysical significance that reached its apex in *Principles of Philosophy*. In the *World*, Descartes begins to connect physical principles with God's creative act, and thus the laws of nature with God's immutability and simplicity. All bodies tend to move in straight lines because God acts in the simplest way possible:

> I shall add as a third rule that, when a body is moving, even if its motion most often takes place along a curved line and, as we said above, it can never make any movement that is not in some way circular, nevertheless each of its parts individually tends always to continue moving along a straight line. This rule rests on the same foundation as the other two, and depends solely on God's conserving everything by a continuous action, and consequently on His conserving it not as it may have been some time earlier but precisely as it is at the very instant He conserves it. So, of all motions, only motion in a straight line is entirely simple and has a nature which may be grasped wholly in an instant. For in order to conceive of such motion it is enough to think that a

---

[50] The definition of "straightness" was an item of particular concern among mathematicians and geometricians during this period, though it evaded a satisfactory resolution. See De Risi (2007).

[51] In the *Meditations*, Descartes concludes that we can be sure of our experience of the physical world, so long as the experience consists of clear and distinct ideas. Thus, our clear and distinct knowledge of motion is ultimately warranted by the direct action of God, whose benevolence prevents Him from deceiving us about the truth of clear and distinct ideas. By the time of the *Principles*, though, it is no longer clear exactly how God warrants our knowledge of motion. That is, it is not clear whether we are to take Descartes to mean that motion is a real property of bodies, a position defended by Garber (1992a), or to mean that God directly endows the intellect with a clear and distinct perception of motion that does not depend in any way on the actual properties of extended things, a position defended by Machamer and McGuire (2009). This debate, however, is tangential to my argument, since, at this point, it only concerns the absolute nature of the intuition of motion, regardless of the ultimate cause of that intuition. In either case, though, the appeal to God to warrant knowledge requires a simple and direct intuition of motion. Since God, a supremely independent being, Himself associates motion with body (in the body or in the intellect), there must be a clearly, distinctly, and immediately known fact of the matter about a body's state of motion. Motion cannot depend on the intellectual compositions of mortal, dependent creatures.

body is in the process of moving in a certain direction, and that this is the case at each determinable instant during the time that it is moving.[52]

Bodies tend to move rectilinearly because rectilinear motion is simple. In the terms of the *Rules*, linear motion is "absolute" – it can be "wholly" and directly grasped in a single instant, without reference to other bodies or other instants. Thus, when God (re)creates the world in each moment he tends to conserve motions as they are "at the very instant" He acts. But only straight motion can be "grasped wholly in an instant." Curved motion requires comparisons to other motions at "some time earlier." As Descartes puts it, "to conceive of circular motion, or any other possible [curved] motion, it is necessary to consider at least two of its instants, or rather two of its parts, and the relation between them."[53] So the simplicity of God's conservation of the universe preserves straight motions, not curved.[54]

Notice that this "third rule" of nature in the *World* is an explicit statement of the kind of conservation principle for directions that is only implicit in the *Optics*. Descartes is here asserting that the direction of motion is conserved. Without the action of some extrinsic, secondary cause, a body will continue moving in the same direction, since God would simply conserve the direction it already possessed. Moreover, to move "in the same direction" is here explicitly coordinated with rectilinear motion. Curvilinear motion is, by contrast, a *change* of motion in successive instants, such that the motion at "some time earlier" is not the same as the motion "at the very instant." Descartes here refers directions to orientations of space. A direction is just a pointing along a straight line, off to infinity. Directions are nowhere related to centers.

The "simplicity" of rectilinear motion depends on Descartes's oriented representation of space. Straight motion is simple precisely because it preserves direction. "It is enough to think," says Descartes, "that a body is in the process of moving in a certain direction" at every instant of its motion. As it moves along a straight path, a body is always moving in a "certain direction" that does not change. In general, though, straight motion only preserves direction in an oriented space, where direction is conceived as self-parallel. Curved motion, including circular motion, changes direction in an oriented framework. In other words, in Descartes's oriented space, the description of curves is not simple. To describe them, one must consider different rectilinear directions in which the body moves during successive parts of its motion.

---

[52] Descartes (1998, 29–30).   [53] Descartes (1998, 30)

[54] Recall that the distinction between rectilinear and all other kinds of motion is simply intuited. The distinction between motion and rest, not addressed here, is more problematic. See Garber (1992b, 307; 1992a, 285–87), Shea (1996, 457–58).

Meanwhile, this conception of curves as "relative" is a direct echo of the precedence given to straight lines in Descartes's geometry. The precedence of rectilinearity in Descartes's geometrical method eventually filtered into the nascent philosophical method found in the *Rules* and the *World*.[55]

The principle of conserved direction or determination, as coordinated with straight lines, is also codified in the *Principles of Philosophy*. There, the "third rule" from the *World* appears as the "second law of nature":

> The second law of nature: that all movement is, of itself, along straight lines; and consequently, bodies which are moving in a circle always tend to move away from the center of the circle which they are describing. ... This rule, like the preceding one, results from the immutability and simplicity of the operation by which God maintains movement in matter; for He only maintains it precisely as it is at the very moment at which He is maintaining it, and not as it may perhaps have been at some earlier time. Of course, no movement is accomplished in an instant; yet it is obvious that every moving body, at any given moment in the course of its movement, is inclined to continue that movement in some direction in a straight line, and never in a curved one.[56]

As in the *World*, God acts to conserve the world in the simplest way possible. This entails that He conserves the "inclination" to move in some direction, which is always along a straight line, since only the straight can be conceived "in an instant." Again, though, this account depends on the specification of directions as orientations of space, not in relation to any center.[57]

The *Principles* makes explicit Descartes's rejection of a (singly) centered representation of space for his fundamental explanations of motion. In a discussion of a body's "external place," Descartes notes that the body's situation with respect to other bodies depends on those other bodies "which we consider to be motionless."[58] But the determination of a body's situation *only* depends on a stipulation on the part of the observer as to what he or she counts as motionless. There are no privileged locations or bodies in the universe to which directions and locations can be referred:

> Moreover, in order to determine that situation [of one body among others] we must take into account some other bodies which we consider to be motionless; and, depending on which bodies we consider, we can say that the same thing simultaneously changes and does not change its place. Thus, when a ship is heading out to sea, a person seated in the stern always remains

---

[55] As Emily Grosholz notes, "the straight line segments of the *Geometry* seem to correspond nicely to the inherently uniform, rectilinear motion of the bits of matter which are the simples in the physics" (1988, 244). See also Slowik (1999b, 2002).

[56] *Principles* I.39 (Descartes 1983, 60–61).   [57] See Grosholz (1986).

[58] *Principles* II.13 (Descartes 1983, 45).

in one place as far as the parts of the ship are concerned, for he maintains the same situation in relation to them. But this same person is constantly changing his place as far as the shores are concerned, since he is constantly moving away from some and toward others. ... [O]f course, we shall determine his place by certain supposedly motionless points in the heavens. Finally, if we think that no truly motionless points of this kind are found in the universe, as will later be shown to be probable; then from that, we shall conclude that nothing has an enduring [French version: fixed and determinate] place, except insofar as it is determined in our minds.[59]

A body's location, that is, is a purely subjective determination relative to an arbitrary choice of relative reference frame. The location of bodies is described only by relation to stipulated fixed reference points, but this is merely a determination of our subjective minds, not an objective fact about the phenomena. There are no "fixed and determinate" points by which locations are to be specified. Descartes's description of location and of motion does not require stipulated fixed points. His theory, that is, represents space as homogeneous.

Similarly, it represents space as isotropic. There are no privileged directions. Any direction in space sets up an orientation. In the *Rules*, Descartes stresses that length, breadth, and depth are concepts applied by the intellect to imaginary representations of physical bodies. There is nothing in bodies or their representations that dictates which "mode or aspect" is to be "measured" as its length, etc.:

> We should note incidentally that there is merely a nominal difference between the three dimensions of body – length, breadth, and depth; for in any given solid it is quite immaterial which aspect of its extension we take as its length, which as its breadth, etc. Although these three dimensions have a real basis at any rate in every extended thing simply *qua* extended, we are no more concerned with them here than with countless others which are either intellectual fictions or have some other basis in things.[60]

Physical bodies, that is, are extended things. It is always possible to "measure" their length, breadth, and depth simply because they are extended. Nothing, however, necessitates that a particular aspect – i.e., a certain direction in the body – is to be conceived as its length, breadth, or depth. There is no feature of a body that the intellect must consider as a particular spatial dimension. On the contrary, the aspect of the body described as its length, breadth, or depth is a matter of arbitrary subjective choice. In other words, the orientation of the space by which the body is to be described is

---

[59] *Principles* II.13 (Descartes 1983, 45).   [60] Descartes (1985–1991, 1:63).

something chosen by the observing and intuiting subject, rather than something discovered in the phenomena.[61]

Thus far, then, the oriented representation of space seems fundamental for Descartes. His fundamental physics – the mechanics of hard bodies – depends on stipulated orientation of space, and this is consonant with his more general metaphysics of material substances and epistemological theory of sensory observation. For Descartes, spatial centers are no longer essential to descriptions of spatial phenomena. Given the influence of Descartes's metaphysics and the "mechanical philosophy" it inspired, this was itself significant. A de-centered, oriented spatial framework became standard as natural philosophers adopted the new Cartesian philosophy.

Descartes dis-oriented

However, Descartes's descriptive frameworks were not always consistent, and there are limits on the generality of the oriented representation of space in Descartes's natural philosophy. In particular, as Descartes's natural philosophy grew more systematic and general, he began to consider phenomena, like gravitation and planetary motion, that exhibit centers of physical force. As a result, centered representations of physical phenomena began to creep back into Descartes's physical theory.

Descartes's fundamental physical principles, the "laws of nature," govern the collisions of perfectly elastic bodies moving in a void. In fact, however, Descartes held that no such void obtains. The universe, rather, is a plenum, so bodies are always in contact with other bodies. The "laws of nature," therefore, are counterfactual. They dictate only what bodies would do if they were not in a plenum.[62] Consequently, bodies do not actually move along straight lines. The motion of one body requires the displacement of some other body in the plenum, but this can only be accomplished if yet a third body is displaced. Thus, all motions are closed loops, where the last moved body takes the place of the first.[63] As Descartes goes on to describe, the universe contains vast numbers of these looped motions, which form vortices of matter. The largest of these are those around stars, which carry planets around them. Smaller vortices, nestled among the former, are found around the planets, and so on, down to small whorls in everyday bodies.

Consider, then, how Descartes applies his fundamental laws of nature to the motion of bodies in a curved path. The inclination of a body towards

---

[61] For more on this point, see Gaukroger (2006, 292).

[62] *Principles* II.53 (Descartes 1983, 69). See Anderson (1976), Shea (1996, 457).

[63] *Principles* II.34 (Descartes 1983, 55–56).

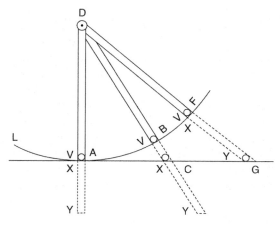

Figure 6.2 Stone in a sling.[64]

rectilinear motion implies that it tends along the tangent of its motion at each instant,

> Thus the stone turning in a sling along the circle *AB*, for example, tends towards *C* when it is at point *A* [in Figure 6.2], if one considers just its agitation in isolation; and it tends circularly from *A* to *B*, if one considers its motion as regulated and determined by the length of the cord which retains it; and finally the same stone tends toward *E* if, ignoring that part of its agitation whose effect is not impeded, the other part of it is opposed to the resistance that this sling continually offers to it.
>
> But, for a distinct understanding of this last point, imagine this stone's inclination to move from *A* to *C* as if it were composed of two other inclinations, one turning along the circle *AB* and the other rising straight up along [*monter tout droit suivant*] the line *VXY*. ... Then, since we know that one of the parts of its inclination, namely that which carries it along the circle *AB*, is in no way impeded by the sling, it is easily seen that the stone meets resistance only in its other part, namely that which would cause it to move along the line *DVXY* if it were unimpeded, and consequently it tends – that is, strives – only to move away from the center *D*.[65]

The tangential inclination, that is, is composed of two others: a circumferential tendency around and a radial tendency away from the center of rotation. If the centrifugal tendency is impeded, such as it is by the sling or by the press of bodies in a plenum, then the only remaining tendency in the

[64] Descartes (1897–1913, 11:46).
[65] Descartes (1998, 54–55). See also the arguments in *Principles* II.39 and III.58 (Descartes 1983, 60–61, 113–14).

body is the tendency to move circularly around the center. Descartes concludes that when the net action on a body is zero (when the internal centrifugal tendency is cancelled by the extrinsic press of surrounding bodies) the resulting motion is circular. Orbital motion is a combination of an imposed tendency – counteracting the centrifugal tendency of the body – and the body's conserved motion. Only here, the actually conserved motion, the component of the body's motion that is preserved from moment to moment, is the circular motion around the center. As in Galileo, this circular motion around the center is neither natural nor forced (i.e., continually caused by some extrinsic action), but merely preserves the earlier state of motion. Thus, in a plenum, circular motion around the center is conserved. It is simply the unconstrained component of a prior motion, and only changes of circular motion need to be explained by an additional action.[66]

The centrifugal tendency of all bodies in a rotating vortex, meanwhile, accounts for both optical and gravitational phenomena. Light is the pressure caused by the centrifugal tendency of the subtlest matter. Gravity is the effect of a swiftly moving medium that displaces gross bodies toward the center because of its greater outward tendency. Descartes thus proposes the reverse of Galileo's account in *De Motu*: all bodies tend away from the center (i.e., "up"), and heavy bodies "float" toward the center.

Notice, however, that this account is the result of a subtle slide into a centered representation of space. The rotation of the vortex introduces a center of rotation, and the tangential tendency is described in relation to that center. Thus, Descartes says that it consists of a component directed away from the center and a component perpendicular to the center. The "direction" of the resulting motion is circularly around, always perpendicular to the center. To continue the "same motion" – that is, to continue moving in the same direction at the same speed – is to move circularly around the center at a uniform rate. In a plenum, the unforced, conserved motion is circular.

Significantly, Descartes does not use the parallelogram rule for the composition of motions or determinations implicitly present in the *Optics* in later work. In the *Principles*, Descartes does say that motions can be decomposed. As one example, he provides a decomposition of one recti-linear motion into two others:

> For one can imagine any line whatever, even a straight one, which is the simplest of all, to have been described by innumerable diverse movements.

[66] See Westfall (1971, 82), Shea (1996, 460–61), Slowik (1999a), Gaukroger (2002, 119; 2006, 294).

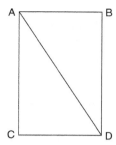

Figure 6.3 Composition of motions in *Principles*.[67]

> For example, if at the same time as the line *AB* [in Figure 6.3] moves toward
> *CD*, its point *A* moves closer to B; the straight line *AD* (which will be
> described by the point *A*) will depend . . . on the two movements of *A* toward
> B and of *AB* toward *CD*, which are straight.[68]

That is, uniform motion of a point along a line that is itself moving
uniformly (but always parallel to itself) produces a resultant rectilinear
motion that is represented as the diagonal of the parallelogram – here a
rectangle, on the unstated assumption that the two motions are perpendicular – with the two component motions represented by the sides.
Nevertheless, Descartes does not present this construction as a special
case. Moreover, as we have seen, he does not decompose the tangential
tendency of the stone in the sling using the parallelogram decomposition,
even though it fits precisely the case he describes here, conceiving of a single
straight motion as a composition of two others. Instead, he uses a decomposition along the lines of another example: the decomposition of the
"exceedingly crooked" motion of a point on a wagon wheel into the circular
motion of the wheel around its axle and its straight motion "along the
length of the route."[69]

   In fact, nowhere in Descartes's writings after the *Optics* does he explicitly
consider parallelogram compositions of oblique motions. In the *Principles*,
for instance, all the laws of motion are applied only to cases of bodies
colliding in the same straight line. There is no suggestion, as there is in the
Optics, of what might happen in the case of an oblique collision in which the
tendency or motion in one direction is combined with a tendency or
motion in another.

[67] Descartes (1897–1913 vol. 9, plate 1, fig. 2).   [68] *Principles* II.32 (Descartes 1983, 55).
[69] *Principles* II.32 (Descartes 1983, 55).

In Descartes's mature physics, then, there is a reversal of Galileo's Archimedean approximation. Fundamentally, the theory of motion does not presuppose privileged centers or directions. The basic, small-scale interactions of individual corpuscles are therefore represented in an oriented framework. Once Descartes begins to address large-scale phenomena in a plenum, however, he switches to a centered representation of space in which the center of the vortex is the stipulated center of the spatial ordering. For Descartes, the small-scale, centerless physics "builds up" into a cosmic, centered theory of vortices. Indeed, Descartes adopts a multiply centered representation of cosmic space, as each vortex is ordered around its own center:

> For, first, because there is no void at all in this new world, it was not possible for all the parts of matter to move in a straight line. Rather, since they were all just about equal and as easily divisible, they all had to form together into various circular motions. And yet, because we suppose that God initially moved them in different ways, we should not imagine that they all came together to turn around a single center, but around many different ones, which we may imagine to be variously situated with respect to one another.[70]

There are "many different" centers in Descartes's universe, though at the smallest scale, there are none at all.

The centered representation of space can be seen throughout Descartes's discussion of celestial physics in the *World* and Book III of the *Principles*. Consider, for instance, his discussion of the fall of terrestrial bodies. Descartes proposes that the earth itself possesses a vortex. But this is described using a centered representation of space:

> Then consider that, since there is no space such as this beyond the circle *ABCD* [around the earth; see Figure 6.4] that is void and where the parts of the heavens contained within that circle are able to go, unless others which are exactly similar replace them simultaneously, the parts of the Earth cannot move away any further than they do from the center *T* either, unless just as many parts of heaven or other terrestrial parts required to fill them come down to replace them. Nor, conversely, can they move closer to the center unless just as many others rise in their place. . . . Now it is evident that, since much more terrestrial matter is contained within this stone than is contained in an amount of air of equal extent . . . the stone should not have the force to rise above it; but on the contrary this amount should rather have the force to make the stone fall downwards.[71]

---

[70] Descartes (1998, 32–33).   [71] Descartes (1998, 49).

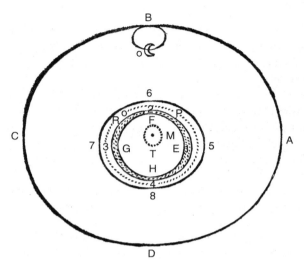

Figure 6.4 Earth and its vortex.[72]

Here, Descartes assumes a central point near (though not quite identical to) the center of the earth, and then specifies directions and locations in relation to it. "Above" means further from the center. "Downwards" is toward the center.

This then leads to the striking and tell-tale description of the moon's behavior as a stasis, rather than a rotation:

> So it [the moon] must remain as if attached to the surface of a small heaven *ABCD* and turn continually with it about *T*. That is what prevents its forming another small heaven around it, which would make it turn again around its own center.[73]

In other words, in Descartes's view, the moon does not rotate "around its own center." The fact that it does not have its own vortex is meant to explain why not. Yet, as with Copernicus's "third motion" of the earth, such a description is only coherent in a centered representation of space. The same face of the moon is always directed to the earth. In a centered representation of space, where the direction of the moon's "face" is related to a radius to the center, this behavior is described as a stasis. In a centered representation of space, the direction remains constant as the moon orbits the earth.

[72] Descartes (1897–1913, 11:74). [73] Descartes (1998, 46).

Incidentally, note that Descartes is never completely clear about the relationship between the actual motion of a body and its "determination" or "tendency" to move in one direction or another. In particular, Descartes never says whether the total "determination," which does include a direction, is in any way related to the "power" that moves bodies or to motion itself. Despite the presence of the decomposition rule for "motions" noted above, it is not clear that Descartes ever considered "motion" as anything other than a scalar quantity. Thus, the *Principles* gives two *separate* conservation principles, one for each of these quantities, as the first two "laws of nature." The third law and its associated rules of collision then treat the two quantities as independent.[74]

Commentators sometimes assert that the first two laws, taken together, seem to express the modern law of inertia: bodies conserve their motions and directions, and thus tend to move uniformly in straight lines.[75] However, one result of the foregoing discussion is that, because of the slide into a centered representation of space for large-scale phenomena, the modern inertial principle in its full generality cannot be attributed to Descartes. The laws themselves are stated in the context of small-scale interactions between bodies where an oriented framework is applied. But in large-scale plena, a centered framework is applied, such that the conservation of direction implies circular motion. Bodies in a vortex both conserve their quantity of motion, in accordance with the first law, and tend along straight lines at each instant, in accordance with the second law, even though they conserve a circular motion. Hence, in the vortex, Descartes's laws are satisfied, but the modern principle is not.

Fermat's orientation of the *Optics*

At this point, the thread returns to the *Optics*. While his mature physics eventually adopted a centered representation of large-scale phenomena, Descartes's early physical theory, as expressed in his *Optics*, contained the germ of a descriptive system that associated his conservation principle with an oriented representation of space, as we have seen. The rectification of the conservation principle was not explicit, but that is not to say it was not apparent. Indeed, Descartes's contemporaries noticed the text's oriented framework, even before the *Optics* emerged from the press, and their

---

[74] See Garber (1992a, 219–29).
[75] For example, Koyré (1965, 69), Blackwell (1966), Westfall (1977, 33–34), Huggett (1999, 103), Barbour (2001, 430), Meli (2008, 656).

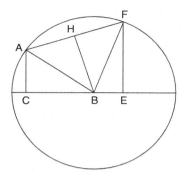

Figure 6.5 Fermat's alternate analysis of reflection.[76]

commentary brought the oriented description of physical phenomena to the fore. Pierre de Fermat was especially perceptive in this respect.

In 1637, as Descartes's *Discourse* and *Essays* were making their way into print, Marin Mersenne, who was shepherding the book through publication as well as making its introduction among the Paris *savants*, asked Fermat to comment on the *Optics*. The result was two critical letters, each of which elicited a response from Descartes. Fermat's first letter already expresses concerns about Descartes's decomposition of motions. Fermat notes that Descartes says that "determination to move in some direction [*vers quelque costé*] can … be divided in all the parts of which one can imagine that it is composed."[77] He then wonders why Descartes chose to decompose the incident determination in the case of reflection (*AB* in Figure 6.1, above) into the components parallel and normal to the surface, as opposed to some other decomposition. Fermat suggests that the incident determination could be decomposed into two others, both oblique to the normal, such as *AH* and *HB* in Figure 6.5. Following Descartes's own construction, the determination that does not encounter the reflecting surface would not be affected, so *AH* would continue through *HF*, while the direction of the determination encountering the "resisting" surface, *HB*, would be reversed. Re-composing the resultant determination, *BF*, gives an angle of reflection different from the angle of incidence. Thus, Fermat shows, Descartes's law of reflection depends on the initial decomposition of determinations into normal and parallel components, which Descartes

---

[76] Descartes (1897–1913, 1:359).

[77] "[I]l [i.e., Descartes] dit que la determination à se mouvoir vers quelque costé peut, aussi bien qu le mouvement & generalement que toute autre quantité, estre divisée en toutes les parties desquelles on peut imaginer qu'ell est composée" (Descartes 1897–1913, 1:358).

claims is merely an arbitrary choice among all the decompositions imaginable. As Fermat puts it,

> of all the divisions of the determination to movement, which are infinite, the author has taken only the one which serves his conclusion, and thus he has accommodated his *medium* [i.e., his argument] to his conclusion.[78]

In effect, Fermat asks why *only* the normal component of an incident determination is reversed. But this is to demand kinematic rules by which determinations are, first, decomposed and, second, transformed in collisions that Descartes never provides, even in his tangential response to Fermat's letter.[79] Fermat subsequently lets the issue drop, since he takes the law of reflection to be non-controversial, but it is significant that he probes Descartes's descriptive framework for motions and determinations from the start.

In the second letter, Fermat directed his criticism against Descartes's treatment of refraction. There, Descartes had extended the analogy of the tennis ball by supposing that refraction is like the result of the ball slowing down or speeding up upon encountering some surface, such as piercing a "weak and loosely woven cloth"[80] or being struck a second time by a racket. Descartes again supposes that only the ball's motion normal to the surface will be affected, and the parallel component unchanged. Thus, the path of the ball can be found by effectively solving for the normal component necessary to make up the resulting speed:

> Then, having described from the center *B* the circle *AFD* [in Figure 6.6], and drawn at right angles to *CBE* the three straight lines *AC*, *HB*, *FE* in such a way that there is twice as much distance between *FE* and *HB* as between *HB* and *AC*, we will see that this ball must tend toward the point *I*. For, since it loses half of its speed by going through the cloth *CBE*, it must take twice as much time to pass below, from *B* to a certain point on the circumference of the circle *AFD*, as it took above to come from *A* to *B*. And since it loses nothing at all of the determination that it had to advance toward the right side, in twice as much time as it took to pass from the line *AC* to *HB*, it must make twice as much headway toward this same side, and as a result arrive at a certain point of the straight line *FE* at the same instant that it arrives at a certain point of the circumference of the circle *AFD*. This would be impossible were it not going toward *I*, inasmuch as that is the only point below the cloth *CBE* where the circle *AFD* and the straight line *FE* intersect.[81]

---

[78] "Il est donc evident que de toutes les divisions de la determination au mouvement, qui sont infinies, l'autheur n'a pris que celle qui luy peut servir pour sa conclusion; et partant il a accommodé son *medium* à sa conclusion" (Descartes 1897–1913, 1:359).

[79] Descartes (1897–1913, 1:450–54). See also Schuster (2000).   [80] Descartes (2001, 77).

[81] Descartes (2001, 78).

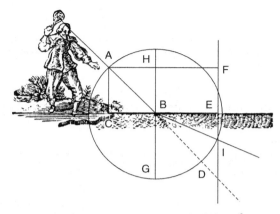

Figure 6.6 Descartes's analysis of refraction.[82]

Since the ball's total speed is reduced by half, it will move twice as far in the parallel direction after striking the cloth before reaching the distance *AB*, which represents the incident movement. The parallel component of determination after refraction generates a motion represented by *BE*, twice the parallel motion before, represented by *CB*. The refracted path, then, is given by the intersection of the line *FE* and the circle *AFD*. Notice, though, that the velocities in the refractive media are in the same proportion as the lines *CB* and *BE*, which are the sines of the angles of incidence and refraction. Made general by this and similar constructions, this yields the sine law of refraction: the ratio of the sines of the angles of incidence and refraction is equal to the ratio of the refractive indices of the media.[83]

In his letter, Fermat calls these arguments "paralogistic." His criticism stems from the fact that Descartes's constructions implicitly require a proportionality between movement and determination, even though Descartes explicitly denies there is one:

> I note first that the author has not remembered the difference he established between determination and the moving force [*force mouvante*], or the speed of movement. For it is very true that the cloth *CBE* weakens the movement of the ball, but it does not impede the continuation of its determination from high to low; and though it would be slower than before, one cannot say that, because the movement of the ball is weakened, the determination which

---

[82] Descartes (1897–1913, 6:97).
[83] Descartes reverses the modern view that light moves slower in denser media with higher refractive indices. For Descartes, a higher refractive index means light moves *faster* (or, more precisely, has a greater tendency to motion) in the material.

makes it go from high to low would change. On the contrary, its determination to move in the line *BI* is just as much composed, in the author's sense, of [the determination] that makes the ball go from high to low and the one that makes it go from left to right, as the original determination to move in the line *AB*.[84]

Descartes, that is, cannot presume that determination is merely an inclination in some direction or another, without any magnitude. For the ball always – before and after the interaction with the surface – possesses a determination in both the normal and parallel directions. Thus, "one cannot say" that the normal component has changed upon meeting the refractive surface. But this means that, taking determinations as *only* directional, the ball should continue in the same direction as before, along *BD*. Fermat concludes, correctly, that in order to reach Descartes's desired conclusion, the determination must have magnitude. In modern terms, determinations are vector quantities, not just directions. In his response to Fermat, Descartes concedes this point.[85]

Taking determinations as directed quantities, as he has shown he must, Fermat notes that the direction of a resultant determination is determined by the proportions between its components. So, for instance, the direction of the incident motion along *AB* is determined by the ratio between the parallel and normal determinations out of which it is composed. This ratio is affected by the interaction of the medium, but the direction of the resulting motion along *BI* can be generated *either* by reducing the normal determination or increasing the parallel one (or both). Descartes gives no clear reason why the parallel determination remains the same while the normal determination changes, when the same effect could be generated by the reverse. Moreover, even allowing that only the normal component changes, Descartes's construction is valid only if the change of determination is related to the change of speed, such that the change of total determination "makes up" the change in total movement. (Incidentally, this is not a straightforward proportion, but requires the change of normal

---

[84] "Ie remarque d'abbord que l'Autheur ne s'est pas souvenu de la différence qu'il avoit establie entre la determination & la force mouvante, ou la vitesse du mouvement. Car il est bien vray que la toile *CBE* affoiblit le mouvement de la balle, mais elle n'empesche pas qu'elle ne continue sa determination de haut en bas; & quoy que se soit plus lentement qu'auparavant, on ne peut pas dire que, parce que le mouvement de la balle est affoibly, la determination qui la faict aller de haut en bas soit changée. Au contraire sa determination a se mouvoir dans la ligne *BI* est aussi bien composée, au sens de l'Autheur, de celle qui la faict aller de haut en bas, & de celle qui la faict aller de la gauche à la droitte, comme la premiere determination a se mouvoir dans la ligne *AB*" (Descartes 1897–1913, 1:466–67).

[85] Descartes admits that "the determination cannot be without some speed, although the same speed can have different determinations, and the same determination can be combined with various speeds" (Descartes 1897–1913, 2:18). See Sabra (1981, 120), Garber (1992a, 192).

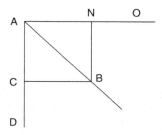

Figure 6.7 Fermat's parallelogram composition of motions.[86]

determination to vary with the cosine of the angle of incidence.) In other words, Fermat notices that the power of direction is proportional to the power of movement, which Descartes denies. Descartes, therefore, "falls again into his first mistake, not distinguishing the determination of the force from the movement."[87]

Finally, Fermat proposes to "plainly destroy"[88] Descartes's sine law by deriving, from what he takes to be Descartes's own premises, a different law of refraction. In fact, the refutation fails, since Fermat is mistaken about Descartes's assumptions. Indeed, this results from yet another confusion about direction, determination, and movement caused by Descartes's failure to clearly articulate the distinctions. Fermat mistakes Descartes's view by taking the change of normal determination to be independent of the total movement. Thus, he takes the change of normal motion to be constant for all incident angles, whereas Descartes supposes that the total refracted speed, in any direction, is the constant quantity.[89] Again, Descartes's view entails that total determination is proportional to total movement, but this is contrary to what he says, and Fermat is understandably confused.[90]

Setting these details aside, though, what is important for my purposes is that, in order to present his refutation, Fermat provides a parallelogram composition of "moving forces." That is, Fermat supplies the rule of vector composition missing in Descartes's analyses. The passage is worth quoting at length:

[86] Descartes (1897–1913, 1:469).
[87] "Voyez comme il retombe dans sa premier faute, ne distinguant pas la determination de la force du mouvement" (Descartes 1897–1913, 1:468).
[88] "Mais pour destruire plainement la proposition" (Descartes 1897–1913, 1:468).
[89] See Sabra (1981, 124).
[90] Sabra, who lays the blame on Fermat (1981, 123–25), is too generous to Descartes, who expressly contradicts his earlier statements. See also Mahoney (1973, 375–90).

Let us consider the two [straight lines] *DA* and *AO* [in Figure 6.7], which contain the angle *DAO*, of whatever size you like;[91] and let us imagine a heavy body at point *A* that descends in the line *ACD*, while at the same time, the line advances toward *AN*, provided that it always makes the same angle with *AO*, and that the point *A* of the same line *ACD* is always in the line *AN*. If the two movements, of the line *ACD* toward *AO* and of the same body in the line *ACD*, are uniform, as we can suppose, it is certain that the composed movement will carry the body always in a straight line, such as *AB*. If you take a point of this [line], such as *B*, from which you draw the lines *BN* and *BC*, parallel to the lines *DA* and *AO*, such that at the time the body reaches *B*, it would have been at *C* had there been only the movement on *ACD*, and it would have been at *N* had there been only the other motion [on *ANO*], and the proportion of the force that carries the body along *AD* to the force that carries it along *AO* is as *AC* to *AN*, which is to say as *BN* to *BC*. This kind of composed motions served Archimedes and the other ancients in the composition of their helixes, where the principle property is that the two moving forces do not at all impede one another, and remain always the same.[92]

Fermat again unambiguously takes motion to be a vector quantity, with both a direction and a magnitude, and he represents two uniform motions as the sides of a parallelogram, *AC* and *AN*. Their combination, he shows, is represented by the diagonal, here *AB*. Moreover, Fermat repeats the construction a second time, with much the same effect. However, this time, he considers the components as "moving forces" with "lines of direction." In other words, he converts the first, kinematic presentation that combines motions into a dynamic presentation that combines forces to produce a motion. For Fermat, the difference is not significant, since he assumes that the "moving force" is simply proportional to the motion it creates.

Note, though, that the parallelogram construction necessarily depends on an oriented representation of space. Fermat takes the line *AO* to orient the space, such that the motion along *ACD* is always the "same" so long as it

---

[91] The fact that the angle *DAO* in Fermat's diagram appears right is incidental. The angle can be "whatever size you like," and he indeed gives a construction in which *DAO* is obtuse in the same letter.

[92] "Considerons les deux *DA* & *AO*, qui comprennent l'angle *DAO*, de quelque grandeur que vous voudrés; & imaginons un grave au point A qui descende dans la ligne *ACD*, en mesme temps que la ligne s'avance vers *AN*, a telle condition qu'elle fasse toujours mesme angle avec *AO*, & que le point *A* de la mesme ligne *ACD* soit tousiours dans la ligne *AN*. Si les deux mouvements, de la ligne *ACD* vers *AO*, et du mesme grave dans la ligne *ACD*, sont uniformes, comme nous les pouvons supposer, il est certain que ce mouvement composé conduira tousiours le grave dans une ligne droitte comme *AB*; dans laquelle si vous prenez un point, comme *B*, duquel vous tiriés les lignes *BN* & *BC*, paralleles aux lignes *DA* & *AO*; lors que le grave sera au point *B*, en un temps esgal, s'il n'y eust eu que l'autre mouvement tout seul, il eust esté au point *N*; et la proportion de la force qui le conduit sur *AD* a sa force qui le conduit vers *AO*, sera comme *AC* a *AN*, c'est-a-dire comme *BN* a *BC*. C'est de cette sorte de mouvements composés que se servent Archimede & les autres anciens en la composition de leurs Helices; desquelles la principalle proprieté est que les deux forces mouvantes ne s'empeschent point mutuellement, ains demeurent tousiours les mesmes" (Descartes 1897–1913, 1:468–69).

"always makes the same angle with *AO*." That is, the direction of the motion stays the "same" if and only if it stays parallel to itself. Parallel lines of the same length, like *AC* and *NB*, thus represent one and the same motion, even when combined with another motion, here along *AO* as *AN* or *CB*. Fermat, then, brings the tacit assumption of an oriented representation of space in Descartes's early physical theory to light. He expressly describes the motion of bodies according to the oriented framework, and he uses that framework to support the parallelogram composition of oblique motions.

Fermat's correspondence with Descartes is an important moment in the history of physics, as it establishes the centerless, oriented framework as the fundamental descriptive framework for physical theory, and it codifies the parallelogram rule for the representation of composed motions. Fermat corrects Descartes's assumption that the "force" of motion, the speed of motion, and its direction could all be treated separately. Fermat combines these all into a single vector quantity, assuming that the "force" of motion is proportional to the motion itself. Fermat also introduces the parallelogram composition of motions into the descriptive apparatus of physical theory. As Fermat humbly comments, the parallelogram representation of "this [composed] movement has not come into wide use."[93] For the first time, the identification of parallel directions is taken as general and fundamental.

There is an important postscript to this episode. Sometime afterwards, Fermat's friend and mentor Gilles Personne de Roberval authored "Observations on the Composition of Movements, and on the Method of Finding the Tangents to Curved Lines."[94] This, too, offers an oriented representation of motions, explicit even in the definitions that begin the treatise, among which are the following:

> Power is a moving force.
> Impression is the action of this power.
> The line of direction of the impression is that by which the power moves the body.
> We call impressions similar or diverse according to whether their lines of direction are parallel among themselves [*lignes de direction sont entre elles paralleles*], or not, etc.[95]

[93] "Mais pource que ce mouvement ne vient pas si bien dans l'usage" (Descartes 1897–1913, 1:469).
[94] "Observations sur la composition des mouvemens, et sur le moyen de trouver les touchantes des lignes courbes." Mersenne sent this to Descartes for comment in 1648 (Descartes 1897–1913, 5:203–08, 661n). Roberval presented it to the Royal Academy in 1668 (Roberval 1693, 67).
[95] "Puissance est une force mouvante.
Impression est l'action de cette puissance.
La ligne de direction de l'impression est celle par laquelle la puissance meut le mobile.
Nous appellons les impressions semblables, ou diverses, suivant que leurs lignes de direction sont entre elles paralleles, ou ne le sont pas, &c" (Roberval 1693, 69).

Roberval explicitly identifies forces with actions along parallel lines. Two forces are in the "same direction" if they are parallel to one another, and they are different if they are not. Roberval expressly sets up a descriptive framework in which parallel pointings are to be identified as the "same direction." Roberval, that is, introduces the oriented representation of space as a fundamental and universal principle. Directions, he says, are to be described without reference to any center.

Roberval immediately follows his definitions with his first theorem, the parallelogram composition of motions:

> If a moving body is carried by two different movements, each straight and uniform, the movement composed of these two will be a movement straight and uniform, different from them, but always in the same plane, such that the straight line the body describes will be the diagonal of a parallelogram, the sides of which will be proportional to the speeds of the two movements; and the speed of the composed [movement] will be to each of the component [movements] as the diagonal to each of the sides.[96]

This proposition directly follows, Roberval says, from the description of directions expressed by his definitions, in which the "same line [of direction] moves always parallel to itself."[97] The oriented representation of space, as in Fermat, supports a parallelogram composition of forces.

Roberval goes on to use the parallelogram construction to criticize, in passing, Descartes's *Optics*, along the same lines as Fermat. He notes, in particular, that Descartes "has confused the terms 'impression' or 'speed' and 'determination', which he however distinguished just a bit before."[98] He also uses the parallelogram composition to correct the derivations found in the text. However, his main interest is the "general method for finding tangents to curves" in mathematics, so he lets the mechanical matter drop. Roberval, like Fermat, treats motion only kinematically. In the his treatise, Roberval does not offer descriptions of real phenomena, even the path of a projectile, let alone causal explanations of changes of directions or motions. Instead, he consigns this line of investigation to a prospectus for an unfulfilled "project for a book of mechanics treating composed movements."[99] Still, Roberval

---

[96] "Si un mobile est porté par deux divers movemens chacun droit & uniforme, le mouvment composé de ces deux fera un mouvement droit & uniforme différent de chacun d'eux, mais toutefois en mesme plan, en sorte que la ligne droite que décrira le mobile fera le diamétre d'un parallelogramme, les costez duquel seront entre eux comme les vîtesses de ces deux mouvemens; & la vîtesse du composé sera à chacun des composans comme le diamétre à chacun des costez" (Roberval 1693, 70).

[97] "la mesme ligne se meut toûjours parallelement a soy-mesme" (Roberval 1693, 71).

[98] "Secondement, expliquant la réfraction de la bale dans l'eau, il a confondu les termes d'impression ou vitesse, & de détermination, lesquels pourtant il avoit distinguez peu auparavant" (Roberval 1693, 75).

[99] Roberval (1693, 112–13).

states as a universal descriptive principle, without qualification as to size, scale, or the phenomena involved, that space is to be represented as oriented, and directions "are parallel among themselves" (*sont entre elles parallèles*).[100] In the hands of Fermat and Roberval, the representation of space is finally and definitively oriented.

It is worth lingering, finally, on Roberval's one and only "axiom," that "the direction of a moving power of a body, which describes the circumference of a circle by its movement [i.e., is moving along the arc of a circle], is the line perpendicular to the extremity of the diameter, at the end where the body is found."[101] Since Roberval has coordinated directions with parallels, and in circular motion the perpendiculars at each point are not parallel, it follows that the "direction changes at each point of the circumference."[102] In other words, Roberval points out that in an oriented representation of space, motion along a curved line, such as a circle, involves a continual *change* of direction. Therefore, orbital motion is a dynamic process, the result of a constant application of the force needed to change the direction. It is not, as Descartes held, a state of static equilibrium, in which all forces are balanced. The importance of this simple statement — orbital motion *changes* direction — cannot be overstated, as we shall see. Equally significant, though, is that it can only be stated as a general truth in the context of a fundamental and universal oriented representation of space.[103]

Conclusion

Descartes's early physics and geometry implicitly contained an oriented representation of space. The fundamental mechanics of colliding hard bodies was described according to an oriented representation of homogeneous and isotropic space. Thus, at the most basic level, stipulated spatial centers are not required by Descartes's physics. He supposed that directions are identifiable in and of themselves, without reference to any center, which is to say that they are parallel to themselves throughout space. As his mature philosophy developed, this oriented description of phenomena became part of his metaphysics. In an oriented representation of space, straight-line

---

[100] Roberval (1693, 69).

[101] "La direction d'une puissance mouvant un mobile, lequel par son mouvement décrit une circonference de cercle, est la ligne perpendiculaire à l'extrémité du diamétre, au bout duquel le mobile se trouve" (Roberval 1693, 69).

[102] "D'où il s'ensuit que cette direction change à chaque point de la circonférence" (Roberval 1693, 70).

[103] See Shea (1996, 463): "Descartes never took the decisive step of identifying change in direction with change in motion."

motion is "simple" – it does not change direction. Thus, the fact that God acts simply explains why bodies tend to move rectilinearly. However, in Descartes's mature theory, the oriented representation of space is supplanted by the centered representations of large-scale plena. Though it is fundamental, the oriented representation of space is not a universal descriptive framework for Descartes.

The oriented representation of space became universally applicable in the hands of Descartes's critics, Fermat and Roberval, responding to Descartes's *Optics*. Fermat, especially, generalized the implicit suggestion in Descartes's own work into an explicit descriptive framework, including the vector representation of motions and forces and their parallelogram composition. Then Roberval, following Fermat, explicitly stated the oriented framework as part of the definitional identifications of his theory of composed motions. Of course, the oriented framework was consonant with Descartes's own fundamental metaphysics of bodies and motion, and Fermat's and Roberval's more detailed kinematics became standard alongside the widespread acceptance of Descartes's philosophy.[104]

Lurking in the background of all this, of course, is the principle of conserved motions. It was noted in Chapter 5 that the explanatory principle only became the modern principle of rectilinear inertia in association with an oriented representation of space. Following Roberval, the oriented representation of space was firmly ensconced as a part of mechanics. Motions were henceforth to be represented as directed linear magnitudes – as vectors – subject to parallelogram compositions. Consequently, conserved motion was coordinated with rectilinear translation. Uniform motion in a straight line was now simple, unchanging motion. It was up to the Cartesian physicists to extend this explanatory principle to actual phenomena.

We have seen how Descartes more or less set aside the mathematical description of phenomena, which he had pursued in his youth, in favor of a more qualitative, explanatory project in his mature *Principles*. That text expounded an all-encompassing metaphysics consisting of extended bodies interacting only by contact action, but it mostly avoided representations of these entities in mathematical terms. Thus, Descartes did not offer mathematical laws to coordinate his explanatory natural philosophy with

---

[104] As we shall see in Chapter 7, the parallelogram rule was published in 1671 in John Wallis's textbook, *Mechanica*. A version of the parallelogram rule is also stated in Jacques Rohault's *Traité de Physique*, also first published in 1671 (Rohault 1671, 105–07). Rohault's book was very popular. Reprinted numerous times, it became the standard physics text into the eighteenth century. See also Costabel (1966).

concrete phenomenal magnitudes – despite the fact that the ontology of extended magnitudes warranted the reality of geometrical descriptions. Instead, this became the primary project of Descartes's immediate successors, who sought Galilean-style quantifications to accompany Descartes's mechanistic ontology.

One significant area of work was the characterization of the Cartesian vortex.[105] In particular, physicists sought a mathematical expression for the centrifugal force acting on bodies in the vortex, which Descartes said was responsible for both light and gravity, and thus played a central role in his physical system. For instance, Christiaan Huygens, the leading theoretical physicist in the generation following Descartes, accepted vortices as the cause of celestial and terrestrial gravitation. However, he thought Descartes had not finished the job of explaining the operation of a vortex. In particular, he felt that Descartes had not satisfactorily shown how the basic physical principles, governing collisions between two particles at a time, gave rise to the centrifugal and centripetal forces in a rotating ensemble of particles:

> We understand the nature of straight movement well enough, and the laws which govern bodies in the exchange of their movements, when they collide. But as much as one considers this sort of movement, and the reflections which arise from [collisions] between the parts of matter, one finds nothing which determines them to tend towards a center.[106]

Huygens accepted the laws governing the motions of colliding bodies, but he did not see how this essentially rectilinear behavior could bring about a centrifugal tendency in the subtle fluid and thus a tendency toward the center in heavy bodies. (In effect, he accused Descartes of replacing the Aristotelians' unexplained tendency toward a center with an unexplained tendency away from a center.) Hence one finds Huygens attempting to work out a complete, mathematical theory of vortex motion, particularly in *De Vi Centrifuga* (completed by 1659, published 1703)[107] and *Discourse de la Cause de la Pesanteur* (published 1690, though also written earlier).

Note that, in a sense, Huygens's attempt to link the explanation of small-scale phenomena, collisions, with that of global- and cosmic-scale phenomena, the vortices, was also an attempt to unify the oriented framework used to represent collisions with the centered representation of space applicable to vortices. Since these two sets of explanations were associated with

[105] See Aiton (1972). [106] *Discours de la Cause de la Pesanteur* (Huygens 1888–1950, 21:451)
[107] The text itself was not published until 1703, but its theorems were appended to *De Horologium Oscillatorium*, published in 1673, a copy of which Huygens presented to Newton. See discussion in Chapter 7, below.

different representations of space, Huygens's unifying project entailed, in part, demonstrating how the oriented framework applied to collisions could "build up" into the centered space associated with vortices. The explanatory synthesis required a descriptive one.

In the end, Descartes's vortical account of terrestrial and celestial phenomena sent his successors into something of a blind alley. The physics of vortices is associated with a centered representation of space, in which motion around the center is described as an unchanging motion, always in the same direction. As a result, the orbit of planets is represented – in the work of Huygens, for example – as a static case of equilibrium. Vortices continue to rotate because there is no net force acting on the bodies in them. Their radial tendencies away from the center are counteracted by the pressure of the medium. But this, among other difficulties, renders the commonalities between the planets' particular motions (expressed by Kepler's laws) inexplicable. Each planet moves as it does because it always has, not because some force is *causing* its specific motion. Huygens was forever perplexed by how vortices could, let alone must, produce elliptical orbits.

Another area of focus was the correction of Descartes's collision rules from Part II of the *Principles*. These were notoriously inconsistent. They predicted wildly divergent outcomes for similar or even identical interactions. By 1656, Huygens had developed a corrected collision rule by applying Galileo's principle that shared motions are unobservable. Significantly, this solution also followed Fermat and Roberval in measuring motions as directed magnitudes – i.e., as vector quantities.[108] In other words, Huygens coordinated the Cartesian conservation principle with a directed magnitude. The conserved quantity became momentum, the vector product of mass or bulk and motion, not, as it had been for Descartes, simply the scalar product or "quantity of motion." For Huygens, the conservation principle stated in the *Principles* applies to a directed motion, as in the modern theory, not speed and direction separately, as in Descartes. He re-described the phenomena to fit with the explanation.

Huygens discussed this solution with some members of the Royal Society upon a visit to England in 1661, where he found an interested audience including Christopher Wren and John Wallis.[109] Later, in 1668, perhaps occasioned by the arrival of a book on the subject by Giovanni Borelli,[110] the secretary of the Society, Henry Oldenburg, solicited papers from Wren, Wallis, and Huygens. All responded with a similar theory, depending on the

---

[108] In *De Motu Corporum ex Percussione*, published in 1703.   [109] Bennett (1975).
[110] *De Vi Percussionis.* See Hall (1966, 28).

conservation of momentum, and their papers were all published the following year.[III] This episode is well known, but I mention it here to demonstrate the widespread interest in mathematical representations of collision and the concurrent acceptance of Fermat's and Roberval's descriptive framework in the 1660s.

Chapter 7 will address the final consolidation of this descriptive framework with explanations using inertial and gravitational principles to explain terrestrial and celestial phenomena alike in Isaac Newton's physical theory.

[III] The papers by Wren and Wallis were published together in the *Philosophical Transactions*. Huygens's paper first appeared in the *Journal des Sçavans*, but it was reprinted in the *Transactions* shortly thereafter (Hall 1966; Blackwell and Huygens 1977).

CHAPTER 7

Incline it to verge: *Newton's spatial synthesis*

Introduction

I near the end of the tale. We saw in Chapter 6 how Descartes made an oriented representation of space, associated with rectilinear inertia, the fundamental spatial framework in his physical theory, thereby reversing Galileo's Archimedean approximation. We also saw how he nevertheless stopped short of applying that framework to celestial phenomena – his vortices were described in relation to their center. Even Fermat and Roberval, who stated the generality of oriented space in principle, did not actually associate it with planetary motions. This fell to Isaac Newton, who applied the oriented framework to the heavens, thereby unifying the terrestrial and the celestial into a single physical system – a physics that did not depend on geometric centers. This synthesis combined the attractive force Newton called gravity – first conceived in an oriented space by Kepler – with the force of inertia – rectified by Galileo and Descartes – using the parallelogram composition of motions – announced by Fermat and Roberval.

It has often been noted that Newton was spurred toward the completion of his theory of universal gravitation, published in 1687 in his *Philosophiae Naturalis Principia Mathematica*, by an epistolary exchange with Robert Hooke in 1679.[1] What is less clear, however, is just what it was about the earlier correspondence that contributed to Newton's ultimate triumph. Indeed, Newton and Hooke themselves debated the latter's contribution in a testy and protracted dispute once the book was published. In 1679, Newton was already mathematically skilled, and he was well-versed in mechanics and astronomy, so he had all the explanatory and analytical resources found in the *Principia* at his disposal. Yet he was unprepared to

---

[1] This story has been told most thoroughly by Ofer Gal (2002). An overview of secondary literature on the topic is provided by Guicciardini (2005). See also Lohne (1960), Westfall (1971, 424–39), De Gandt (1995, 139–58), Brackenridge and Nauenberg (2002).

answer Hooke's simple question about the shape of a planetary orbit under the influence of an inverse-square force. Newton had followed Descartes in associating a centered representation of space with planetary motions. Hooke's key suggestion was that this way of describing the action of an attractive force was inappropriate, and that planetary motion should be described in relation to an orientation. Applying this oriented representation of space opened the door to an application of the parallelogram rule to analyze the interaction of inertial and attractive forces. This analysis, in turn, became the heart of Newton's mathematical treatment – set down as the first proposition of the *Principia*.

Hooke's query

In November 1679, Hooke authored a cordial but tentative letter to Newton, then Lucasian Professor at Cambridge.[2] Hooke was fulfilling his official duties as Secretary of the Royal Society, re-establishing contact with a wayward Fellow who had been distant from the Society's activities for several years. Hooke was wary, since Newton's withdrawal from the Society had been partly his own doing – Newton had been aggrieved by Hooke's criticism of his papers on optics earlier in the decade. Hence, the letter is apologetic, attributing any animosity to the intrigues of others,[3] and careful to guarantee secrecy if Newton should desire it. "Differences in opinion," Hooke writes, "should not be the occasion of Enmity."

The letter itself asks Newton for comment on some theories and observations discussed by the Fellows in London, and seeks any ideas Newton might have to communicate to the group. In particular, Hooke seeks Newton's help with his own idea of "compounding the celstiall motions of the planetts of a direct motion by the tangent & an attractive motion towards the centrall body."[4]

For several years, Hooke had been trying to convince his peers that the Cartesian vortex theory of planetary motions was inadequate. The problem, he noted, was precisely the descriptive inconsistency discussed in Chapter 6. Descartes's fundamental explanatory principles, the conservation principle and the collision rules, are stated in association with an oriented representation of space. Hence, bodies tend to move in straight lines, and an external force is required to bend them into other paths. However, Descartes

---

[2] Turnbull (1960, 2:297–300).
[3] Though he is unnamed, the reference is to Henry Oldenburg, from whom Hooke inherited the post of Secretary in 1677.
[4] Turnbull (1960, 2:297).

described planetary motions in vortices using a centered representation of space. On this account, the centrifugal tendency of the planet is counterbalanced by the resistance of the medium, such that there is no net force, and therefore no change of motion. But in the centered representation, the unchanging motion is a circular revolution around the center. Hence, for Descartes, all that is required to set a planet in orbit is the initial impetus to set it (and the surrounding vortex) moving. Once the equilibrium is established, no further force is necessary to keep it in a curved path.

Hooke saw that the fundamental, small-scale oriented framework should be applied to planetary motion, too. The "same" motion always in the "same" direction does not preserve its relation to a center, but remains equally deflected from an orientation. As a result, a circular orbit is not the same motion throughout, but a continual *change* of direction, requiring the constant action of a non-zero external force. As Hooke argued in a 1666 address to the Royal Society:

> I have often wondered, why the planets should move about the sun according to Copernicus's supposition, being not included in any solid orbs (which the antients possibly for this reason might embrace) nor tied to it, as their center, by any visible strings; and neither depart from it beyond such a degree, nor yet move in a strait line, as all bodies, that have but one single impulse, ought to do: For a solid body, moved in a fluid, towards any part, (unless it be protruded aside by some near impulse, or be impeded in that motion by some other obviating body; or that the medium, through which it is moved, be supposed not equally penetrable every way) must persevere in its motion in a right line, and neither deflect this way nor that way from it. But all the celestial bodies, being regular solid bodies, and moved in a fluid, and yet moved in circular or elliptical lines, and not strait, must have some other cause, besides the first impressed impulse, that must bend their motion into that curve.[5]

The planets are just solid bodies, Hooke says, so they should obey the same laws that govern small solid corpuscles. They should, that is, "persevere" in a straight line. The curved orbits, meanwhile, require the continuous application of "some other cause, besides the first impressed impulse" to "bend their motion into that curve." Hooke goes on to suggest that the "second cause of inflecting a direct motion into a curve may be from an attractive property of the body placed in the center; whereby it continually endeavours to attract or draw it to itself."[6] Thus, as he puts it to Newton, the celestial motion is compounded "of a direct motion by the tangent & an attractive motion towards the centrall body."

[5] Birch (1756, 2:91).   [6] Birch (1756, 2:91).

Hooke illustrated his idea with a conical pendulum – a pendulum set moving obliquely to the axis of suspension. Like planets, such pendulums move in ellipses, and Hooke suggested that inertial "endeavour" was along the tangent, while the continuous "endeavour" toward the center served to turn the motion inward, "inflecting" it into a curve. However, as Hooke well knew, the dynamics of a pendulum and those of the planets were not the same. Most importantly, "the conatus of returning to the center in a pendulum is greater and greater, according as it is farther and farther removed from the center, which seems to be otherwise in the attraction of the sun; as I may afterwards farther explain."[7] The central force, that is, is directly proportional to the distance to the center in the case of a pendulum, but seems to diminish in some other proportion to the distance for the planets, as Hooke hopes to "farther explain." The trouble was that Hooke was an insufficiently skilled mathematician to work out the mathematics of the force law causing the "inflection."[8] He asked his more adept peers for help,[9] but by 1679, Hooke had still not reached a solution. Hence his query to Newton.

Newton's early thoughts on orbits

As it happened, Newton was a good person to ask. He was known to be mathematically astute, as his manuscripts on fluxions and infinite series had been circulating since the early 1670s. Moreover, since the beginning of his days as a Cambridge undergraduate in 1661, Newton had pursued a keen interest in theoretical dynamics, in particular orbital dynamics. Though untutored in the subject,[10] he came under the dominant influence of Descartes and Galileo, both of whom he cites in his notebooks. In particular, Newton worked carefully through Descartes's *Principles*, paralleling the work that was going on elsewhere. Thus, independently of Huygens and the rest, Newton attempted to apply the kind of quantitative treatment one finds in Galileo's work to the theory of collisions and vortex motion.

One of the first entries in a bound notebook, dating from around 1665 and known as the *Waste Book*, is an attempt to measure the force needed to keep a body in a circular orbit. Newton approaches this problem by considering a body bouncing around inside an immovable spherical

---

[7] Birch (1756, 2:92).

[8] Hooke may have not been far off. He produced a geometrical solution in 1685, though this may have been after seeing (or hearing about) one of Newton's early *De Motu* papers, which contained the key composition of motions by the parallelogram rule (Pugliese 1989; Nauenberg 1994; Gal 2005, 530; Nauenberg 2005).

[9] Especially Christopher Wren (Lohne 1960, 14–16; Bennett 1975).   [10] Whiteside (1970, 6).

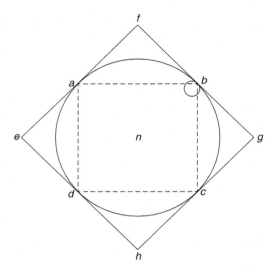

Figure 7.1 Body rebounding in a spherical shell.[11]

shell, following regular-polygonal paths. At each vertex, the body is deflected away from the inner surface of the shell toward the next vertex. Newton shows that the total resistance exerted by the shell in a complete revolution is to the ball's "movement" as the perimeter of the orbit is to the radius of its circumscribing circle.[12] The same proportion, therefore, will hold in the limit as the number of sides goes to infinity, so that the path coincides with a circle:

> [B]y the same proceeding if the Globe *b* [in Figure 7.1] were reflected by each side of a circumscribed polygon of 6, 8, 12, 100, 1000 sides etc. the force of all the reflections is to the force of the bodys motion as the sume of those sides to the radius of the circle about which they are circumscribed. And so if [the] body were reflected by the sides of an equilaterall circumscribed polygon of an infinite number of sides (i.e. by the circle it selfe) the force of all the reflections are to the force of the bodys motion as all those sides (*id est* the perimeter) to the radius.[13]

In a circular orbit, the force required to keep the body moving in a circle is to the body's motion as the circumference is to the radius, that is, as 2π. This yields, in turn, a crude measure of the force: the force exerted on the

---

[11] Herivel (1965, 130).   [12] Herivel (1965, 7–10).   [13] Herivel (1965, 130).

revolving body in the time it passes through an arc equal to the radius (i.e., $1/2\pi$ of a complete orbit) is equal to the force necessary to create a "movement" in a similar body equal to that of the revolving body. That is, the force acting on the body through that portion of the orbit would produce a speed in another body equal to the speed of the orbiting body.

This is not a particularly useful result, and the proof is conceived in ways Newton will later have reason to correct. For one thing, the force is proportional to the motion, not to its change, as Newton later will realize. Moreover, the "movement" of the body is just a product of bulk and speed – the direction is independent of the quantity of motion, as Descartes held. Thus, the body has a constant motion throughout its revolution, while the reflections against the inside of the spherical shell serve only to change the direction of the motion, not its quantity.

Even so, this early essay contains indications of Newton's thinking worth noting. First, Newton is trying to reduce orbital motion to Descartes's collision dynamics.[14] Descartes had represented a similar case as a body rotating in a sling. But a sling exerts a continuous force, not an impact, so it is difficult to coordinate this description with the collision rules at the heart of the physics. For Newton, the counteracting force is represented by an immovable shell, so that the orbit is caused by an elastic impact, thereby linking more directly the basic explanatory principles in Descartes's physics with the phenomenon of orbital motion. Second, Newton's method of approximating to the limit is already apparent. Newton approximates the action of a continuous force by a sequence of discrete, instantaneous impulses. He then takes the limit as the separation of these impulses goes to zero. As it happens, this will be the method he follows in the *Principia*.

Newton's explanatory principles eventually developed beyond Descartes's. In a later entry in the *Waste Book*, there is a re-statement of the Cartesian inertial principle:

Axiomes. And Propositions
1. If a quantity once move it will never rest unless hindered by some externall caus.
2. A quantity will always move on in the same straight line (not changing the determination nor the celerity of its motion) unless some externall cause divert it.[15]

---

[14] Newton was an early devotee of the mechanical philosophy, having read Descartes, Gassendi (in Charleton's translation), Boyle, Hobbes, and other mechanists as an undergraduate (Westfall 1980, 89).
[15] Herivel (1965, 141).

Aside from the parenthetical insertion, this repeats the import of Descartes's first two laws of nature. First, motion is conserved, and cannot be destroyed unless a contrary force is applied. A separate, second principle says that direction is conserved insofar as bodies tend to move in straight lines, and a force is required to deflect motion into some other path.[16] But Newton's parenthesis adds something distinctive to Descartes's conservation principles. It connects them, specifying that conserved motion changes neither direction ("determination") *nor* speed ("celerity"). Like Fermat, Roberval, and others, Newton realizes that speed and direction are not conserved separately, as for Descartes, but as one.[17] The conserved quantity is a directed magnitude. So, for instance, an elastic reflection does not conserve the "quantity of motion," changing only "determination," but is itself a changed motion. In other words, Newton coordinates the conservation principle with uniform rectilinear translation. Motion conserved is uniform motion in a straight line.

Later in the *Waste Book*, Newton states this explicitly as a consolidated inertial principle:

> Ax: 100. Every thing doth naturally persevere in that state in which it is unlesse it bee interrupted by some externall cause, hence axiome 1st and 2d [i.e., those quoted above] and A body once moved will always keepe the same celerity, quantity and determination of its motion.

Here, the parenthetical elaboration becomes the principle itself. "Celerity, quantity [which amount to the same thing] and determination" of motion are conserved.

Note also that Newton's second "axiom" identifies unique directions or "determinations" with straight lines. Motion in the same direction is motion along a straight line. This implies, therefore, that Newton is here associating the conservation principle with an oriented representation of space. Directions are to be described in relation to rectilinear orientations, for it is only in such a framework that an arbitrary straight line is always described as being in the same direction. He describes direction throughout space, not just at a place, in relation to a line, not a center. It follows, then, that Newton adopted the inertial principle of conserved motion and associated it with an oriented representation of space in his earliest physical thinking. Newton had the modern inertial principle from the start. In this, at least, Cartesian influence was strong and significant.

Later, Newton would depart from Descartes's physical principles, however. In particular, he retreated from Descartes's insistence on contact

---

[16] See *Principles* II.37–39 (Descartes 1983, 59–60).   [17] Whiteside (1970, 10).

action. In Cartesian physics, bodies can only be set in motion by the acquisition of some quantity of motion from other bodies in contact with them. Newton was eventually more ecumenical. He admitted "forces" generally as the causes of motion, measuring a "force" by the change of motion it produced, regardless of the causal process actually responsible. Thus, Newton's "forces" *might* be contact actions or not – it made no difference to the physical theory – and in the case of gravity, he famously "feigned no hypotheses."[18] (This feature of Newton's explanatory innovation, as controversial as it was, is not germane to the following discussion, and I will leave further commentary to the abundant literature.)

At the descriptive level, on the other hand, Newton's representation of orbital motions did not easily escape Descartes's slide into a centered framework. *All* Newton's treatments of orbital motion prior to 1679 are framed in a centered representation of space. We have already seen that Newton's first treatment of orbital motion presumed that a circular motion would be conserved in the absence of a net force. In a later manuscript known as "On Circular Motion," probably completed before 1669, Newton revisits the measurement of the centrifugal tendency in a circular orbit:

> The endeavour [*conatus*] from the center of a body *A* [in Figure 7.2] revolving in a circle *AD* toward *D* is of such a magnitude that in the time [corresponding to movement through] *AD* (which I set very small) it would carry it away from the circumference to a distance *DB*: since it would cover that distance in that time if only it were to move freely along the tangent without hindrance to its endeavour.[19]

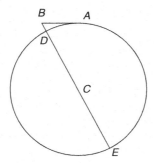

Figure 7.2 Measure of centrifugal endeavor.[20]

---

[18] Newton (1999, 392, 943).   [19] Herivel (1965, 195, the third bracketed insertion is Herivel's).
[20] Herivel (1965, 193).

Here, Newton follows Descartes in supposing the body's inertial tendency along the tangent is composed of the centrifugal tendency *DB* and the circular motion *AD*. Thus, if the centrifugal tendency is removed by the counteraction of some force, the circular motion remains, yielding the orbit. To calculate the quantity of that centrifugal tendency, Newton assumes that *DB* is proportional to the square of the time taken for the body to rotate through *AD* (Galileo's law of free fall), and by taking the limit as the distance *AD* goes to zero, Newton shows that the total centrifugal tendency in an entire orbit is proportional to the square of the velocity divided by the radius.[21] This is an ingenious result, correct as far as it goes.[22] However, it again depends on a centered descriptive framework. The circular motion is considered conserved in the absence of net forces, once the centrifugal "*conatus*" and constraining force are in equilibrium. Circular motion is the "same" all the way around.

Newton's "gross blunder"[23]

The point of all this is to show that Newton was not unprepared to respond to Hooke's overture in 1679. He had considered the dynamics of orbital motion in some detail. Still, his response was not inclined to reconciliation. Newton notes the "kindness" of Hooke's letter, but says he has "shook hands with Philosophy." Being "taken of wth other business," he declines "Philosophicall commerce" with the Royal Society and expresses ignorance of the hypotheses Hooke mentions.

Yet Newton could not help himself, and, excuses made, he proceeds to comment on some of what Hooke had related, even proposing an experiment "concerning ye descent of heavy bodies for proving ye motion of ye earth":

> Suppose then in a very calm day a Pistol Bullet were let down by a silk line from the top of a high Building or Well, the line going through a small hole made in a plate of Brass or Tinn fastened to ye top of ye Building or Well & yt ye bullet when let down almost to ye bottom were setled in water so as to cease from swinging & then let down further on an edge of steel lying north & south . . . The steel being so placed underneath, suppose the bullet be then drawn up to ye top & let fall by cutting clipping or burning the line

---

[21] Brackenridge and Nauenberg (2002, 92).

[22] Huygens published this proportion, without proof, in an appendix to his *Horologium Oscillatorium* in 1673. A presentation copy was sent to Newton, who especially noted the appendix in his letter of thanks (Turnbull 1960, 1:290).

[23] Westfall (1980, 384).

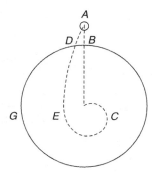

Figure 7.3 Newton's sketch of a body falling to the center.[24]

of silk, & if it fall constantly on ye east side of ye steel it will argue ye diurnall motion of ye earth.[25]

Of course, this is none other than the fall from a high place described in Galileo's *Dialogo*. Newton, like Sagredo, contends that the fall of a body to the east of the point over which it was dropped would prove the rotation of the earth.

Indeed, Newton's explanation is the same as Sagredo's. The falling body has more eastward motion at the start of its fall than the place beneath, since it is further from the axis of rotation:

> Suppose then *BDG* [Figure 7.3] represents the Globe of ye Earth carried round once a day about its center *C* from west to east according to ye order of ye letters *BDG*; & let *A* be a heavy body suspended in the Air & moving round with the earth so as perpetually to hang over ye same point thereof *B*. Then imagin this body *B* let fall & it's gravity will give it a new motion towards ye center of ye Earth without diminishing ye old one from west to east, by reason that before it fell it was more distant from ye center of ye earth then the parts of ye earth at wch it arrives in its fall, will be greater then the motion from west to east of ye parts of ye earth at wch ye body arrives in it's fall: & therefore it will not descend in ye perpendicular *AC*, but outrunning ye parts of ye earth will shoot forward to ye east side of the perpendicular describing in it's fall a spiral line *ADEC*, quite contrary to ye opinion of ye vulgar who think that if ye earth moved, heavy bodies falling would be outrun by its parts & fall on the west side of ye perpendicular.[26]

The falling body conserves the greater motion it has at the start of its fall and falls to the east, ahead of the earth's rotation.[27]

---

[24] Herivel (1965, 239).   [25] Turnbull (1960, 2:302).   [26] Turnbull (1960, 2:301).

[27] I do not know if Newton got his idea from Galileo, though Newton probably read Thomas Salusbury's 1670 English translation of the *Dialogo*.

Clever as it is, Newton's proposal reveals that he is still wedded to a centered representation of orbital motions. As for Galileo, the motion conserved here is the curvilinear translation from west to east. It remains the same, "undisturbed" by the "new" radial motion toward the center, because it preserves its relation to the center. If the "new" motion were not added, the body would have continued orbiting the center in a circle, always perpendicular to the center. Hence also Newton's supposition that the trajectory of the body will be a spiral – the combination of a circular motion around with a radial motion inward. The fall, that is, is away from the original circular motion. At least in this case, Newton describes the phenomenon using a centered spatial framework, just as he had in his youthful considerations on the subject.

It was now Hooke's turn to let a philosophical inclination and argumentative nature get the better of politesse. Newton had repeated Descartes's mistake by suggesting a spiral path of the falling body, and Hooke could not help pointing it out. In his reply, Hooke expresses the Society's intention to carry out the suggested experiment, but he corrects Newton's prediction of the trajectory:

> But as to the curve Line which you seem to suppose it to Desend by (though that was not then at all Discoursed of) Vizt a kind of spirall which after sume few revolutions Leave it in the Center of the Earth my theory of circular motion makes me suppose it would be very differing and nothing att all akin to a spirall but rather a kind of Elleptueid. . . . Let *ABDE* [in Figure 7.4] represent the plaine of the equinox limited by the superficies of the earth: *C* the center thereof to which the lines of Gravitation doe all tend. . . . I conceive the curve that will be described by this descending body *A* will be *AFGH* and that the body *A* would never approach neerer the Center *C* then *G* were it not for the Impediment of the medium as Air or the like but would continually proceed to move round in the Line *AFGHAFG* &c.[28]

Hooke does not explain in any detail why he thinks the path will be ellipsoidal, but the reasoning is clear enough. Instead of simply attracting the falling body to the center, the force of gravity bends the path inward from the tangent. Hence, the body will not fall into the center, but, passing by, reach a new apex on the opposite side, where the tangential motion is again directed perpendicularly to the center, at which point the process repeats. In the absence of a resisting medium, moreover, the motion of the body would *just* be an ellipse.

[28] Turnbull (1960, 2:305).

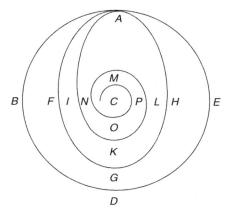

Figure 7.4 Hooke's sketch of an ellipsoid spiral.[29]

To his credit, Newton quickly understood the import of Hooke's suggestion. For one thing, he had understood from early in his career that rectilinear translation is conserved, and that the laws of motion are properly applied in an oriented representation of space. He was therefore equipped to recognize the inconsistency in his association of the inertial principle with a centered framework and, thus, a circular motion in his letter to Hooke. Indeed, he realized that Hooke was right: an extrinsic force does not simply cancel a centrifugal component of a body's motion, but bends its trajectory away from the tangent.[30]

Newton's next letter acknowledges Hooke's correction. "Your acute Letter having put me upon considering thus far ye species of this curve," Newton writes, "I might add something about its description."[31] The curve, he explains, would not be a spiral, but oscillate about the center, supposing the force to be constant:

> I agree with you yt ye body ... if its gravity be supposed uniform it will not
> descend in a spiral to ye very center but circulate with an alternate ascent &

---

[29] Herivel (1965, 241).

[30] I am not claiming that Hooke gave Newton the key to orbital dynamics by shifting the emphasis to centripetal, as opposed to centrifugal, force – at least not directly. I mean to suggest only that Hooke's representation of the phenomenon was superior to Newton's. It was a better explanatory fit with the physical principles at work, particularly rectilinear inertia. Significantly, Leibniz later disagreed. He argued that the centered representation of the orbit fit better with the available explanation, because the orbit was explained by the action of a vortex, which was itself described using a centered representation of space. See Meli (2005, 537).

[31] Turnbull (1960, 2:308).

descent made by it's *vis centrifuga* & gravity alternately overballancing one another.[32]

The terminology here is a bit awkward, but Newton means that the inertial tendency along the tangent and the gravitational tendency to the center combine to produce a trajectory that does not end at the center. The centripetal "gravity" bends the inertial motion inward, but can never turn it directly toward the center. As a result, the body will pass by the center and, the centrifugal tendency now dominating, reach another apex beyond, just as Hooke had suggested.

This becomes clearer in Newton's argument against Hooke's claim of an ellipsoid path. In an elliptical orbit, the tangents of the motions at each apse are parallel to each other. In other words, when the body reaches a point opposite from where it was released, the direction of its motion must be turned exactly 180 degrees. At quadrature, halfway to the opposite apse and even with the center of the ellipse, the motion must be perpendicular to the original motion, turned 90 degrees. This, Newton argues, cannot be so in the case Hooke describes:

> Yet I imagin ye body will not describe an Ellipsoeid but rather such a figure as is represented by *AFOGHIKL* [in Figure 7.5] &c. Suppose *A* ye body, *C* ye center of ye earth, *ABDE* quartered with perpendicular diameters *AD*, *BE*, wch cut ye said curve in *F* & *G*; *AM* ye tangent in wch ye body moved before it began to fall & *GN* a line drawn parallel to yt tangent. When ye body

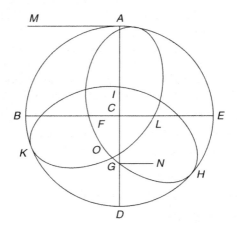

Figure 7.5 Newton's sketch of a fall in constant gravity.[33]

---

[32] Turnbull (1960, 2:307).   [33] Herivel (1965, 243).

descending through ye earth (supposed previous) arrives at G, the determination of its motion shall not be towards N but towards ye coast between N & D. For ye motion of ye body at G is compounded of ye motion it had at A towards M & of all ye innumerable converging motions successively generated by ye impresses of gravity in every moment of it's passage from A to G. . . . The innumerable & infinitly little motions (for I here consider motion according to ye method of indivisibles) continually generated by gravity in its passage from A to F incline it to verge from GN towards D, & ye like motions generated in its passage from F to G incline it to verge from GN towards C. But these motions are proportional to ye time they are generated in, & the time of passing from A to F (by reason of ye longer journey & slower motion) is greater then ye time of passing from F to G. And therefore ye motions generated in AF shall exceed those generated in FG & so make ye body verge from GN to some coast between N & D.[34]

The path of the falling body is composed of the initial rectilinear motion from A towards M and "the innumerable & infinitly little motions" caused by a continuously acting force of gravity. These "little motions" serve to change the *direction* of the original motion, "inclining it to verge" inward toward D and then back toward A again. Newton thinks that Hooke is supposing that the force is constant, so the curvature produced is proportional only to time – i.e., the number of "little motions" accumulated. But since the times spent travelling to quadrature at F and then from F to the opposing apse at G are unequal, the motion cannot be turned a perfect 180 degrees, i.e., along GN. Hence the body cannot move in an ellipse, but must move in some other curve, as Newton sketches.

The details of Newton's argument need not detain us,[35] except to note the complete reconception of direction in Newton's treatment from one letter to the next. Whereas in his first letter, the body's trajectory was composed of just two motions – the circular motion around and the radial fall to the center – the trajectory is now the result of "innumerable" motions. Circular motion had counted as a single motion in a single direction. Now it is a continual turning caused by the innumerable "inclinations to verge" in a new direction, away from that parallel to the one before. Newton, that is, has applied an oriented representation of space in order to describe the phenomenon in which motions not parallel to one another are motions in different directions and therefore different motions. Hooke's correction has rectified orbital motion. From now on, Newton will apply an oriented representation of space to all physical phenomena at all scales: from microscopic collisions to planetary motion.

---

[34] Turnbull (1960, 2:307–08).   [35] See De Gandt (1995, 151–55), Brackenridge and Nauenberg (2002).

Application of the parallelogram rule

In his response to Hooke, Newton had assumed that the force was constant throughout the interior of the planet, where he assumed the body was moving.[36] However, in his riposte, Hooke explains that he was thinking of an inverse-square force in which the "Attraction always is in a duplicate proportion to the Distance from the Center Reciprocall."[37] Hooke also supposes, attributing the view to Kepler,[38] that this is the force of attraction acting on planets, so the case in question is actually that of planetary motion, not subterranean fall. If this is so, Hooke claims, the orbit will be an ellipsoid, if not an actual ellipse:

> And that with Such an attraction the auges [apses] will unite in the same part of the Circle and that the neerest point of accesse to the center [i.e., the perigee] will be opposite to the furthest Distant [the apogee].[39]

In other words, the nearest and furthest approaches to the center will lie along an axis through the center, and the orbit will be some kind of ellipsoidal oval. But, and this was always Hooke's problem, all he could muster by way of argument for the claim was that the force should be inversely proportional to the distance (by Kepler's third law) and that planetary orbits are elliptical (by Kepler's first law). He could not *prove* that an inverse-square force would produce an elliptical orbit. For this, he needed better mathematics, which is why he called upon others to address his "hypotheses." As he put the challenge to Newton in the last substantive letter of their exchange:

> It now remains to know the proprietys [properties] of a curve Line (not circular nor concentricall) made by a centrall attractive power which makes the velocitys of Descent from the tangent Line or equall straight motion at all Distances in a Duplicate proportion to the Distances Reciprocally taken. I doubt not but that by your excellent method you will easily find out what that Curve must be, and its proprietys, and suggest a physicall Reason of this proportion.[40]

Hooke hopes that Newton can solve the geometrical properties of motion in an inverse-square force. Given the force, what is the path? Hooke begs only

---

[36] In fact, on the assumption of a constant force, Newton's diagram is remarkably similar to the actual path, despite the sketchiness of his argument. Brackenridge and Nauenberg (2002) endeavor to show that Newton's diagram was a careful construction. I am inclined to believe that Newton's thoughts were still intuitive at this juncture. See also Lohne (1960, 27–28).

[37] Turnbull (1960, 2:309).

[38] A relatively natural assumption perhaps picked up from Ismaël Boulliau's criticism of Kepler (Lohne 1960, 18).

[39] Turnbull (1960, 2:309).   [40] Turnbull (1960, 2:313).

"a word or two of you Thoughts" on the subject. Newton, for his part, did not immediately oblige.

As we have seen, the early manuscripts reveal that Newton's reticence was not for a complete lack of thoughts. Nevertheless, Newton was stumped by Hooke's query. Hooke required Newton to consider how a force might affect the *direction* of a body's motion, which, since he only considered circular motion in a centered framework, Newton had always assumed was conserved. Also, Hooke was asking, given an inverse square force, what is the orbit? All of Newton's early work inquired in the opposite direction. He considered a circular orbit as given, and tried to work out the force required to produce it. So Hooke had posed a new problem Newton could not answer: how can the composite action of inertial motion and the motion caused by a centripetal force be represented in a geometrically tractable way? How, that is, can the orbit be constructed? And what orbit would an inverse-square force create?

This is a question about the composition of motions, and we have already seen that composed motions in an oriented space can be represented by the parallelogram rule. In fact, Newton knew this. A version appears in the *Waste Book*. In one note, he states:

> If the body *b* [in Figure 7.6] move in the line *bd* and from the point *d* two lines *da, dc* be drawne the motion of the body *b* from *ad* is to its motion from *dc* as *ab* parallel to *dc* is to *cb* parallel to *ad*.[41]

That is, the motion of the body along *bd* can be decomposed into motions along *da* and *dc*. This decomposition rule is immediately followed by the inverse rule for compositions:

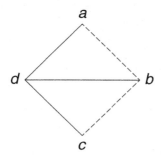

Figure 7.6 Parallelogram construction in the *Waste Book*.[42]

[41] Herivel (1965, 182).   [42] Herivel (1965, 182).

Coroll 1. the body *b* receiving two divers forces from *a* and *c* and the force from *ba* is to the force from *bc* as *ba* to *bc* then draw *ad* parallel to *bc* and *cd* parallel to *ab* and the body *b* shall be moved in the line *bd*.[43]

In other words, if two forces separately move a body away "from" the perpendiculars *ba* and *bc*, then the resulting combined motion will be along the diagonal of the completed rectangle, *bd*. Note, though, that the motion along *da* is motion "from" – i.e., normal to – *dc*, and *vice versa*. Thus, this only describes a decomposition of motion into *perpendicular* components. It is not a general statement of the parallelogram rule.

A more comprehensive statement of the parallelogram rule appears in a manuscript Newton titlted "The Laws of Motion," where it appears as the third "rule":

If a body *A* [in Figure 7.7] move towards *B* with the velocity *R*, and by the way hath some new force done to it which had the body rested would have propelled it towards *C* with the velocity *S*. Then making *AB:AC::R:S*, and completing the Parallelogram *BC* the body shall move in the Diagonall *AD* and arrive at the point *D* with this compound motion in the same time it would have arrived at the point *B* with its single motion.[44]

The combination of two independent motions, proportional to and in the directions of *AB* and *AC*, is the motion proportional to and in the direction of *AD*, the diagonal of the completed parallelogram.

It is not entirely clear how Newton arrived at the parallelogram rule. For one thing, the dating of "The Laws of Motion" paper is not certain. However, one plausible source is the work of John Wallis, Savilian Professor of Geometry at Oxford, and one of the Fellows of the Royal Society who had successfully corrected Descartes's rules of collision, with Wren and Huygens, in 1669. During the late 1660s, Wallis was writing for the Royal Society a compendium textbook on physics: the *Mechanica; sive, de Motu, Tractatus Geometricus*, published in three parts, in 1670–71. This

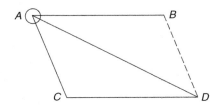

Figure 7.7 Parallelogram rule in *Laws of Motion*.[45]

[43] Herivel (1965, 182).   [44] Herivel (1965, 209).   [45] Herivel (1965, 209).

was meant to represent the state of the art of mathematical physics, and was probably composed with full knowledge of advances on the continent, such as the work of Fermat and Roberval.

The parallelogram rule appears as Proposition 6 of Part III of the *Mechanica*, published in 1671:

> If two motive causes in two directions create an impetus in a mobile, following two straight lines making an angle, the speed of each to the other in equal proportion to these lines, as given lengths of the sides of a parallelogram; then the mobile is moved along the diagonal of the parallelogram, its speed to those given as the diagonal is to the respective sides.[46]

This, of course, is the rule in full generality. While there is no direct evidence that Newton read Wallis before he wrote the "Laws of Motion" paper, all three parts of the *Mechanica* were in Newton's library. Newton also thanked a correspondent for sending the second part when it was published,[47] making it likely he would have sought out the third upon its appearance. At the very least, Wallis's text shows that the parallelogram rule was known in England by Newton's contemporaries.

Of course, as noted extensively above, the parallelogram rule presumes an oriented representation of space, since it supposes that parallel directions, and thus parallel motions, are similar. But in 1679, following the suggestion by Hooke, Newton began to apply an oriented descriptive framework to orbital motion. This made it possible to use the parallelogram rule to answer Hooke's question. Specifically, Newton could compose a body's inertial motion with the motion caused by a centripetal force according to the parallelogram rule. In fact, that is precisely what Newton proceeded to do.

The *De Motu* tracts and the *Principia*

In early 1684, Christopher Wren, the astronomer Edmond Halley, and Hooke entered into a discussion regarding planetary orbits. They agreed that the force attracting the planets to the sun decreased in proportion to the square of the distance, and that such a force created elliptical orbits. Yet they could not prove the connection. Wren even offered a reward for such a proof delivered within two months, which went unclaimed. A short time

---

[46] "Si Mobile, ob duas causas Motrices, duos concipiat directos impetus; putà secundum duas rectas positione datas, angulum facientes; Celeritatibus in se aequalibus, ad invicem verò eisdem rectis, ut parallelogrammi lateribus longitudine datis, proportionalibus: feretur Mobile per Parallelogrammi diagonium, ea celeritate quae fit ad datas, ut diagonium illud ad respectiva latera" (Wallis 1670–1671, 3:654).

[47] Harrison (1978, 259).

later, Halley thought to ask Newton and visited him in Cambridge. What curve, he asked, is produced by an inverse-square force? An ellipse, Newton famously replied, probably recalling his 1679 exchange with Hooke. Indeed, he told the surprised and delighted Halley, he had calculated the orbit.[48] Newton recreated his proof within a few months, and it was delivered to the Royal Society in November.[49] With the encouragement and support of Halley, Newton eventually published a full elaboration of this preliminary insight: the *Principia*.

All this remarkable work, from the 1684 *De Motu* manuscripts written in the aftermath of Halley's visit to the *Principia* itself, crucially depend on the parallelogram composition of an inertial motion and a centripetal attraction in an oriented representation of space. In the first *De Motu* manuscript, the rule for composing forces and motions is "Hypothesis 3": "A body is carried in a given time under the combined action of [two] forces so far as it would be carried by the forces acting separately in succession for equal times."[50] This "rather obscure formulation"[51] is intended to be the parallelogram rule, and it is used as such in the first theorem of the tract. A later version adds a lemma making the rule explicit: "Lemma 1. A body acted on simultaneously by [two] forces describes the diagonal of a parallelogram in the same time as it would the sides if the forces acted separately."[52] It also appears as "Hypothesis 3" in another manuscript likely written in the same period:

> Hyp. 3. Motions imprest in two different lines, if those lines be taken in proportion to the motions and completed into a parallelogram, compose a motion whereby the diagonal of the Parallelogram shall be described in the same time in which the sides thereof would have been described by those compounding motions apart.[53]

In the *Principia*, meanwhile, the parallelogram rule appears as Corollary 1 to the second Law of Motion:

> A body acted on by [two] forces acting jointly describes the diagonal of a parallelogram in the same time in which it would describe the sides if the forces were acting separately.[54]

As for the forces being composed, Newton assumes that one is the rectilinear inertia of the body. In the *De Motu* tracts, this appears as "Hypothesis 2" or "Law 1": "By its innate force alone a body will always proceed

---

[48] This story was told in 1727 by a friend of Newton and Halley, Abraham de Moivre, to Newton's heir and biographer, John Conduitt. See, e.g., Whiteside (1970, 18n41), Newton (1999, 12n3).
[49] This is a well-known episode. See, for instance, De Gandt (1995, 3–9), Cohen (1999, 11–17).
[50] Herivel (1965, 278).   [51] Herivel (1965, 290n6).   [52] Herivel (1965, 299–300).
[53] Herivel (1965, 246).   [54] Newton (1999, 417).

uniformly in a straight line provided nothing hinders it."[55] This is also the first Law of Motion in the *Principia*: "Every body perseveres in its state of being at rest or of moving uniformly straight forward, except insofar as it is compelled to change its state by forces impressed."[56] That is, the undisturbed motion of a body is a rectilinear translation. To deflect from a straight line is to change direction and thus to change the state of motion, which requires the exertion of some external force. Again, directions are parallel to themselves.

Finally, this inertial motion is composed with the motion caused by a centripetal force in the first theorem of the *De Motu* papers, which is repeated almost verbatim as the first proposition of the *Principia*:

> Let the time be divided into equal parts, and in the first part of the time let a body by its inherent force describe the straight line *AB* [in Figure 7.8]. In the second part of the time, if nothing hindered it, this body would (by law 1) go straight on to *c*, describing line *Bc* equal to *AB*, so that – when radii *AS*, *BS*, and *cS* were drawn to the center – the equal areas *ASB* and *BSc* would be described. But when the body comes to *B*, let a centripetal force act with a single but great impulse and make the body deviate from the straight line *Bc* and proceed in the straight line *BC*. Let *cC* be drawn parallel to *BS* and meet *BC* at *C*; then when the second part of the time has been completed, the body (by corol. 1 of the laws) will be found at *C* in the same plane as triangle *ASB*.[57]

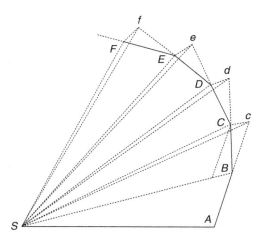

Figure 7.8 Parallelogram construction in *Principia*, Proposition 1.[58]

[55] Herivel (1965, 299). See also Herivel (1965, 277).   [56] Newton (1999, 416).
[57] Newton (1999, 444–45).   [58] Newton (1687, 37).

A body moving inertially along *AB* is subjected to a centripetal force at *B*, which adds a motion toward the center along *BS*. The composition of these two motions is given by Corollary 1 of the Laws of Motion – the parallelogram rule – such that the resulting motion of the body in the given instant is the diagonal, *BC*. At *C*, another centripetal impulse is given, adding to the inertial motion acquired in the second instant, *BC*, resulting in the motion *CD*, and so on.

This construction finally answers Hooke's challenge. The representation allows Newton to get a mathematical handle on how a centripetal force can bend an inertial trajectory into an orbit. He can geometrically measure how force changes the motion in each instant, from *AB* to *BC* to *CD*. The theorem itself proceeds to prove that the areas of the triangles formed by the radii to the center in each instant are all equal. By taking the limit as the instants become infinitesimal, Newton proves that the "areas which bodies made to move in orbits describe by radii drawn to an unmoving center of forces lie in unmoving planes and are proportional to the times."[59] Newton proves, that is, Kepler's area law for all centripetal forces.

The area law is central to Newton's analysis because it provides a geometrical measure of time – time is directly proportional to the area swept out by the radii to a body in a central force field. This allows, in turn, a comparison between forces. By setting areas equal, one can derive the motion produced by a force in equal times. Thus, the geometrical properties of orbital figures become measures of the force that produces them, and in subsequent theorems, Newton shows that an elliptical orbit is indicative of an inverse-square force, finally establishing the connection between the one and the other.[60] By measuring the amount of fall produced by a force in a given time, Newton also proves that the inverse-square attractive force acting on the moon is identical to terrestrial gravitation, and that it is found universally – acting on the bodies in the solar system. In other words, the parallelogram composition is the heart of the proof of universal gravitation.

Centerless space

The development of Newton's *Principia* has been well described by others, and there is no profit in rehearsing it here, but it remains to emphasize the

---

[59] Newton (1999, 444).

[60] An ellipse is also characteristic of a force that is directly proportional to the distance. Note that Newton actually solves the so-called "inverse problem." Halley had asked for the orbit given the force law. Newton derives the force law given the orbit.

oriented representation of space in the key theorem. The representation in Proposition 1 assumes that the two distinct motions in each instant do not change – the external centripetal force is only exerted at the beginning of an instant, and no force acts once the impulse is received. Yet the motions of the moving body remain parallel to each other everywhere throughout the instant, such that, in the absence of the other motion, the body would move from one side of a parallelogram to the other. The "same" motion *just means* self-parallel uniform rectilinear translation. The redescription of the planetary motions using an oriented representation of space makes Newton's final proof possible.[61]

Notice that, in effect, Newton has employed his own version of Galileo's Archimedean approximation. In actuality, all centripetal motions are convergent. The force always acts toward the center. This is what is represented in the limit of Newton's construction, when the instants are vanishingly small. Yet in the approximation, when the instants are finite, the centripetal motion remains parallel to itself in each instant. In other words, the inertial motion is combined with a descent that is everywhere parallel to itself – just as in Galileo, where the inertial horizontal motion is combined with a self-parallel vertical fall. This approximation, dependent on an oriented representation of the (small) space, has the same effect – it makes the physical situation mathematically tractable.

There is also a trace of Kepler's solution to the problem of the versed sines here. In Newton's representation, the orbiting body continues its motion due to its (Cartesian) linear inertia, which takes the place of Kepler's *anima motrix*.[62] To this movement is added a motion to the center, caused by the action of the centripetal force, which is the evolution of Kepler's *vis insita*. The path of the body is then derived from a composition of the two motions. Newton's analysis, however, relies on the assumption that the two motions of the body – one inertial, the other gravitational – remain parallel to themselves throughout the instant in question. In other words, the motions are not directed toward any presupposed center, but are directed along presupposed, self-parallel orientations – the parallel actions are the *same* action. Newton, like Kepler, assumes that the force moving the body toward the center respects an orientation, not a center. The attractive force, always acting toward the center, is continually acting in *different* directions.

---

[61] For further discussion of the role of spatial geometry in Newton, see Stein (1967), DiSalle (1995, 2006), Huggett (2012).

[62] Newton knew of Keplerian astronomy from Thomas Streete's *Astronomia Carolina* (1661) (Westfall 1980, 94).

This assumption of an oriented space allows Newton to treat the motion of the planets using the same rectilinear framework used to represent collisions, at least in each instant of the orbit. This Newtonian synthesis of small-scale and cosmic space depends, in part, on the fact that the spatial framework used to represent inertia, derived from Descartes, has the same oriented structure as the one Newton uses to represent the gravitational force, as in Kepler. The common oriented framework renders the forces commensurate.[63]

Newton has thus unified the small-scale oriented space of contact collisions with the cosmic space of planetary orbits. By treating all phenomena using a single descriptive framework, Newton could use one set of explanations in all parts of space and at all spatial scales. In other words, the descriptive synthesis allowed Newton to assimilate all phenomena, both celestial and terrestrial, into one explanatory scheme – the Newtonian Synthesis. The shift to an oriented representation of space, for both terrestrial and celestial phenomena, was an essential and enabling feature of Newton's remarkable physical system.

Once Newton adopted the oriented, isotropic representation of space, points lost their causal efficacy. It was no longer possible to explain a body's fall by appealing to a unique geometric center, since the representation of space rendered such a point conceptually unavailable. Likewise, it became necessary to explain why planets remained in their orbit without assuming they innately respected a central point. An explanation based on an object's tendency toward, away from, around, or along some geometric entity became incoherent in an oriented space, where all such entities are arbitrarily determined.

This was the ultimate answer to the Averroist question that had motivated Copernicus. Averroës had wondered where the center of the universe was, for Aristotelian physics depended on where bodies were situated with respect to that center. That spatial relationship, and thus the center itself, possessed physical efficacy: bodies naturally moved toward, away from, or around that center. In Newtonian physics, however, centers are not physically operative in and of themselves, *qua* geometric points. A center might represent a body, but bodies themselves move with respect to other bodies, in response to physical forces exerted between those bodies. Physical theory no longer required the specification of a unique center.

---

[63] For the relation between Newtonian and Cartesian space, see McGuire (1983). Note that Newton's views on space developed through his career. His early *De Gravitatione* privileges closed geometric solids, including spheres, as the basis of spatial descriptions. Later, Newton bases his treatment of space on straight lines. See Newton (1962). For a discussion of Newton's metaphysics of space, see Janiak (2008, ch. 5).

In the modern era, the links between description and explanation have become more explicit, especially in the context of general relativity. To solve the Einstein field equations is just to determine the representation of space. For instance, the affine structure from a solution specifies which directions are to be counted as identical. This representation of space then explains the inertial and gravitational behavior of bodies – inertial movement is just the movement along the geodesics in the affine structure. Description and explanation continue to interact, but now they do so more explicitly. Even so, general relativity assumes that the micro-structure of space is homogeneous, isotropic, and self-parallel. It assumes, that is, a fundamentally oriented representation of space.

Where is the center? There are no centers.

CHAPTER 8

Conclusion: methodological morals

It remains to draw some morals. Of course, the persuasiveness of my conclusions depends upon the reader's reception of what has come before, but I hope to have earned some measure of sympathy.

Little more needs to be said about the epistemological and historical claims made in the introduction. The historical narrative substantiates the layered model of scientific theories I have proposed: theories comprise both explanatory principles and a descriptive framework that coordinates the principles with the phenomena. In a physical theory, the descriptive framework contains a representation of space that specifies how the spatial features of phenomena are to be described. Representations of space, moreover, were central to the theoretical developments of the early modern period. What had been described by referring to a stipulated center at the beginning of the seventeenth century was described in relation to a given orientation at its end – the centered Aristotelian cosmos had given way to the oriented space of modern physics. Most importantly, parallel directions were identified such that simple and unchanging motion was associated with uniform rectilinear translation. This shift was integral to the notable advances in physical theory at the center of the Scientific Revolution. The advent of the Keplerian account of celestial motions, of the modern principle of rectilinear inertia, and of Newton's theory of universal gravitation all essentially depended on adopting an oriented representation of space. Thus, the story of the Scientific Revolution is, in large part, a story about representations of space.

Beyond this, though, there is an opportunity for broader observations addressing the historiographical method I have followed. The first point is an obvious one: there really was a revolution in physics and astronomy during the early modern period. In the century and a half between 1543 (the date of Copernicus's *De Revolutionibus*) and 1687 (that of Newton's *Principia*), understanding of the physical world underwent a drastic revision. Aristotelian physics, and the Ptolemaic astronomy based on it, had long prevailed as the dominant account of natural facts. This theory constituted a remarkably coherent and powerful edifice, which could successfully accommodate all manner of terrestrial and celestial phenomena. Yet in a very short time, this entire theoretical structure was overturned and replaced by a recognizably modern physics. A completely new understanding of the world emerged in which little, if anything, of the old remained.

Historians have looked at the rapidity and totality of the theoretical shifts involved and concluded that an account of the period in terms of explanatory progress is impossible. After all, this "Copernican Revolution" was Thomas Kuhn's archetype of a "paradigm shift" – the conceptual frameworks marking its beginning and end were so different as to constitute different worlds.[1] How is it possible to trace a narrative connection between endpoints that are so fundamentally discontinuous? Such changes seem unaccountable. They must involve illogical leaps or "conversion experiences." Furthermore, the reasoning goes, if a paradigm shift is really just a conversion experience, then it cannot be explained in epistemic terms. One might be able to show the practical, political, or social causes of such a drastic reconceptualization of natural understanding, but one cannot say that the new theory was adopted because it provided better explanations than the old. Because the origin and end of the change are completely discontinuous, there is no rational basis for a comparison – neither for the historical actors nor for modern historians. This line of thought has engendered a predominant style in recent history of science, which eschews intellectual causes in favor of extrascientific factors in accounts of scientific change. Scholars with this perspective deny that there was a *scientific* revolution – a revolution *in science*.[2]

A consideration of representations of space might seem at first only to reinforce this position. How could one, it might be asked, hope to explain the change of something as basic as the meaning of "up" and "down," or of what counts as "the same motion"?

But the success of my narrative, I hope, has demonstrated that historians of science can construct coherent narratives of revolutionary scientific change in epistemic terms. On my account, the origin and end of the theoretical development are indeed discontinuous, but they are connected by a sequence of continuous steps from one intermediate theory to the next. By distinguishing distinct explanatory and descriptive layers within a scientific theory, I have shown how theoretical changes at one level could be made while the other level remains fixed – a process I have called reciprocal

---

[1] Kuhn (1957; 1996, esp. ch. 10).   [2] See Miller (2011b).

iteration. Authors alternately adjusted their explanatory principles and their descriptive coordinations as they attempted to improve their explanations of observed phenomena. New descriptive coordinations were accepted if they better accommodated the same explanatory principles to the phenomena; and new explanatory principles were accepted if they better accounted for the same descriptions of phenomena. A succession of changes at both levels might eventually render a newer theory incomparable with a predecessor, but changes at each level remain both explicable and accountable as explanatory progress.

As a result, it is possible to tell the story of the early modern revolution in physics and astronomy as a revolution *in science*. One can explain the developments as a sequence of attempts to improve theoretical explanation. Though the actors involved were certainly sensitive to practical, political, and social concerns, one is not *compelled* to appeal to such factors to account for a scientific revolution. A coherent account can be based on scientific considerations alone.

The other side of the same coin bears a message for historians of philosophy. If one can offer an explanation of the scientific revolution I have described in scientific terms, there is also no compulsion to fall back on metaphysical considerations in order to account for its novel conception of space and associated theoretical innovations. The authors responsible for the shift in descriptive coordinations in early modern physics and astronomy were not *primarily* concerned with the substantial properties of space. They altered their descriptions of space primarily for the benefit of theoretical explanation, not for speculative consistency. What mattered was the epistemology of space – how it was understood within physical theories – not its metaphysics. The authors in the period evinced little interest in earlier philosophical accounts of space, and whatever investigations of the nature of space (or body, or motion) they did pursue were ancillary to the physics. As I noted in the introduction, the history of changing representations of space is the development of empirical theories within physics and astronomy in response to particular explanatory and empirical problems. The oriented representation of space came about close to the phenomenal ground, so to speak, not in the metaphysical clouds.

This shows, in turn, that historians of philosophy can be and should be more circumspect with respect to empirical science. In attempting to make sense of the history of philosophy, scholars have tended to emphasize the historical analogues of contemporary philosophy over those of modern science. Thus, for instance, authors who engaged in more speculative theorizing, such as Leibniz or Spinoza, have attracted more attention than those who toiled closer to the phenomena and generally refrained from systematic philosophy, like Galileo. The same is true for the more philosophical work of authors who also engaged in empirical research, such as Descartes. Yet the Scientific Revolution was an essential catalyst for the consequent revolutions in philosophy, leading to the Enlightenment and beyond. Certainly many of the philosophical innovations by Descartes, Leibniz, Spinoza, Malebranche, Locke, Berkeley, Hume, Kant, and others were directly inspired by the new ways of explaining nature. Thus, it seems that the history of empirical science is significantly understudied by historians of philosophy. Newton's stature has increased in the past few years, but Copernicus, Kepler, and Galileo, at least, also deserve more prominent places in the philosophical canon.

The process of reciprocal iteration also highlights the importance of each author's *dynamic* role in intellectual developments. Making sense of early modern physics requires an examination of how theories change, both within the work of each author and between successive authors. Resolving the discontinuities of the period into a continuous sequence of theoretical shifts demands close attention to the intellectual moves each player made. But this approach also stands in contrast to the usual method in the history of philosophy. Historians of philosophy – or, more generally, philosophers interested in philosophical history – tend to survey the work of an individual author in an attempt to systematize disparate pronouncements into a single viewpoint. This treats the author as a static corpus and elides the development of his or her ideas. Scholars thus tend to see variations within an author's work as discrepancies to be reconciled rather than developments to be accounted for. I do not wish to paint with too broad a brush. There are many historians of philosophy, especially recently, who emphasize the diachronic progression of ideas across authors' careers. And in any case, a thorough understanding of any individual's general way of thinking is an invaluable counterpart to attempts to account for particular changes of mind. Yet there is much to be gained by further emphasizing change within the views of individual authors and by expanding historical attention across multiple authors in order to tell a wider story of intellectual development. The illumination of how Galileo's work progressed and how it fit with Descartes's, for instance, is just as important as the study of Galileo or Descartes alone.

The focus on individuals also tends to encapsulate scholars in the conceptual frameworks particular to each author. Naturally, this aids systematization of the author's work and helps avoid anachronism. Hence, many historians strive to remain faithful to the explicit conceptual apparatus – the "actors' categories" – peculiar to each author. However, this encapsulation can obscure important connections. Conceptual frameworks vary even between successive thinkers, and are certainly variable across any significant length of time. Thus, a coherent story spanning the entire seventeenth century could not have been told in the terms of its individual actors alone. It was necessary to articulate an analytical framework that transcended them. In this case, I had to identify a unit of analysis – representation of space – that could plausibly be identified between texts and between authors. By seeking the representations of space implicit in the work of each author, I could tie their positions together and show the development of a single concept across the entire period. If the use of representation of space as a means of historical investigation is an anachronism, it is a fruitful and necessary one, and not to be ruled out of hand.

This last point stresses the importance of the integrated history and philosophy of science as the scholarly methodology I have tried to follow. I argued for an epistemology of scientific knowledge and change *at the same time* as I tried to tell a story about a historical episode. Indeed, I could not have pursued one of these ends without the other. The coherence of the historical narrative would have been unachievable without the philosophical hypotheses by which it was constructed. The historical narrative, meanwhile, provided the evidence for the philosophical thesis. This was not mere bootstrapping – a tautological and ahistorical "rational reconstruction." The history and the philosophy together withstood scrutiny of the historical evidence by careful textual interrogation. An inability to use the epistemological framework to construct a coherent narrative comporting with the evidence would have told against both. Recalcitrant data could have called – and may yet call – the entire enterprise into question. Conversely, the strength of the story I have told shows that integrated history and philosophy of science can be profitably used to produce illuminating scholarship. If the foregoing has been at all successful, then it has demonstrated the usefulness of integrated history and philosophy of science.

References

Acloque, Paul 1982. "Histoire des Expériences pour la Mise en Évidence du Mouvement de la Terre," *Cahiers d'Histoire et de Philosophie des Sciences* 4 (new series): 1–141.

Aiton, Eric J. 1969. "Kepler's Second Law of Planetary Motion," *Isis* 60: 75–90.

1972. *The Vortex Theory of Planetary Motion*. New York: Elsevier.

1973. "Infinitesimals and the Area Law," in Fritz Krafft, Karl Meyer, and Bernhard Sticker (eds.), *Internationales Kepler-Symposium, Weil der Stadt 1971*. Hildesheim: Gerstenberg.

1981. "Celestial Spheres and Circles," *History of Science* 19: 75–114.

Amico, Giovanni Battista 1536. *De Motibus Corporum Coelestium Iuxta Principia Peripatetica Sine Eccentricis et Epicyclis*. Venice: Ioanne Patavino et Venturino Roffinello.

Anderson, Wallace E. 1976. "Cartesian Motion," in Peter K. Machamer and Robert G. Turnbull (eds.), *Motion and Time, Space and Matter*. Columbus: Ohio State University Press, pp. 200–23.

Aristotle 1984. *The Complete Works of Aristotle*, edited by Jonathan Barnes. Princeton: Princeton University Press.

Barbour, Julian B. 2001. *The Discovery of Dynamics: A Study from a Machian Point of View of the Discovery and the Structure of Dynamical Theories*. Oxford: Oxford University Press.

Barker, Peter 1999. "Copernicus and the Critics of Ptolemy," *Journal for the History of Astronomy* 30: 343–58.

Barker, Peter, and Goldstein, Bernard R. 1994. "Distance and Velocity in Kepler's Astronomy," *Annals of Science* 51: 59–73.

2001. "Theological Foundations of Kepler's Astronomy," *Osiris* 16: 88–113.

Beeckman, Isaac 1939–1953. *Journal Tenu par Isaac Beeckman de 1604 à 1634*, edited by Cornelis De Waard. 4 vols. Le Haye: Martinus Nijhoff.

Bennett, Jim A. 1975. "Hooke and Wren and the System of the World: Some Points Towards An Historical Account," *British Journal for the History of Science* 8: 32–61.

Birch, Thomas 1756. *The History of the Royal Society of London for Improving of Natural Knowledge*. 4 vols. London: A. Millar.

Blackwell, Richard J. 1966. "Descartes' Laws of Motion," *Isis* 57: 220–34.

Blackwell, Richard J., and Huygens, Christiaan 1977. "Christiaan Huygens' *The Motion of Colliding Bodies*," *Isis* 68: 574–97.

Blair, Ann 2008. "Natural Philosophy," in Katherine Park and Lorraine Daston (eds.), *The Cambridge History of Science, Volume 3: Early Modern Science*. Cambridge: Cambridge University Press, pp. 365–406.

Boner, Patrick J. 2006. "Kepler's Living Cosmology: Bridging the Celestial and Terrestrial Realms," *Centaurus* 48: 32–39.

2008. "Life in the Liquid Fields: Kepler, Tycho and Gilbert on the Nature of the Heavens and Earth," *History of Science* 46: 275–97.

Bos, Henk 1981. "On the Representation of Curves in Descartes' *Géométrie*," *Archive for History of Exact Sciences* 24: 295–338.

2001. *Redefining Geometrical Exactness: Descartes' Transformation of the Early Modern Concept of Construction*. New York: Springer.

Bowen, Alan C. 2002. "Simplicius and the Early History of Greek Planetary Theory," *Perspectives on Science* 10: 155–67.

2007. "The Demarcation of Physical Theory and Astronomy by Geminus and Ptolemy," *Perspectives on Science* 15: 327–58.

Brackenridge, J. Bruce, and Nauenberg, Michael 2002. "Curvature in Newton's Dynamics," in I. Bernard Cohen and George E. Smith (eds.), *The Cambridge Companion to Newton*. Cambridge: Cambridge University Press, pp. 85–137.

Brigandt, Ingo 2010. "The Epistemic Goal of a Concept: Accounting for the Rationality of Semantic Change and Variation," *Synthese* 177: 19–40.

Brown, Harvey R. 2005. *Physical Relativity: Space-Time Structure from a Dynamical Perspective*. Oxford: Oxford University Press.

Burtt, Edwin A. 1954. *The Metaphysical Foundations of Modern Physical Science*. Garden City, NY: Doubleday.

Butterfield, Herbert 1957. *The Origins of Modern Science*. London: G. Bell.

Büttner, Jochen 2008. "Big Wheel Keep on Turning," *Galilaeana* 5: 33–62.

Camerota, Michele, and Helbing, Mario 2000. "Galileo and Pisan Aristotelianism: Galileo's 'De Motu Antiquiora' and the Quaestiones de Motu Elementorum of the Pisan Professors," *Early Science and Medicine* 5: 319–65.

Carnap, Rudolf 1950. "Empiricism, Semantics, and Ontology," *Revue Internationale de Philosophie* 4: 20–40.

Caspar, Max 1959. *Kepler*, translated by C. Doris Hellman. London: Abelard-Schuman.

Chang, Hasok 2004. *Inventing Temperature: Measurement and Scientific Progress*. Oxford: Oxford University Press.

Chen-Morris, Raz 2001. "Optics, Imagination, and the Construction of Scientific Observation in Kepler's New Science," *Monist* 84: 453–86.

Clagett, Marshall 1959. *The Science of Mechanics in the Middle Ages*. Madison: University of Wisconsin Press.

Clarke, Desmond M. 1996. "The Concept of *Vis* in Part III of the Principia," in Jean-Robert Armogathe and Giulia Belgioioso (eds.), *Descartes: Principia Philosophiae (1644–1994)*. Naples: Vivarum, pp. 321–39.

Clavelin, Maurice 1983. "Conceptual and Technical Aspects of the Galilean Geometrization of the Motion of Heavy Bodies," in William R. Shea (ed.), *Nature Mathematized*. Dordrecht: D. Reidel, pp. 23–50.

Cohen, I. Bernard 1999. *A Guide to Newton's Principia*. Berkeley: University of California Press.

Copernicus, Nicolaus 1543. *De Revolutionibus Orbium Coelestium, Libri VI*. Nuremburg: Iohannes Petreus.

　　1976. *On the Revolutions of the Heavenly Spheres*, translated by A. M. Duncan. London: David and Charles.

　　1978. *On the Revolutions*, translated by Edward Rosen, edited by Jerzy Dobrzycki. Baltimore: Johns Hopkins University Press.

　　2002. *On the Revolutions of the Heavenly Spheres*, translated by Charles Glen Wallis, edited by Stephen Hawking. Philadelphia: Running Press.

Costabel, Pierre 1966. "Varignon, Lamy, et le Parallélogramme des Forces," *Archive Internationales d'Histoire des Sciences* 19: 103–24.

Davidson, Donald 1967. "Causal Relations," *Journal of Philosophy* 64: 691–703.

Davis, A. E. L. 1992. "Kepler's 'Distance Law' – Myth Not Reality," *Centaurus* 35: 103–20.

　　2003. "The Mathematics of the Area Law: Kepler's Successful Proof in *Epitome Astronomiae Copernicanae* (1621)," *Archive for History of Exact Sciences* 57: 355–93.

De Gandt, François 1995. *Force and Geometry in Newton's Principia*, translated by Curtis Wilson. Princeton: Princeton University Press.

De Risi, Vincenzo 2007. *Geometry and Monadology: Leibniz's* Analysis Situs *and Philosophy of Space*. Basel: Birkhäuser Verlag.

Dear, Peter 1995. *Discipline and Experience: The Mathematical Way in the Scientific Revolution*. Chicago: University of Chicago Press.

　　1998. "Method and the Study of Nature," in Daniel Garber and Michael Ayers (eds.), *The Cambridge History of Seventeenth-Century Philosophy*. Cambridge: Cambridge University Press, pp. 147–77.

Descartes, René 1897–1913. *Oeuvres de Descartes*, edited by Charles Adam and Paul Tannery. 13 vols. Paris: Léopold Cerf.

　　1983. *Principles of Philosophy*, translated by Valentine Rodger Miller and Reese P. Miller. Dordrecht: D. Reidel.

　　1985–1991. *The Philosophical Writings of Descartes*, edited and translated by John Cottingham, Robert Stoothoff, Dugald Murdoch, and Anthony Kenny. 3 vols. Cambridge: Cambridge University Press.

　　1998. *The World and Other Writings*, translated by Stephen Gaukroger. Cambridge: Cambridge University Press.

　　2001. *Discourse on Method, Optics, Geometry, and Meteorology*, translated by Paul J. Olscamp. Indianapolis: Hackett.

Di Bono, Mario 1995. "Copernicus, Amico, Fracastoro and Ṭūsī's Device: Observations on the Use and Transmission of a Model," *Journal for the History of Astronomy* 26: 133–54.

Dijksterhuis, E. J. 1961. *The Mechanization of the World Picture*, translated by C. Dikshoorn. Princeton: Princeton University Press.

DiSalle, Robert 1995. "Spacetime Theory as Physical Geometry," *Erkenntnis* 42: 317–37.

2006. *Understanding Space-Time*. Cambridge: Cambridge University Press.

Domski, Mary 2009. "The Intelligibility of Motion and Construction: Descartes' Early Mathematics and Metaphysics, 1619–1637," *Studies in History and Philosophy of Science* 40: 119–30.

2013. "Descartes' Mathematics," in Edward N. Zalta (ed.), *The Stanford Encyclopedia of Philosophy*. http://plato.stanford.edu/archives/fall2013/entries/descartes-mathematics/.

Donahue, William H. 2008. "Astronomy," in Katherine Park and Lorraine Daston (eds.), *The Cambridge History of Science, Volume 3: Early Modern Science*. Cambridge: Cambridge University Press, pp. 562–95.

Drake, Stillman 1970. *Galileo Studies*. Ann Arbor: University of Michigan Press.

1978. *Galileo at Work*. Chicago: University of Chicago Press.

1986. "Reexamining Galileo's Dialogue," in William A. Wallace (ed.), *Reinterpreting Galileo*. Washington, D.C.: Catholic University of America Press, pp. 155–78.

1999. *Essays on Galileo and the History and Philosophy of Science*, edited by Noel M. Swerdlow and Trevor Harvey Levere. 3 vols. Vol. 2. Toronto: University of Toronto Press.

Drake, Stillman, and Drabkin, I. E. 1969. *Mechanics in Sixteenth-Century Italy*. Madison: University of Wisconsin Press.

Dreyer, J. L. E. 1953. *A History of Astronomy from Thales to Kepler*. New York: Dover.

Dugas, René 1941. "Sur l'Origine du Théorème de Coriolis," *Revue Scientifique Illustrée* (*Revue Rose*) 79: 267–70.

1988. *A History of Mechanics*, translated by J. R. Maddox. New York: Dover Publications.

Duhem, Pierre 1913. *Études sur Léonard de Vinci III: Les Précurseurs Parisiens de Galilée*. Paris: Hermann.

1969. *To Save the Phenomena, an Essay on the Idea of Physical Theory from Plato to Galileo*, translated by Edmund Doland and Chaninah Maschler. Chicago: University of Chicago Press.

Earman, John 1989. *World Enough and Space-Time*. Cambridge: MIT Press.

Epicurus 1987. "Letter to Herodotus," in A. A. Long and D. N. Sedley (eds.), *The Hellenistic Philosophers*. New York: Cambridge University Press.

Feldhay, Rivka 1995. "Producing Sunspots on an Iron Pan," in Henry Krips, J. E. McGuire, and Trevor Melia (eds.), *Science, Reason, and Rhetoric*. Pittsburgh: University of Pittsburgh Press, pp. 119–44.

1998. "The Use and Abuse of Mathematical Entities," in Peter Machamer (ed.), *The Cambridge Companion to Galileo*. Cambridge: Cambridge University Press, pp. 80–145.

Ferguson, Kitty 2002. *Tycho and Kepler: The Unlikely Partnership that Forever Changed Our Understanding of the Heavens*. New York: Walker and Company.

Field, J. V. 1988. *Kepler's Geometrical Cosmology*. Chicago: University of Chicago Press.

Finocchiaro, Maurice A. 1980. *Galileo and the Art of Reasoning*. Dordrecht: D. Reidel.

2001. "Aspects of the Controversy about Galileo's Trial (from Descartes to John Paul II)," in José Montesinos and Carlos Solís (eds.), *Largo Campo di Filosofare: Eurosymposium Galileo 2001*. La Orotava, Tenerife: Fundación Canaria Orotava de Historia de la Ciencia, pp. 491–512.

Fracastoro, Girolamo 1584. "Homocentricorum, sive de Stellis," in *Hieronymi Fracastorii Veronensis Opera Omnia*. Venetiis: Apud Juntas, pp. 1–48.

Franklin, Allan 1976. *The Principle of Inertia in the Middle Ages*. Boulder: Colorado Associated University Press.

Fredette, Raymond 2001. "Galileo's *De Motu Antiquiora*: Notes for a Reappraisal," in José Montesinos and Carlos Solís (eds.), *Largo Campo di Filosofare: Eurosymposium Galileo 2001*. La Orotava, Tenerife: Fundación Canaria Orotava de Historia de la Ciencia, pp. 165–81.

Freudenthal, Gad 1983. "Theory of Matter and Cosmology in William Gilbert's *De magnete*," *Isis* 74: 22–37.

Friedman, Michael 1983. *Foundations of Space-Time Theories: Relativistic Physics and Philosophy of Science*. Princeton: Princeton University Press.

1999. "Geometry, Convention, and the Relativized A Priori: Reichenbach, Schlick, and Carnap," in *Reconsidering Logical Positivism*. Cambridge: Cambridge University Press, pp. 59–70.

2001. *Dynamics of Reason*. Stanford: CSLI Publications.

2008. "Descartes and Galileo: Copernicanism and the Metaphysical Foundations of Physics," in Janet Broughton and John Carriero (eds.), *A Companion to Descartes*. Malden, MA: Blackwell, pp. 69–83.

Furley, David J. 1976. "Aristotle and the Atomists on Motion in a Void," in Peter K. Machamer and Robert G. Turnbull (eds.), *Motion and Time, Space and Matter*. Columbus: Ohio State University Press, pp. 83–100.

Gabbey, Alan 1971. "Force and Inertia in Seventeenth-Century Dynamics," *Studies in History and Philosophy of Science* 2: 1–67.

Gal, Ofer 2002. *Meanest Foundations and Nobler Superstructures: Hooke, Newton and the Compounding of the Celestial Motions of the Planets*. Boston: Kluwer Academic Publishers.

2005. "The Invention of Celestial Mechanics," *Early Science and Medicine* 10: 529–34.

Gal, Ofer, and Chen-Morris, Raz 2005. "The Archaeology of the Inverse Square Law: (1) Metaphysical Images and Mathematical Practices," *History of Science* 43: 391–414.

2012. "Nature's Drawing: Motion as Mathematical Order in Kepler and Galileo," *Synthese* 185: 429–66.

Galilei, Galileo 1890–1909. *Le Opere di Galileo Galilei*, edited by A. Favaro. 20 vols. Florence: Barbèra.

1957. *Discoveries and Opinions of Galileo*, translated by Stillman Drake. New York: Doubleday.

1960a. "On Mechanics," in I. E. Drabkin and Stillman Drake (eds.), *On Motion, and On Mechanics*. Madison: University of Wisconsin Press, pp. 133–86.

1960b. "On Motion," in I. E. Drabkin and Stillman Drake (eds.), *On Motion and On Mechanics*. Madison: University of Wisconsin Press, pp. 13–114.

1967. *Dialogue Concerning the Two Chief World Systems*, translated by Stillman Drake. Berkeley: University of California Press.

1989. *Two New Sciences*, translated by Stillman Drake. Toronto: Wall and Emerson.

1997. *Galileo on the World Systems*, edited and translated by Maurice A. Finocchiaro. Berkeley: University of California Press.

Galilei, Galileo, and Fredette, Raymond 2000. *De Motu Antiquiora*. http://echo.mpiwg-berlin.mpg.de/content/scientific_revolution/galileo/englishtranslation

Galilei, Galileo, and Scheiner, Christoph 2010. *On Sunspots*, edited and translated by Eileen Reeves and Albert Van Helden. Chicago: University of Chicago Press.

Galuzzi, Massimo 1980. "Il Problema delle Tangenti nella 'Géométrie' di Descartes," *Archive for History of Exact Sciences* 22: 36–51.

Garber, Daniel 1992a. *Descartes' Metaphysical Physics*. Chicago: University of Chicago Press.

1992b. "Descartes' Physics," in John Cottingham (ed.), *The Cambridge Companion to Descartes*. Cambridge: Cambridge University Press, pp. 286–334.

2001. *Descartes Embodied*. Cambridge: Cambridge University Press.

2008. "Physics and Foundations," in Katherine Park and Lorraine Daston (eds.), *The Cambridge History of Science, Volume 3: Early Modern Science*. Cambridge: Cambridge University Press, pp. 21–69.

Gaukroger, Stephen 1995. *Descartes: An Intellectual Biography*. Oxford: Clarendon Press.

2002. *Descartes' System of Natural Philosophy*. Cambridge: Cambridge University Press.

2006. *The Emergence of a Scientific Culture: Science and the Shaping of Modernity, 1210–1685*. Oxford: Oxford University Press.

Gilbert, William 1600. *De Magnete, Magneticisque Corporibus, et de Magno Magnete Tellure, Physiologia Nova*. London: Peter Short.

1651. *De Mundo Nostro Sublunari Philosophia Nova*. Amstelodami: Ludovicum Elzevirium.

1958. *De Magnete*, translated by P. Fleury Mottelay. New York: Dover Publications.

Gingerich, Owen 1975. "'Crisis' Versus Aesthetic in the Copernican Revolution," *Vistas in Astronomy* 17: 85–95.

1992. "Johannes Kepler and the Rudolphine Tables," in *The Great Copernicus Chase*. Cambridge, MA: Sky Publishing, pp. 123–31.

2003. "The Galileo Sunspot Controversy: Proof and Persuasion," *Journal for the History of Astronomy* 34: 77–78.

2004. *The Book Nobody Read: Chasing the Revolutions of Nicolaus Copernicus*. New York: Walker and Company.

2013. "Galileo's Copernican Conversion," in John W. Hessler and Daniel De Simone (eds.), *Galileo: Starry Messenger*. Delray Beach, FL: Levenger, pp. 146–52.

Gingerich, Owen, and Van Helden, Albert 2011. "How Galileo Constructed the Moons of Jupiter," *Journal for the History of Astronomy* 42: 259–64.

Giusti, Enrico 1998. "Elements for the Relative Chronology of Galilei's *De Motu Antiquiora*," *Nuncius* 13: 427–61.

Goldstein, Bernard R. 1967. "The Arabic Version of Ptolemy's Planetary Hypotheses," *Transactions of the American Philosophical Society* 57: 3–55.

2002. "Copernicus and the Origin of his Heliocentric System," *Journal for the History of Astronomy* 33: 219–35.

Goldstein, Bernard R., and Bowen, Alan C. 1983. "A New View of Early Greek Astronomy," *Isis* 74: 330–40.

Goldstein, Bernard R., and Hon, Giora 2005. "Kepler's Move from Orbs to Orbits: Documenting a Revolutionary Scientific Concept," *Perspectives on Science* 13: 74–111.

Grant, Edward 1978. "Cosmology," in David C. Lindberg (ed.), *Science in the Middle Ages*. Chicago: University of Chicago Press, pp. 265–302.

1981. *Much Ado About Nothing: Theories of Space and Vacuum from the Middle Ages to the Scientific Revolution*. Cambridge: Cambridge University Press.

Grosholz, Emily R. 1986. "A Case Study in the Application of Mathematics to Physics: Descartes' *Principles of Philosophy*, Part II," *PSA: Proceedings of the Biennial Meeting of the Philosophy of Science Association* 1986: 116–24.

1988. "Geometry, Time and Force in the Diagrams of Descartes, Galileo, Torricelli and Newton," *PSA: Proceedings of the Biennial Meeting of the Philosophy of Science Association* 1988: 237–48.

2007. *Representation and Productive Ambiguity in Mathematics and the Sciences*. Oxford: Oxford University Press.

Guicciardini, Niccolò 2005. "Reconsidering the Hooke–Newton Debate on Gravitation: Recent Results," *Early Science and Medicine* 10: 510–17.

Hahm, David E. 1976. "Weight and Lightness in Aristotle and His Predecessors," in Peter K. Machamer and Robert G. Turnbull (eds.), *Motion and Time, Space and Matter*. Columbus: Ohio State University Press, pp. 56–82.

Hall, A. Rupert 1965. "Galileo and the Science of Motion," *British Journal for the History of Science* 2: 185–99.

1966. "Mechanics and the Royal Society, 1668–70," *British Journal for the History of Science* 3: 24–38.

Hamm, Elizabeth Anne 2011. Ptolemy's Planetary Theory: An English Translation of Book One, Part A of the *Planetary Hypotheses* with Introduction and

Commentary. PhD Thesis, Institute for the History and Philosophy of Science and Technology. Toronto: University of Toronto.

Harrison, John 1978. *The Library of Isaac Newton*. Cambridge: Cambridge University Press.

Hattab, Helen 2007. "Concurrence or Divergence? Reconciling Descartes's Physics with his Metaphysics," *Journal of the History of Philosophy* 45: 49–78.

Heilbron, J. L. 1979. *Electricity in the 17th and 18th Centuries*. Berkeley: University of California Press.

2012. "Robert Westman on Galileo and Related Matters," *Perspectives on Science* 20: 379–88.

Hempel, Carl G. 1965. *Aspects of Scientific Explanation and Other Essays in the Philosophy of Science*. New York: Free Press.

Henry, John 2001. "Animism and Empiricism: Copernican Physics and the Origin of William Gilbert's Experimental Method," *Journal of the History of Ideas* 62: 99–119.

Herivel, John 1965. *The Background to Newton's* Principia: *A Study of Newton's Dynamical Researches in the Years 1664–84*. Oxford: Clarendon Press.

Hesse, Mary B. 1960. "Gilbert and the Historians (II)," *British Journal for the Philosophy of Science* 11: 130–42.

Hooper, Wallace 1998. "Inertial Problems in Galileo's Preinertial Framework," in Peter Machamer (ed.), *The Cambridge Companion to Galileo*. Cambridge: Cambridge University Press, pp. 146–74.

Huggett, Nick (ed.) 1999. *Space from Zeno to Einstein: Classic Readings with a Contemporary Commentary*. Cambridge, MA: The MIT Press.

2012. "What did Newton mean by 'Absolute Motion'?" in Andrew Janiak and Eric Schliesser (eds.), *Interpreting Newton*. Cambridge: Cambridge University Press, pp. 196–218.

Humphreys, Paul W. 1989. "Scientific Explanation: The Causes, Some of the Causes, and Nothing But the Causes," in Philip Kitcher and Wesley C. Salmon (eds.), *Scientific Explanation*. Minneapolis: University of Minnesota Press, pp. 283–306.

Huygens, Christiaan 1888–1950. *Oeuvres Complètes*. 22 vols. La Haye: M. Nijhoff.

Jammer, Max 1954. *Concepts of Space*. Cambridge, MA: Harvard University Press.

Janiak, Andrew 2008. *Newton as Philosopher*. Cambridge: Cambridge University Press.

Jardine, Nicholas 1976. "Galileo's Road to Truth and the Demonstrative Regress," *Studies in History and Philosophy of Science* 7: 277–318.

1979. "The Forging of Modern Realism: Clavius and Kepler Against the Sceptics," *Studies in History and Philosophy of Science* 10: 141–73.

1984. *The Birth of History and Philosophy of Science: Kepler's* A Defence of Tycho Against Ursus. Cambridge: Cambridge University Press.

Joy, Lynn S. 2008. "Scientific Explanation from Formal Causes to Laws of Nature," in Katherine Park and Lorraine Daston (eds.), *The Cambridge History of Science, Volume 3: Early Modern Science*. Cambridge: Cambridge University Press, pp. 70–105.

Kant, Immanuel 1998. *Critique of Pure Reason*, translated by Paul Guyer and Allen W. Wood. New York: Cambridge University Press.

Kelly, Suzanne 1965. *The De Mundo of William Gilbert*. Amsterdam: Menno Hertzberger and Company.

Kepler, Johannes 1604. *Ad Vitellionem Paralipomena Quibus Astronomiae Pars Optica Traditur*. Frankfurt: Apud Claudium Marnium et Haeredes Ioannis Aubrii.

   1937–. *Johannes Kepler Gesammelte Werke*, edited by Bayerische Akademie der Wissenschaften. Munich: C. H. Beck.

   1981. *Mysterium Cosmographicum: The Secret of the Universe*, translated by A. M. Duncan. New York: Abaris.

   1992. *New Astronomy*, translated by William H. Donahue. Cambridge: Cambridge University Press.

   1995. *Epitome of Copernican Astronomy and Harmonies of the World*, translated by Charles Glenn Wallis. Amherst, MA: Prometheus Books.

   2000. *Optics: Paralipomena to Witelo & Optical Part of Astronomy*, translated by William H. Donahue. Santa Fe, NM: Green Lion Press.

Kitcher, Philip 1978. "Theories, Theorists and Theoretical Change," *The Philosophical Review* 87: 519–47.

Koestler, Arthur 1968. *The Sleepwalkers*. New York: Macmillan.

Koyré, Alexandre 1955. "A Documentary History of the Problem of Fall From Kepler to Newton," *Transactions of the American Philosophical Society* 45: 329–95.

   1957. *From the Closed World to the Infinite Universe*. Baltimore: Johns Hopkins University Press.

   1965. *Newtonian Studies*. London: Chapman and Hall.

   1966. *Études Galiléennes*. Paris: Hermann.

   1967. "Giambattista Benedetti, Critic of Aristotle," in Ernan McMullin (ed.), *Galileo: Man of Science*. New York–London: Basic Books, pp. 98–117.

   1973. *The Astronomical Revolution: Copernicus, Kepler, Borelli*, translated by R. E. W. Maddison. Ithaca, NY: Cornell University Press.

Kozhamthadam, Job 1994. *The Discovery of Kepler's Laws*. Notre Dame: University of Notre Dame Press.

Kuhn, Thomas S. 1957. *The Copernican Revolution: Planetary Astronomy in the Development of Western Thought*. Cambridge, MA: Harvard University Press.

   1996. *The Structure of Scientific Revolutions*. 3rd edn. Chicago: University of Chicago Press.

Lakoff, George 1987. *Women, Fire, and Dangerous Things: What Categories Reveal About the Mind*. Chicago: University of Chicago Press.

Lange, Marc 2011. "Why Do Forces Add Vectorially? A Forgotten Controversy in the Foundations of Classical Mechanics," *American Journal of Physics* 79: 380–88.

Lenoir, Timothy 1979. "Descartes and the Geometrization of Thought: The Methodological Background of Descartes' *Géométrie*," *Historia Mathematica* 6: 355–79.

Levin, Michael E. 1976. "The Extensionality of Causation and Causal-Explanatory Contexts," *Philosophy of Science* 43: 266–77.

Lindberg, David C. 1976. *Theories of Vision from al-Kindi to Kepler*. Chicago: University of Chicago Press.

1986. "The Genesis of Kepler's Theory of Light: Light Metaphysics from Plotinus to Kepler," *Osiris* 2: 4–42.

Lohne, Johannes 1960. "Hooke Versus Newton: An Analysis of the Documents in the Case on Free Fall and Planetary Motion," *Centaurus* 7: 6–52.

Lucretius 1987. "De Rerum Natura," in A. A. Long and D. N. Sedley (eds.), *The Hellenistic Philosophers*. New York: Cambridge University Press.

Ludlow, Peter 2004. "Descriptions," in Ed Zalta (ed.), *Stanford Encyclopedia of Philosophy*. http://plato.stanford.edu/archives/fall2013/entries/descriptions/.

Machamer, Peter K. 1978. "Aristotle on Natural Place and Natural Motion," *Isis* 69: 377–87.

1995. "Comment: A New Way of Seeing Galileo's Sunspots (and New Ways to Talk Too)," in Henry Krips, J. E. McGuire, and Trevor Melia (eds.), *Science, Reason, and Rhetoric*. Pittsburgh: University of Pittsburgh Press, pp. 145–52.

Machamer, Peter K., and McGuire, J. E. 2009. *Descartes's Changing Mind*. Princeton: Princeton University Press.

Mahoney, Michael S. 1973. *The Mathematical Career of Pierre de Fermat (1601–1665)*. Princeton: Princeton University Press.

Maier, Anneliese 1982. *On the Threshold of Exact Science*, translated by Steven D. Sargent. Philadelphia: University of Pennsylvania Press.

Mancosu, Paolo 1996. *Philosophy of Mathematics and Mathematical Practice in the Seventeenth Century*. New York: Oxford University Press.

2008. "Descartes and Mathematics," in Janet Broughton and John Carriero (eds.), *A Companion to Descartes*. Malden, MA: Blackwell, pp. 103–23.

Manders, Kenneth 2006. "Algebra in Roth, Faulhaber, and Descartes," *Historia Mathematica* 33: 184–209.

Martens, Rhonda 2000. *Kepler's Philosophy and the New Astronomy*. Princeton: Princeton University Press.

Maull, Nancey L. 1980. "Cartesian Optics and the Geometrization of Nature," in Stephen Gaukroger (ed.), *Descartes: Philosophy, Mathematics and Physics*. Sussex: Harvester Press, pp. 253–73.

McGuire, J. E. 1983. "Space, Geometrical Objects and Infinity: Newton and Descartes on Extension," in William R. Shea (ed.), *Nature Mathematized*. Dordrecht: D. Reidel, pp. 69–112.

McLaughlin, Peter 2000. "Force, Determination and Impact," in Stephen Gaukroger, John Schuster, and John Sutton (eds.), *Descartes' Natural Philosophy*. London: Routledge, pp. 81–112.

McMullin, Ernan 1967. "Introduction: Galileo, Man of Science," in Ernan McMullin (ed.), *Galileo, Man of Science*. New York: Basic Books, pp. 1–51.

Meli, Domenico Bertoloni 2005. "Who Is Afraid of Centrifugal Force?" *Early Science and Medicine* 10: 535–43.

2008. "Mechanics," in Katherine Park and Lorraine Daston (eds.), *The Cambridge History of Science, Volume 3: Early Modern Science*. Cambridge: Cambridge University Press, pp. 632–72.

Miller, David Marshall 2008. "O Male Factum: Rectilinearity and Kepler's Discovery of the Ellipse," *Journal for the History of Astronomy* 39: 43–63.

2011a. "Friedman, Galileo, and Reciprocal Iteration," *Philosophy of Science* 78: 1293–305.

2011b. "The History and Philosophy of Science History," in Seymour Mauskopf and Tad Schmaltz (eds.), *Integrating History and Philosophy of Science*. Dordrecht: Springer, pp. 29–48.

Moody, Ernest A. 1951. "Galileo and Avempace: The Dynamics of the Leaning Tower Experiment," *Journal of the History of Ideas* 12: 163–93, 375–422.

1966. "Galileo and his Precursors," in Carlo L. Golino (ed.), *Galileo Reappraised*. Berkeley: University of California Press, pp. 23–43.

Murdoch, John E., and Sylla, Edith D. 1978. "The Science of Motion," in David C. Lindberg (ed.), *Science in the Middle Ages*. Chicago: University of Chicago Press, pp. 206–64.

Murschel, Andrea 1995. "The Structure and Function of Ptolemy's Physical Hypotheses of Planetary Motion," *Journal for the History of Astronomy* 26: 33–61.

Nadler, Steven 1998. "Doctrines of Explanation in Late Scholasticism and in the Mechanical Philosophy," in Daniel Garber and Michael Ayers (eds.), *The Cambridge History of Seventeenth-Century Philosophy*. Cambridge: Cambridge University Press, pp. 513–52.

Nauenberg, Michael 1994. "Hooke, Orbital Motion, and Newton's *Principia*," *American Journal of Physics* 62: 331–50.

2005. "Hooke's and Newton's Contributions to the Early Development of Orbital Dynamics and the Theory of Universal Gravitation," *Early Science and Medicine* 10: 518–28.

Naylor, R. H. 1980. "Galileo's Theory of Projectile Motion," *Isis* 71: 550–70.

Nerlich, Graham 1976. *The Shape of Space*. Cambridge: Cambridge University Press.

1994. *What Spacetime Explains: Metaphysical Essays on Space and Time*. Cambridge: Cambridge University Press.

Neugebauer, O. 1957. *The Exact Sciences in Antiquity*. Providence: Brown University Press.

Newton, Isaac 1687. *Philosophiae Naturalis Principia Mathematica*. London: Joseph Streater.

1962. "De Gravitatione et Aequipondio Fluidorum," in A. Rupert Hall and Marie Boas Hall (eds.), *Unpublished Scientific Papers of Newton*. Cambridge: Cambridge University Press.

1999. *The Principia: Mathematical Principles of Natural Philosophy*, translated by I. Bernard Cohen and Anne Whitman. Berkeley: University of California Press.

Osler, Margaret J. 2008. "Descartes's Optics: Light, the Eye, and Visual Perception," in Janet Broughton and John Carriero (eds.), *A Companion to Descartes*. Malden, MA: Blackwell, pp. 124–41.

Panofsky, Erwin 1956. "Galileo as a Critic of the Arts: Aesthetic Attitude and Scientific Thought," *Isis* 47: 3–15.

Pav, Peter Anton 1966. "Gassendi's Statement of the Principle of Inertia," *Isis* 57: 24–34.

Pedersen, Olaf 1978. "Astronomy," in David C. Lindberg (ed.), *Science in the Middle Ages*. Chicago: University of Chicago Press, pp. 303–37.

Persson, Anders O. 2005. "The Coriolis Effect: Four Centuries of Conflict between Common Sense and Mathematics, Part I: A History to 1885," *History of Meteorology* 2: 1–24.

Plato 1997. *Complete Works*. Indianapolis: Hackett Publishing.

Poincaré, Henri 1905. *Science and Hypothesis*. London: Walter Scott.

Ptolemy, Claudius 1984. *The Almagest*, translated by G. J. Toomer. New York: Springer.

Pugliese, Patri J. 1989. "Robert Hooke and the Dynamics of Motion in a Curved Path," in Michael Hunter and Simon Schaffer (eds.), *Robert Hooke: New Studies*. Woodbridge, Suffolk: The Boydell Press, pp. 181–206.

Putnam, Hilary 1962. "The Analytic and the Synthetic," in Herbert Feigl and Grover Maxwell (eds.), *Scientific Explanation, Space, and Time*. Minneapolis: University of Minnesota Press, pp. 358–97.

Quine, W. V. O. 1951. "Two Dogmas of Empiricism," *The Philosophical Review* 60: 20–43.

Rabouin, David 2010. "What Descartes Knew of Mathematics in 1628," *Historia Mathematica* 37: 428–59.

Reichenbach, Hans 1920. *Relativitätstheorie und Erkenntnis Apriori*. Berlin: Springer.

1958. *Philosophy of Space and Time*, translated by Maria Reichenbach and John Freund. Mineola, NY: Dover Publications.

Renn, Jürgen 2004. "Proofs and Paradoxes: Free Fall and Projectile Motion in Galileo's Physics," in Peter Damerow, Gideon Freudenthal, Peter McLaughlin, and Jürgen Renn (eds.), *Exploring the Limits of Preclassical Mechanics*. New York: Springer, pp. 135–278.

Ribe, Neil M. 1997. "Cartesian Optics and the Mastery of Nature," *Isis* 88: 42–61.

Roberval, Gilles Personne de 1693. *Divers Ouvrages de M. de Roberval*. Paris: Academie Royale.

Rohault, Jacques 1671. *Traité de Physique*. Paris: Denys Thierry.

Rosen, Edward 1937. "The Commentariolus of Copernicus," *Osiris* 3: 123–41.

Roux, Sophie 2006. "Découvrir le Principe d'Inertie," in Sarah Carvallo and Sophie Roux (eds.), *Du Nouveau dans les Sciences*. Grenoble: Université Pierre Mendès France, pp. 449–512.

Ruffner, J. A. 1971. "The Curved and the Straight: Cometary Theory from Kepler to Hevelius," *Journal for the History of Astronomy* 2: 178–94.

Sabra, A. I. 1981. *Theories of Light from Descartes to Newton*. Cambridge: Cambridge University Press.

1984. "The Andalusian Revolt against Ptolemaic Astronomy: Averroes and al-Biṭrūjī," in Everett Mendelsohn (ed.), *Transformation and Tradition in the Sciences*. Cambridge: Cambridge University Press, pp. 133–54.

Salmon, Wesley C. 1989. "Four Decades of Scientific Explanation," in Philip Kitcher and Wesley C. Salmon (eds.), *Scientific Explanation*. Minneapolis: University of Minnesota Press, pp. 3–219.

Sasaki, Chikara 2003. *Descartes's Mathematical Thought*. Dordrecht: Kluwer Academic Publishers.

Schmaltz, Tad M. 2008. *Descartes on Causation*. Oxford: Oxford University Press.

Schuster, John 2000. "Descartes Opticien: The Construction fo the Law of Refraction and the Manufacture of Its Physical Rationales, 1618–29," in Stephen Gaukroger, John Schuster, and John Sutton (eds.), *Descartes' Natural Philosophy*. London: Routledge, pp. 258–312.

Scriven, Michael 1988. "Explanation, Predictions, and Laws," in Joseph C. Pitt (ed.), *Theories of Explanation*. Oxford: Oxford University Press, pp. 51–74.

Shank, Michael H. 1998. "Regiomontanus and Homocentric Astronomy," *Journal for the History of Astronomy* 39: 157–66.

Shapere, Dudley 1964. "The Causal Efficacy of Space," *Philosophy of Science* 31: 111–21.

1974. *Galileo: A Philosophical Study*. Chicago: University of Chicago Press.

Shea, William R. 1972. *Galileo's Intellectual Revolution*. New York: Science History Publications.

1991. *The Magic of Numbers and Motion*. Canton, MA: Science History Publications.

1996. "The Difficult Path to Inertia: the Cartesian Step," in Jean-Robert Armogathe and Giulia Belgioioso (eds.), *Descartes: Principia Philosophiae (1644–1944)*. Naples: Vivarum, pp. 451–70.

Skinner, Quentin 1988. "A Reply to My Critics," in James Tully (ed.), *Meaning and Context: Quentin Skinner and His Critics*. Cambridge: Polity Press, pp. 235–59.

Sklar, Lawrence 1974. *Space, Time, and Spacetime*. Berkeley: University of California Press.

Slowik, Edward 1999a. "Descartes and Circular Inertia," *Modern Schoolman* 77: 1–11.

1999b. "Descartes, Spacetime, and Relational Motion," *Philosophy of Science* 66: 117–39.

2002. *Cartesian Spacetime: Descartes' Physics and the Relational Theory of Space and Motion*. Dordrecht: Kluwer.

Smith, A. Mark 1987. "Descartes's Theory of Light and Refraction: A Discourse on Method," *Transactions of the American Philosophical Society* 77: 1–92.

Stein, Howard 1967. "Newtonian Space-Time," *Texas Quarterly* 10: 174–200.

Stephenson, Bruce 1994. *Kepler's Physical Astronomy*. Princeton: Princeton University Press.

Stevin, Simon 1586. *De Beghinselen der Weeghconst*. Leiden.

1955. *The Principal Works of Simon Stevin*, edited by Ernst Crone, E. J. Dijksterhuis, R. J. Forbes, M. G. J. Minnaert, and A. Pannekoek. Amsterdam: C. V. Swets and Zeitlinger.

Suter, Rufus 1952. "A Biographical Sketch of Dr. William Gilbert of Colchester," *Osiris* 10: 368–84.

Swerdlow, Noel M. 1973. "The Derivation and First Draft of Copernicus's Planetary Theory: A Translation of the Commentariolus with Commentary," *Proceedings of the American Philosophical Society* 117: 423–512.

1999. "Regiomontanus's Concentric-Sphere Models for the Sun and Moon," *Journal for the History of Astronomy* 30: 1–23.

2004. "An Essay on Thomas Kuhn's First Scientific Revolution, 'The Copernican Revolution'," *Proceedings of the American Philosophical Society* 148: 64–120.

2012. "Copernicus and Astrology, with an Appendix of Translations of Primary Sources," *Perspectives on Science* 20: 353–78.

Swerdlow, Noel M., and Neugebauer, O, 1984. *Mathematical Astronomy in Copernicus's* De Revolutionibus. New York: Springer.

Tabarroni, Giorgio 1983. "Giovanni Battista Guglielmini e la Prima Verifica Sperimentale della Rotazione Terrestre (1790)," *Angelicum* 60: 462–86.

Toulmin, Stephen, and Goodfield, June 1961. *The Fabric of the Heavens: The Development of Astronomy and Dynamics*. Chicago: University of Chicago Press.

Turnbull, H. W. (ed.) 1960. *The Correspondence of Isaac Newton, Vol. II (1676–1687)*. Cambridge: Cambridge University Press for the Royal Society.

Van Dyck, Maarten 2006. "Gravitating Towards Stability: Guidobaldo's Aristotelian-Archimedean Synthesis," *History of Science* 44: 373–407.

Van Fraassen, Bas C. 2008. *Scientific Representation: Paradoxes of Perspective*. Oxford: Oxford University Press.

Vilain, Christiane 2008. "Circular and Rectilinear Motion in the *Mechanica* and in the Sixteenth Century," in Walter Roy Laird and Sophie Roux (eds.), *Mechanics and Natural Philosophy before the Scientific Revolution*. Dordrecht: Springer, pp. 149–72.

Voelkel, James R. 2001. *The Composition of Kepler's* Astronomia Nova. Princeton: Princeton University Press.

Wallace, William A. 1967. "The Concept of Motion in the Sixteenth Century," *Proceedings of the American Catholic Philosophical Association* 41: 184–95.

1968. "The Enigma of Domingo de Soto: *Uniformiter difformis* and Falling Bodies in Late Medieval Physics," *Isis* 59: 384–401.

1981. *Prelude to Galileo: Essays on Medieval and Sixteenth-Century Sources of Galileo's Thought*. Dordrecht: D. Reidel.

1988. "Randall Redivivus: Galileo and the Paduan Aristotelians," *Journal of the History of Ideas* 49: 133–49.

1990. "The Dating and Significance of Galileo's Pisan Manuscripts," in Trevor Harvey Levere and William R. Shea (eds.), *Nature, Experiment, and the Sciences*. Dordrecht: Kluwer Academic Publishers, pp. 3–50.

1998. "Galileo's Pisan Studies in Science and Philosophy," in Peter Machamer (ed.), *The Cambridge Companion to Galileo*. Cambridge: Cambridge University Press, pp. 27–52.

Wallis, John 1670–1671. *Mechanica, sive De Motu, Tractatus Geometricus*. London: Gulielmi Godbid.

Weisheipl, James A. 1967. "Galileo and His Precursors," in Ernan McMullin (ed.), *Galileo: Man of Science*. New York–London: Basic Books, pp. 85–97.

Westfall, Richard S. 1966. "The Problem of Force in Galileo's Physics," in Carlo L. Golino (ed.), *Galileo Reappraised*. Berkeley: Univerisity of California Press, pp. 67–95.

1971. *Force in Newton's Physics: The Science of Dynamics in the Seventeenth Century*. London: Macdonald.

1972. "Circular Motion in Seventeenth-Century Mechanics," *Isis* 63: 184–89.

1977. *The Construction of Modern Science: Mechanisms and Mechanics*. Cambridge: Cambridge University Press.

1980. *Never at Rest: A Biography of Isaac Newton*. Cambridge: Cambridge University Press.

Westman, Robert S. 1975. "The Melanchthon Circle, Rheticus, and the Wittenberg Interpretation of the Copernican Theory," *Isis* 66: 164–93.

1980. "The Astronomer's Role in the Sixteenth Century: A Preliminary Study," *History of Science* 18: 105–47.

2011. *The Copernican Question: Prognostication, Skepticism, and Celestial Order*. Berkeley: University of California Press.

Whiteside, D. T. 1970. "Before the *Principia*: The Maturing of Newton's Thoughts on Dynamical Astronomy, 1664–1684," *Journal for the History of Astronomy* 1: 5–19.

Wilson, Curtis 1968. "Kepler's Derivation of the Elliptical Path," *Isis* 59: 4–25.

Woodward, James 1993. "A Theory of Singular Causal Explanation," in David-Hillel Ruben (ed.), *Explanation*. Oxford: Oxford University Press, pp. 246–74.

Yavetz, Ido 1998. "On the Homocentric Spheres of Eudoxus," *Archive for History of Exact Sciences* 52: 221–78.

Zilsel, Edgar 1940. "Copernicus and Mechanics," *Journal of the History of Ideas* 1: 113–18.

1941. "The Origins of William Gilbert's Scientific Method," *Journal of the History of Ideas* 2: 1–32.

Index

Lightning Source UK Ltd.
Milton Keynes UK
UKOW04f0325050218
317379UK00016B/317/P